COHERENCE, CONSONANCE, AND CONVERSATION

The Quest of Theology, Philosophy, and Natural Science for a Unified World-View

S. Brian Stratton

University Press of America,® Inc.
Lanham • New York • Oxford

Copyright © 2000 by
University Press of America,® Inc.
4720 Boston Way
Lanham, Maryland 20706

12 Hid's Copse Rd.
Cumnor Hill, Oxford OX2 9JJ

Library of Congress Cataloging-in-Publication Data

Stratton, S. Brian
Coherence, consonance, and conversation ; the quest of theology,
philosophy, and natural science for a unified world-view / S. Brian Stratton.
p.   cm.
Originally presented as the author's thesis (doctoral)—Princeton
Theological Seminary.
Includes bibliographical references and index.
I. Religion and science. I. Title.
BL240.2.S77   2000   261.5'5—dc21   00-061584 CIP

ISBN 0-7618-1817-0 (cloth: alk. ppr.)
ISBN 0-7618-1818-9 (ppr. alk. ppr.)

⊚™ The paper used in this publication meets the minimum
requirements of American National Standard for Information
Sciences—Permanence of Paper for Printed Library Materials,
ANSI Z39.48—1984

To Lee Osborne Scott

And so, Lord, do thou, who dost give understanding to faith, give me, so far as thou knowest it to be profitable, to understand that thou art as we believe; and that thou are that which we believe. And, indeed, we believe that thou art a being than which nothing greater can be conceived.

St. Anselm, *Proslogion*, Chapter II

Contents

Acknowledgments

Coherence, Consonance, and Conversation: The Quest of Theology, Philosophy, and Natural Science for a Unified World-View was originally presented in a slightly different form as my doctoral dissertation at Princeton Theological Seminary. I am grateful to Professors Wentzel van Huyssteen and Diogenes Allen for their encouragement, guidance, and suggestions which helped clarify and improve my thought. I am, of course, responsible for any inadequacies which remain.

My sincerest appreciation must go to my wife, Carol, who endured the long process of my writing a dissertation only to have to continue to live with this project as it was prepared for publication. I must also thank my son, William, for his sacrifice of hours of play-time with Dad while I finished the book. For their sakes I wish this were a more impressive work, but perhaps they will not be too disappointed if it at least helps to further the discussion of the important question of the relationship between theology, philosophy, and natural science.

Acknowledgment is also made for permission to quote from the following sources:

To Oxford University Press for material quoted from Thomas F. Torrance's *Theological Science*, copyright 1969. Used by permission.

To Harper Collins Publishers for material quoted from Ian Barbour's *Religion in an Age of Science*, copyright 1990. Used by permission.

To Macmillan Press Ltd. for material quoted from W. H. Austin's *The Relevance of Natural Science to Theology*, copyright 1976. Used by permission.

Preface

The theologian Tertullian once asked the question, "What has Athens to do with Jerusalem?" to express his reservations about the value of Greek philosophy for Christian theology, and no doubt the pagan philosophers who claimed to be inspired by Greek thought with whom he quarreled would have (for very different reasons) agreed. "What has Princeton University's Science Department and its Institute for Advanced Studies to do with Princeton Theological Seminary?" could serve as a similar question for contemporary theologians and scientists who understand the relationship between theology and natural science to be one of conflict or irrelevance.

An exciting new option is available today, and there is a place which serves as a nice symbol for the new possibilities available to those exploring the relationship between theology and natural science. The seminary's Center for Theological Inquiry, an institute founded for advanced theological studies, is dedicated in part to fostering a dialogue between theologians and natural scientists. This dialogue attracts and involves willing representatives from both fields, for important developments in philosophy, science, and the philosophy of science have created the opportunity for a new openness to the Christian faith, and many theologians and scientists agree it is now possible to move from "hostility" and an "uneasy truce" between theology and science to a positive dialogue between the two disciplines.

This book is offered as a contribution to the dialogue and focuses specifically on the question of *how* the two disciplines should be related to one another. I reject approaches which see the two as hostile or irrelevant to each other, and I argue that theology, philosophy, and natural science should be understood to be in an ongoing dialogue which eventually results in a harmonious world-view. However, I do not think there is an easy way to do this, for the ongoing interaction of theology and natural science to produce a coherent world-view is a process that is never completed since both disciplines are constantly developing new insights and have a number of significant issues that are far from settled.

In order at the outset to put the position to be argued in as precise a form as possible some discussion of the terms to be used and the outline to be followed is required.

Chapter One discusses the important developments in philosophy, science, and the philosophy of science which have led to the failure of scientism and open the possibility of harmonizing theology and natural science into a coherent world-view. I argue scientism has failed due to: (1) the collapse of Logical Positivism, (2) the broadening of the conception of scientific rationality as evidenced in the dispute over the nature of scientific explanation and theory acceptance, (3) the problematic relation of scientific theories to reality as evidenced in the debate over scientific realism, (4) the self-refuting nature of scientism, and (5) the limitations of natural science. After completing this discussion, it should be clear that one of the major obstacles to the consonance of theology and science within a coherent world-view has been removed.

Chapter Two discusses another position which would undermine the harmonious interaction of theology and science; namely, the view that natural science is irrelevant to theology. I examine the ways science has been thought to be relevant to theology, argue that the claim that science is irrelevant to theology has failed to make its case, and suggest good reasons for theologians to view science as relevant to theology. In addition, I argue that theologians must seek consonance and coherence within their world-views, and I propose some guidelines for how natural science and theology should interact when incorporating the two within one's noetic structure and world-view. By "noetic structure" is meant the set of propositions one believes together with the epistemic relations that hold among the believer and his or her propositions. A "world-view" is a smaller set of related beliefs within a noetic structure which constitutes a conceptual scheme by which one consciously or unconsciously places or fits everything he or she believes and by which he or she interprets and judges reality. By "coherence" is meant that the beliefs one holds should be consistent with one another; that is, one's scientific, philosophical, and theological beliefs should fit with one another and not contradict one another in the claims made about the world. "Consonance," a term borrowed from Ernan McMullin, is used to mean that there should be an accord or harmony reached between what the theologian says about the world as God's creation and what the scientist says about the world in his or her scientific descriptions. Furthermore, more than a mere consistency between the two disciplines will be advocated, for I think that theology and science can interact with one another. By "interaction" is meant that theology and natural science can engage in a mutually enriching open dialogue or conversation. Theology and natural science can make fruitful heuristic and methodological suggestions to one another, but there are some important mistakes often made in relating the two disciplines which should be avoided. After this discussion, the proposed guidelines will be applied to the approaches for integrating theology and science proposed by Ian Barbour and Thomas Torrance.

There is probably little need to justify the choice of either Barbour or Torrance, for both figures have been pioneers in exploring the dialogue between science and theology, and their influence on other thinkers working in this area is considerable. However, the juxtaposition of the two may appear at first sight to be surprising, for Barbour has developed his approach to the relationship between theology and science in the direction of the metaphysics of process theology while Torrance's work follows in the theological legacy of Karl Barth. In spite of these obvious differences, the two do share certain ideas and concerns, for both reject the narrow understanding of rationality that once dominated the philosophy of science and are opposed in principle to any attempt to reduce theology to science or science to theology. In addition, both advocate critical realism in theology and science, and both hold that theology and science can contribute to a unified view of reality. Barbour and Torrance disagree, however, about the nature of the world-view to which theology and science contribute and how the unity of the two disciplines is to be accomplished. The explorations of these two different approaches and methods promise to bring the most important issues in the discussion of the relation between theology and science to the forefront and to suggest possible future directions for the conversation.

Chapter Three carefully examines the method and application of Ian Barbour's approach, which he calls "integration." Barbour develops a theology of nature which views science and religion as contributing to one another indirectly in the search for a consistent metaphysics, and he finds process philosophy to be the best candidate for an adequate conceptual scheme. Barbour's work has much to commend it, especially his use of informal criteria as a way of evaluating scientific theories and religious beliefs, but I argue his approach is ultimately unsuccessful.

Chapter Four thoroughly analyzes the approach to relating theology and science developed by Thomas Torrance. Torrance believes methodological parallels exist between theology and science, and he understands the possibility for both a harmonization of and an enriching dialogue between theology and science to take place at the points where contingent reality points to the transcendent reality of God. Torrance's work has received a number of negative reviews, but I find these criticisms for the most part unsuccessful. I argue that Torrance's overall approach to the relationship between theology and science is the most convincing option currently available, and his model seems to be the most fruitful for exploring the ongoing dialogue between theology and science even though it has some areas in need of further development. The book closes with some suggestions for the future direction of the conversation between theology and natural science and a discussion of some unresolved problems which remain in Torrance's position.

Chapter 1

The Failure of Scientism and the Limitations of Science

Introduction

Many of the early discussions of the relation between Christian theology and natural science were dominated by descriptions such as "conflict," "warfare," and "struggle."[1] On one side were those who defended scientism, or the view that the scientific method was the only reliable path to knowledge;[2] on the other side were those who held that any scientific theory which contradicted a literal reading of the Bible could not be true.[3] Each side waged bitter campaigns against its respective opponent, and the two most famous battles (actually trials, those of Galileo and Scopes) have left a seemingly indelible mark on the *popular* understanding of the way the two disciplines interact.[4] Christianity's cultural image fared badly in these confrontations, and religion increasingly became the symbol of irrationality and superstition. Science, on the other hand, already having established itself as the dominant cultural influence in the modern world,[5] continued its rise in respect due to the rapid progress it made in its explorations, and came to be seen by many as *the* standard for rationality and truth.

Theologians responded to this cultural change in a variety of ways. Fundamentalists adopted an offensive posture toward science, attacking the theory of evolution and offering a position known as "creation science"as an alternative; however, this position commands no respect from biologists in the scientific community and is even seen by most scientists as a threat to their work, thus alienating scientists and religious believers even further and intensifying the "conflict" or "warfare" model of understanding the relationship between theology and science.[6] Other theologians adopted a defensive posture to meet the challenge presented by science by claiming that theology and science were two independent and autonomous disciplines that are irrelevant to one another. Proponents of this view opted for an "uneasy truce" between theology and science,[7] but they did little to overcome the separation between the two disciplines, and theology, for those who were willing to grant it any cognitive status at all, continued to be viewed in a subordinate position to the truth and method for arriving at truth found in science. Other philosophers, such as the Logical Positivists, went so far as to assert theological claims were neither true nor false but meaningless, for they could not meet the standards of the Verification Principle which the Positivists asserted to be true to the methods of science. For many intellectuals, the war between theology and science appeared to be over, and all that remained for science to do was to bury the dead.

To those who claimed the end of theology and the death of God perhaps only one word of reminder need be said – resurrection. Important developments in philosophy, science, and the philosophy of science have led to the collapse of scientism and to a new openness for faith and the claims made by Christian theology, and it is also possible for theologians to move from an "uneasy truce" between the disciplines to a coherence and consonance of world-view which also recognizes an open and mutually enriching dialogue between theology and science. This chapter will discuss the developments which have led to the failure of scientism and a recognition of the limits of science, and the following chapter will address the question of the irrelevance of natural science to theology in order to show how this new harmonious relationship is possible.

The Collapse of Scientism

Scientism is the view which claims that science is the very paradigm of truth and rationality. According to this view, if something does not square with currently well-established scientific beliefs, if it is not within the domain of entities appropriate for scientific investigation, or if it is not amenable to scientific methodology, then it is neither true nor rational.[8] Only science is true and rational; everything else is mere belief or opinion, and it is science which tells us how the world really is. This view is often coupled with scientific materialism to make two assertions: (1) the scientific method is the only reliable path to knowledge; and (2) matter (or matter and energy) is the fundamental reality in the universe.[9] Scientism is widely held in Western culture, and it is popularized by such figures as Carl Sagan in his television series and book *Cosmos*.[10] Scientism, if correct, precludes any coherent vision of theology and science within a consistent world-view on the part of the theologian unless he or she gives up claims to rationality or views religious beliefs as simply poetic expressions or myths which do not refer to anything which actually exists, and, while some theologians have been willing to take this step, the vast majority of Christians do indeed claim that God exists and has acted in God's Son Jesus Christ for the redemption of the world. For these Christians, the claims of scientism do present a challenge to their beliefs, and scientism's current prevalence has so influenced Western culture that it simply cannot be ignored.

Scientism, no matter how widely held, is false. New developments in philosophy, science, and the philosophy of science show just how inappropriate scientism's claims are and reveal some key limitations to the natural sciences. This section will discuss the developments which lead to the collapse of scientism and will include: (1) the collapse of Logical Positivism, (2) the broadening of the conception of scientific rationality as evidenced in the dispute over the nature of scientific explanation and theory acceptance, (3) the problematic relation of scientific theories to reality as evidenced in the debate over scientific realism, and (4) the self-refuting nature of scientism. The second section will discuss the limits of natural science.

The Collapse of Logical Positivism

One of the most important factors in the collapse of scientism is the demise of Logical Positivism.[11] The positivists asserted that scientific discourse provides the norm for all meaningful language, and no statement is meaningful unless it could meet the criterion of the Verification Principle of meaning, which states that the only meaningful statements are either propositions or sentences which in principle are capable of having something observable count for or against their truth, or that they are analytic, that is, they express abstract logical relations such as being true by virtue of the terms involved.[12] Statements from ethics, metaphysics, and theology were said not to be true or false, but were nonsense, meaningless pseudo-statements devoid of cognitive significance. Thus, positivism presented an intellectually sophisticated form of scientism which undermined any credibility for religious beliefs.

Positivism failed, despite its influence on and dominance of philosophy from the 1920s to the 1940s, for it became increasingly clear to philosophers that the positivist outlook was an inadequate philosophy of science and that it was ultimately incoherent.[13] First, positivism's account of scientific explanation was inadequate, for it failed to do justice to the role of the theoretical in scientific explanation. Second, positivism was unable to construct an inductive logic of confirmation which was adequate for application to real scientific tasks.[14] And third, and most important, the Verification Principle, the foundation of positivism, fails for three important reasons. First, it was unable to give a description of what is considered meaningful scientifically, for some basic principles of science are not empirically testable, such as the presupposition of the uniformity of nature. Second, the Verification Principle is incoherent for it is self-refuting.[15] It is not empirically testable and is instead a philosophical claim about meaning and the connection of meaning to empirical matters, nor is it analytic, and if the Verification Principle is neither analytic nor empirically testable then it is meaningless on its own terms and need not be further considered, or else meaningfulness does not depend on empirical verification or analyticity, in which case the principle is false and therefore once again not a cause for concern. And third, revisions of the Verification Principle were unsuccessful for they were either too restrictive (would eliminate science and the Verification Principle itself as meaningless) or too inclusive (would allow for metaphysical and religious assertions to be meaningful).[16] Positivism's failure dealt a severe blow to perhaps the most sophisticated version of scientism.

The Broadening of the Conception of Scientific Rationality

The second important factor in the defeat of scientism is the broadening of the concept of rationality to be found in the contemporary philosophy of science. While the current state of the philosophy of science appears to be a mass of unresolved problems and disagreements, there is a recognition of certain points of agreement within the emerging mainstream of opinion. These developments help to create a new openness for theology and undermine scientism, and include the broadening of the conception of scientific rationality concerning: (1) the nature of scientific explanation, and (2) the confirmation of scientific theories.

The Nature of Scientific Explanation

The first of these developments is the collapse of the consensus on the nature of scientific explanation. Scientism claims science provides the clear standard for what constitutes rational explanation, and, if this is the case, then one should be able to give an account of just what constitutes the clear standard for rational explanation; however, there is much disagreement among philosophers of science as to what a scientific explanation is. The nature of scientific explanation is much more complicated than those who defend scientism would have us believe, and in order to demonstrate this I will give a sketch of the leading conceptions of scientific explanations and the problems associated with each, beginning with the highly influential "covering-law" model of scientific explanation.[17]

The "Covering-law" Model of Scientific Explanation

The covering-law model of scientific explanation, developed by Carl Hempel and Paul Oppenheim, dominated the philosophy of science in such a way that it is commonly considered the classical view of scientific explanation.[18] According to this model, scientific explanations are deductive or inductive arguments and are to be understood as logical inferences.[19] These arguments consist of a conclusion, called the *explanandum*, describing the phenomenon to be explained, and a set of premises, called the *explanans*, describing the facts and laws provided to account for the explanandum. Like other deductive or inductive arguments, the aim of scientific explanations is to provide strong grounds for believing that the phenomenon described in the explanandum (the conclusion) was to be expected. In other words, explanation is logically equivalent to prediction, and explaining an event is always equivalent to showing that it could have been predicted from its antecedents. Thus, the scientist's goal is to show that an event is an instance of a general law; that is, the event can be inferred from the law plus information about previous conditions.

In addition, scientific explanations can be distinguished from other arguments by the nature of their premises. The explanans are testable by experiment or observation, and they are made up of scientific laws, which may be universal laws (which attribute a certain characteristic to all members of a class), statistical laws (which attribute a certain characteristic only to a specified proportion of the members of a class), or a combination of the two.

According to Hempel, the type of law used in the explanans and the type of inference used in the argument provide the basis for dividing scientific explanations into three classes: (1) deductive-nomological explanations, which are deductive explanations that include only universal laws in their explanans (for example, All water boils at 100 degrees centigrade; This is water; Therefore, it will boil at 100 degrees centigrade); (2) deductive-statistical explanations, which are deductive explanations that include at least one statistical law in their explanans (for example, 50% of radioactive substance a will decay in time c; This is b grams of a; Therefore, 50% of b will decay in time c); and (3) inductive-statistical explanations, which are inductive explanations using at least one statistical law in their explanans (for example, 99% of all headache sufferers have an easing of symptoms after taking aspirin; Alcasan took aspirin for his headache; Therefore, Alcasan is highly likely to have an easing of his symptoms).[20]

Despite the fact that Hempel's model was considered to be *the* account of scientific explanation, a number of substantial criticisms have been leveled against it. Michael Scriven has argued that subsumption under general laws capable of making predictions is not a sufficient condition for scientific explanation.[21] For example, Scriven points out that the theory of natural selection is an accepted scientific explanation, yet few would claim from it that one could have predicted the course of evolution. He argues that causality is indispensable in contemporary scientific practice and needs to be included in a theory of explanation, and he adds that the notion of causality is essentially pragmatic, referring to the solution of a range of particular problems raised in a particular context.[22]

Furthermore, Israel Scheffler has argued that one might make a reliable prediction from past experience, but it would not count as an explanation if no intelligible reasons for the occurrence of the predicted events are offered.[23] The old sayings "red sky in the morning,, rain in the evening" formulated as a general law would, even if always valid, provide no explanation of rain. Explanation is more than the empirical confirmation of prediction; some insight into the theoretical structures that can account for the success of predictions is required. Thus, scientific explanation is not achieved merely by formulating a valid deductive argument whose premises include general laws.

The Causal Conception of Explanation

One of the leading alternatives to Hempel's model is the causal conception of scientific explanation argued initially by Michael Scriven and currently defended by Wesley Salmon.[24] In this model, the explanation of a phenomenon essentially involves locating and identifying its cause or causes, and a scientific explanation not only assumes events under laws but also offers understanding of the causal network underlying the events.

According to Salmon's view, scientific explanations may sometimes suggest the elements out of which a deductive or inductive argument can be constructed, and an argument may sometimes exhibit explanatory relations, but a scientific explanation is not itself an argument. The aim of a scientific explanation is not to show that the phenomenon to be explained was expected (as in the covering-law model); rather, its aim is to show how the phenomenon in question were brought about, that is, how it fits under universal or statistical regularities that can be causally explained. One gives a scientific explanation of an event when one presents both the set of factors statistically relevant to it and the causal network underlying those regularities and the event itself.

Salmon gives an example of a scientific explanation in his discussion of why a particular soldier got leukemia. Such an explanation involves: (1) giving the statistically relevant factors (e.g., soldier S was 2 kilometers from the hypo center of an atomic explosion and was unsheltered, the explosion was a one-megaton explosion), (2) giving statistical regularities relevant to (1) (e.g., the probability of a person's getting leukemia given that a person is 2 kilometers from a one-megaton explosion is 1/1000, a number much higher than the national average), and (3) listing the causal processes and interactions underlying the statistical regularities (e.g., a causal process like the fact that high radiation released in a nuclear explosion traverses the space between the explosion and soldier S, strikes the cells of S, interacts with those cells, is absorbed by them, and initiates a process leading to leukemia).[25]

The causal conception of explanation is able to move beyond the equation of explanation with prediction, but it has its difficulties as well. The primary problem with the causal conception of scientific explanation is that an adequate treatment of causation is required for the theory to hold up, and no treatment of causation has emerged which has been able to claim wide enough support to settle the matter conclusively. Logical difficulties with causation have been a vexing problem requiring philosophers to awaken from dogmatic slumbers ever since Hume, and philosophers of science proposing a causal conception of explanation cannot afford to be somnambulists, especially in light of the recent challenges to causation raised by Nelson Goodman.[26] Salmon attempts to give an adequate explanation of causality which would answer Hume, but his arguments have been subjected to a wide range of substantial criticisms.[27] If a causal conception of scientific explanation is to succeed, it must find a way to develop a conception of causality that can convincingly answer the challenges posed by Hume and Goodman.

The Pragmatic Conception of Scientific Explanation

A third model of scientific explanation is the pragmatic conception of Bas van Fraassen. In his highly influential work *The Scientific Image*,[28] van Fraassen argues that scientific explanation is providing a constructive empirical account of an event which involves identifying certain salient factors, and for van Fraassen salience is determined by pragmatic concepts of relevance and of contrasting explanations.

According to van Fraassen, a request for an explanation is to be analyzed as a "why-question," and any scientific explanation can be analyzed as an answer to a "why-question." A why-question is specified by three factors: (1) the topic, (2) the contrast class, and (3) the explanatory relevance relation. The topic is the item about which one asks the why-question. The contrast-class is a set of propositions containing the topic and the alternatives to the topic, and it is determined by the context of the event needing explanation. It is normally obvious to the questioner and therefore usually not be explicitly described. The explanatory relevance relation is the respect in which a reason is requested, and it is this relation which determines what shall count as a possible answer or explanation. The explanatory relevance relation is determined by the context of the one asking the question.

Van Fraassen's conception of explanation can be illustrated by applying it to Gregor Mendel's pioneering work in genetics.[29] Mendel crossed pure-breeding varieties of peas with contrasted characteristics like round versus wrinkled seed form, yellow versus green pods, and tall versus dwarf stature. He then allowed the hybrid offspring (the F1 generation) to self-fertilize to produce a second generation (F2), and Mendel observed that this experiment always obtained the same results. The F1 generation consisted of plants with one of the two contrasted characteristics, and Mendel called the characteristic produced in the hybrids the dominant characteristic. The F2 generation consisted of plants of which three-fourths had the dominant characteristic and of which one-fourth had the other characteristic, which Mendel called recessive. Mendel explained this development by suggesting: (1) that each different characteristic of his pea plants was associated with a different internal factor, (2) that fertilization combined factors segregated into different pollen and egg cells, and (3) that the combination of such factors was random. When the F1 hybrids resulting from crossbreeding pure tall (TT) and dwarf (dd) pea plants were self-fertilized, equal numbers of T-factors and d-factors segregated into different pollen and egg cells which entered randomly into all possible combinations (TT Td dT dd) in equal numbers, thereby producing the observed 3:1 ratio of dominant to recessive characteristics in the F2 generation.

Van Fraassen's account of scientific explanation applied to Mendel's work would look as follows. The why-question for Mendel would be "Why is it the case that the F2 generation of pea plants consists of plants of which three-fourths have the dominant characteristic of tall stature and one-fourth the recessive trait of dwarf stature?" The topic of the question would be the proposition "The F2 generation of plants consists of plants of which three-fourths have the dominant characteristic of tall stature and one-fourth the recessive characteristic of dwarf stature." The contrast class could consist of alternatives to the topic such as "The F2 generation all has the dominant characteristic," "The generation all has the recessive characteristic," and so forth. The explanatory relevance relation in Mendel's case is a request for the events leading up to the F2 generation ratio, but in a different circumstance one could ask the question with a different explanatory relevance relation and thus require a different satisfying answer, such as "Why is it the case that the F2 generation consists of plants of which three-fourths have the dominant characteristic and one-fourth the recessive characteristic when I prefer the taste of the peas grown on dwarf plants to those grown on the tall?"

The answer to Mendel's question (or any scientific explanation), according to van Fraassen, will take the form "P because A," with P being the topic of the question and A the relevant set of related statements. What is or is not a good answer to a question is determined by pragmatic features, and van Fraassen suggests three criteria for evaluating answers relative to the knowledge contexts in which their questions have arisen. First, A should be acceptable or likely to be true. Second, A should make the topic stand out as more probable than other members of the contrast class (P rather than Q, R, S, etc.). And third, A should (1) be more probable than other possible answers to the question at issue, (2) favor P to a greater extent than other possible answers, and (3) not be made wholly or partially irrelevant by other answers.

Van Fraassen's pragmatic conception of scientific explanation has won a number of adherents, but it has also been challenged by a large number of critics who see van Fraassen's theory as reductionistic. Clark Glymour, for example, makes the point that there are clearly pragmatic concerns present in scientific explanation, but these do not have any pertinence as to whether or not there are objective unpragmatic relations between theories and statements of empirical phenomena. Explanation is not entirely interest-dependent, and it should not be reduced to pragmatic concerns.[30] In addition, Alan Musgrave has argued that van Fraassen's conception is deficient for it equates explanation with an empirically adequate account of the world and thus runs into the following problems: (1) it is difficult for descriptive empirical conceptions of scientific explanation to account for science's novel predictive success, and (2) the goal of scientific explanation is to understand, not merely describe, the world. Thus, he finds van Fraassen's position too narrow to serve as an adequate conception of scientific explanation.[31]

The Nature of Scientific Explanation: Conclusion

Two things are clear from this survey: (1) the consensus surrounding the covering-law model of explanation has dissolved, and (2) no alternative model has taken its place as the generally accepted standard account of explanation. These developments undermine scientism, for, in order for scientism to be correct, a clear description of scientific explanation must be given. A number of philosophers of science are at work trying to meet the objections to the causal conception and the pragmatic conception, but more time and debate is required to tell if either of these options will prevail of if a new conception will carry the day. Philosophers of science do agree, however, that an adequate conception of scientific explanation must be broadened from the logicism of the classical model to take pragmatic factors into account, and there is an increasing movement within the philosophy of science toward careful attention to the actual practice of scientists.[32] It is increasingly acknowledged that explanation takes place within a particular context, and explanatory claims cannot be evaluated apart from the empirical problem or situation that they intend to explain. Explanation requires reference to the framework one uses in interpreting a given situation, and pragmatic factors do play some part in scientific explanation. The introduction of these pragmatic factors further weakens scientism's case for the distinctive and superior means of rationality found in the sciences. This becomes especially clear in the current debate over the confirmation of scientific theories, especially since the work of Thomas Kuhn.

The Confirmation of Scientific Theories

The goal of science is explanation, and scientists have at their disposal a collection of laws and theories used to explain what they observe. However, before an explanation can be accepted it must show that it is worthy of acceptance, and a look at the history of science reveals that at any given time a number of alternative hypotheses have been offered to explain the same phenomena. How is a scientist to know which, if any, of the hypotheses to accept? What is the method by which theories are found acceptable or unacceptable? The answers to these questions are not obvious, and philosophers of science have developed no fewer than seven major approaches to the question of theory testing. I will give a brief exposition of these approaches in order to demonstrate how the emerging mainstream in the philosophy of science undermines the claims made by scientism.

Justificationism

Many of the classical philosophers of science proposed the hypothetic-deductive model of the confirmation of scientific hypotheses, and the approach to theory testing which uses this model is often referred to as justificationism or verificationism.[33] In the model used in this approach, scientists deduce from a hypothesis that they want to test an observable consequence of that hypothesis. They then run an experiment to see if the hypothesis holds. If it does not hold, they know the hypothesis is false, but if it does hold, then the scientists have a confirming instance of the hypothesis. As more confirming instances of the hypothesis are found, the probability or degree of confirmation for the hypothesis rises, and when a sufficient number and variety of confirming instances are accumulated, the scientists are justified in accepting the hypothesis as true. Since theories have an infinite number of observational consequences to be compared with the results of observation and experiment, they can never be shown to be definitely true; however, they can be shown to be probably true as repeated positive instances of observational consequences increase in number, and the observation of a single negative consequence is often enough to falsify a theory. Hempel's well-known example of this approach is an inductive argument that generalizes from a number of positive instances of black ravens to the conclusion "All ravens are black."[34]

Justificationism does appear to have a simplicity about it which makes it appear to be a fruitful way of analyzing how theories are tested; however, justificationism came to be attacked on its fundamental principle -- that theories can be validated by confirming instances. Critics pointed out that neither the truth, nor the probable truth, nor the degree of confirmation of a theory can be validly inferred from positive observational instances, for these instances represent too small a proportion of the infinite set of observational consequences of the theory. No theory can ever be validated by confirming instances, for there can never be enough of these instances to make the theory probable.[35]

Falsificationism

Falsificationism, an approach to theory testing developed by Karl Popper, displaced justificationism.[36] Falsificationists agree with critics of justificationism that true observational consequences cannot furnish scientists with valid support for claiming a theory is true or even probably true, but they hold that false observational consequences can furnish scientists with valid support for claiming a theory is false, for a true theory cannot have false consequences. Scientific testing is to be understood as a method for *eliminating false theories* by observation and experiment rather than discovering true theories (hence the name falsificationism). Theories that are corroborated (not eliminated in the testing process) are tentatively accepted because, unlike falsified theories, they may be true. Furthermore, Popper draws a sharp line of demarcation between scientific and nonscientific theories, for the former are falsifiable but the latter are not.

Popper and falsificationism have been criticized on a number of counts. Imre Lakatos has presented one of the most important cases against falsificationism.[37] The decisive point Lakatos argues is that Popper has a simplistic view of how data falsifies a theory, for the history of science is replete with examples of failed predictions where scientists persisted in pursuing the theory and ultimately found ways of reconciling the theory with the evidence.[38] All scientific theories generate some anomalies, and the generation of anomalies is not by itself a sufficient condition for rejecting a theory. Popper's view presupposes much too simple a link between theory and world.

However, one cannot perpetually disregard contrary evidence, and therefore there is a serious methodological problem concerning disconfirmation. Lakatos's solution is to propose a model of scientific explanation and theory testing in which the proper unit of appraisal is the "scientific research programme." It is rational to continue to tinker with a theory and the auxiliary assumptions associated with it as long as the research programme is generally progressive. Before turning to Lakatos's position, however, it will be necessary to discuss conventionalism, for Lakatos incorporates some elements of this approach into his theory of scientific research programmes.

Conventionalism

Conventionalism was developed by Pierre Duhem, a highly influential physicist, historian, and philosopher of science.[39] Duhem's work predated that of Popper (Duhem lived from 1861-1916), but his theory became more influential after the breakdown of Logical Positivism.[40] According to Duhem, theories are not chosen on empirical grounds, for if one has sufficient ingenuity empirical data can be accommodated by almost any conceptual framework. Theories are chosen by convention, on the basis of considerations like simplicity or coherence.

For Duhem, scientific theories are correlative devices which group together experimental laws. A hypothesis is always part of a theory, and it is used to make predictions only along with other parts of the theory. To test a theory consequences must be derived from it that can be compared with observation and experiment, but these consequences derive not from the hypothesis tested in isolation (as in justificationism and falsificationism), but from the hypothesis in correlation with a whole system of relevant theories. If the derived consequence is false, what deductively follows is not the falsity of the hypothesis under test but the falsity of a correlation of hypotheses, one of which is the hypothesis at issue.

In addition, a theory does not represent a group of laws merely by stating a conjunction (or adding together) of the laws, for the relationship is more complex than that, and it allows great range to the imagination of the theorist. A theory is a device for calculating, and nothing matters except that the results of its calculations square with the scientist's observations. The failure of a prediction indicates some inadequacy in the hypothesis in question or in some other hypothesis in the theory assumed in making the prediction, but it does no more than locate the inadequacy.

It shows conclusively something is wrong, but it does not tell the scientist where to look for that something nor what must be rejected or modified. In order to do this, the scientist must confront a whole theory-system of which the hypothesis is a part, and he or she must ultimately rely on convention when deciding between theories, for inductive generalizations from empirical observation alone cannot establish a scientific law due to their reliance on theoretical considerations at every step of the way.

Research Programmes

Lakatos incorporated elements of conventionalism into his methodology of scientific research programmes, but he amended the conventionalist account of theory testing in a number of ways. Lakatos agreed that a negative experimental result cannot falsify a theory, but only a whole system of theories (that is, a correlation of a theory under test and a set of auxiliary hypotheses). A theory can be saved from negative experimental results by suitable revisions of auxiliary hypotheses, but Lakatos adds that a clearer standard than simplicity, coherence, economy, or so forth, must be imposed on the revisions by which a theory is to be saved if theory acceptance is not to be purely arbitrary.[41]

Lakatos suggests that each revision made in a theory's auxiliary hypotheses to save that theory from a negative experimental result should render that theory and its auxiliary hypotheses capable of predicting all the facts they had previously predicted, with the addition of the previously anomalous fact and at least one new fact. In this way, saving a theory with the help of auxiliary hypotheses that satisfy this standard will represent scientific progress, while saving a theory with the help of auxiliary hypotheses that do not satisfy this standard will represent scientific degeneration. In addition, the degree of progress will be measured by the degree to which a theory and its auxiliary hypotheses lead to the discovery of new facts. Then, any scientific theory will be appraised together with its auxiliary hypotheses (as in conventionalism), and also together with its predecessors (not in conventionalism), so that one may see what sort of change has been brought about. Thus, the unit of appraisal will be a series of theory-systems, rather than a single theory-system (as in conventionalism) or a single theory (as in justificationism an falsificationism).

According to Lakatos, the history of science shows that series of theory-systems tend to be characterized by a remarkable continuity evolving from the scientific research programmes set out at their start. Research programmes consist of: (1) a hard core, which is a set of theoretical assumptions; (2) a negative heuristic, which is a directive that bids scientists to develop auxiliary hypothesis to save the central theoretical assumptions from negative experimental results; and (3) a positive heuristic, which is the suggestions for developing auxiliary hypotheses. If a research programme's development leads to scientific progress, it is successful, and if its development leads to scientific degeneration, it is unsuccessful. And, if unsuccessful, the hard core may have to be abandoned. Lakatos claims that the main problems of theory assessment cannot be satisfactorily explored except within this framework of scientific research programmes.

The methodology of scientific research programmes, like the other approaches discussed thus far, has been subjected to a considerable amount of criticism. First, a number of critics have raised the complaint that actual developments in the history of science will not support Lakatos's programme.[42] Second, Ernan McMullin challenges the claim that a reconstructed history can serve as evidence for a methodology for such a use is guilty of question-begging or circular reasoning.[43] Third, W. H. Newton-Smith has pointed out that it is much more difficult to make a sharp distinction between a hard core and auxiliary hypotheses as than Lakatos seems to think, and he also argues that Lakatos's programme is inconsistent.[44] And fourth, Paul Feyerabend has made the point that Lakatos's programmes give no concrete advice about when a research programme should be abandoned, and this means that continuing or abandoning a programme is a decision that is no more rational or irrational than another, thus collapsing Lakatos's case for the distinctiveness of science's rationality.[45] Due to these and other criticisms, the methodology of scientific research programmes has given way for the most part to other approaches to theory testing, though many current philosophers of science want to retain something like Lakatos's distinction between a "hard core" and "auxiliary hypotheses."

Kuhn's Criteria: Value Judgments and Theory Choice

Thomas Kuhn, the most influential (and controversial) philosopher of science on the contemporary scene, has argued that each of the four approaches discussed thus far fail to give an adequate account of theory testing, and he has proposed his own sociological approach.[46] Kuhn's problem with each of the other approaches is that each of these models make the question of theory assessment look far simpler and more straightforward than it really is.

According to Kuhn, there are at least five criteria of theory assessment. First, there is the criterion of accuracy. A theory's consequences should be in qualitative and quantitative agreement with the results of existing experiments and observations. Second, there is the criterion of consistency. A theory should be consistent with itself and other currently accepted theories applicable to related aspects of nature. Third, there is the criterion of scope. A theory's consequences should extend far beyond the particular observations, laws, or subtheories it was initially designed to explain. Fourth, there is the criterion of simplicity. A theory should bring order to phenomena that in the theory's absence would be individually isolated and, as a set, confused. And fifth, there is the criterion of fruitfulness. A theory should disclose new phenomena or previously unnoted relationships among phenomena already known.

These criteria of theory assessment are individually imprecise, and scientists may legitimately differ about their application to concrete cases. Furthermore, when applied together the criteria may conflict with one another. As a result, scientists fully committed to the same criteria of theory assessment may reach different conclusions when choosing between competing theories. The shared criteria of theory assessment function as *values that influence* theory choice rather than *rules that determine* theory choice, and they must be fleshed out by individual idiosyncratic factors to explain the particular theoretical choices that particular scientists make within a particular context to address a particular problem. In addition, the criteria are only fixed in a rough sense, for both their application and the relative weights attached to them have varied markedly over time and with the particular field of scientific specialization, and many of these variations have been associated with particular changes of theory.

As one can see, Kuhn does not think that a system of inductive logic can be developed for the evaluation of theories, and he adds that the only reasonable method for evaluating scientific theories is to consider the judgment of the appropriate scientific community. However, Kuhn argues that the imprecision, conflict, incompleteness, and variation in the criteria used by scientists in theory assessment do not justify the view that theory choice is a product of purely subjective taste or scientific fashionableness. If the shared criteria do not supply all the guidance one would like to have (in the sense of providing rules which produce unequivocal results), then it may be the nature, rather than the limits, of objectivity that is shown. Theory assessment is not as straightforward as the other approaches mentioned earlier have claimed, and the move from one theory to another often involves a Gestalt-like shift on the part of the scientific community. It is at this point that Kuhn's by now famous (or infamous) concept of the paradigm comes into play.[47] According to Kuhn, when one looks at the development of scientific change, one must distinguish between periods of "normal" and periods of "revolutionary" science. Normal science is a conservative enterprise of "puzzle solving activity" which involves: (1) increasing the precision of the agreement between observations and calculations based on a generally accepted paradigm, (2) extending the scope of the paradigm to cover additional phenomena, (3) determining the values of universal constants, (4) formulating quantitative laws which further articulate the paradigm, and (5) deciding which alternative way of applying the paradigm to a new area of interest is most satisfactory.[48] Normal science proceeds undisturbed until enough anomalies develop to create a crisis for the old paradigm. When the crisis occurs, science enters a revolutionary stage with the development of a viable competing paradigm. The old paradigm is not rejected on the basis of a comparison of its consequences and empirical data; rather, this comes about in a three-term relation which involves an established paradigm, a rival paradigm, and the observational evidence. If the new paradigm can solve the problems that led to the crisis in the old one, produces greater quantitative precision, predicts phenomena unsuspected under the old one, and generates the sense that the new way of looking at the world is neater, more fitting, or simpler, then the scientific community will gradually shift to the new model for its activities, and a scientific revolution will have taken place, even if many of the followers of the old paradigm will die off rather than undergo conversion.[49] Thus, paradigm replacement resembles a Gestalt-like shift or a conversion.

The outcome of a paradigm-clash is not fortuitous, however. Although competing paradigms are incommensurable, paradigm replacement has its own standards of rationality. Choosing the new paradigm may involve a decision made on "faith,"[50] but the decision is not irrational; rather, what is needed is a broader conception of rationality than that allowed by those influenced by Logical Positivism.

Kuhn's use of the term "paradigm" was equivocal, and critics immediately jumped on this weakness.[51] In a broad sense, Kuhn's use of paradigm refers to a "disciplinary matrix" or the "entire constellation of beliefs, values, techniques, and so on shared by the members of a given community."[52] A standard example of a paradigm in this broad sense is found in the work of Newton, whose paradigm included symbolic generalizations (mathematical equations), metaphysical commitments (such as matter in deterministic motion was a fundamental and revealing feature of nature), values (the importance of accuracy in prediction, measurability of results, and the observability of subject matter in experiment), and exemplars. An exemplar is a paradigm in a narrow sense and is an influential presentation of a scientific theory as a problem solution demonstrated in an archetypal experiment.[53] Shapere argued that paradigm used in the broad sense was too vague to be a useful tool of historical analysis, and paradigm in the narrow sense hardly merited the term "revolution." Kuhn conceded in the second edition that his use had been equivocal,[54] but he maintained that historical and sociological inquiry may reveal both exemplars and disciplinary matrices. He predicted that one result of such inquiry will be the identification of a large number of relatively small groups, and he conceded that a revolution may occur within one of these micro-communities without causing an upheaval in science. He also allowed for the replacement of one paradigm by another without the occurrence of a prior crisis within the micro-community, and he augmented the possible responses to a crisis situation to include the shelving of an anomaly for future consideration. And finally, Kuhn conceded that the pursuit of "normal science" within a micro-community may be accompanied by a debate over the metaphysical commitments that are basic to the disciplinary matrix of a science.[55] By making these concessions and modifications, Kuhn was able to give an answer which cleared up many of the concerns expressed about ambiguities present in his use of the term "paradigm."

Other critics have attacked Kuhn's claim that paradigms are incommensurable, and it was this feature of Kuhn's work which led to the charge that he was a radical relativist. One of the difficulties is that Kuhn's exposition of incommensurability was ambiguous, and some critics took him to mean that it was impossible to translate the language of one scientific paradigm intelligibly to another or that competing paradigms cannot be compared to one another, and this claim, as Donald Davidson has shown, is clearly false.[56] Kuhn denied he was a relativist, and he has tried to clarify what he meant by incommensurability to answer his critics. Kuhn did say that some kinds of comparison between paradigms are possible, but translating from one paradigm to another will be difficult, just as it is difficult to translate from language to another, and he adds there is no complete comparative procedure that is normal for all paradigms.[57] One paradigm does not stand in a simple matching relationship with another, and Kuhn suggests that it is probably impossible for a single mind to hold two competing paradigms before itself and do a point-by-point comparison.[58] All our perceptions of the world are paradigm-dependent, but we are not caught in relativism, for there is something "out there" which is independent of us and does not change when our paradigms change; however, because all our information about the world comes through perception, our world is "jointly determined by nature and a paradigm,"[59] and our world will change when our paradigms change. This remains confusing,[60] especially since Kuhn wants to distance himself from scientific realism, and Kuhn's lack of clarity does undermine his position. Because of this, there has been a movement away from many of Kuhn's views in the philosophy of science; however, Kuhn's claim of incommensurabilty is just one part of his overall attempt to show that theory change will not follow a set of logical rules, but will be governed by the criteria of values mentioned earlier, such as accuracy, consistency, scope, simplicity, and fruitfulness. These criteria, according to Kuhn, do enable one to justify the decision that one has found a good paradigm to replace another,[61] and this part of his argument is not dependent on the notion of incommensurability. Thus, while Kuhn's notion of incommensurability remains troublesome and subject to criticism, his point that values play an important role in theory choice remains a valuable contribution to the philosophy of science which has been acknowledged by a growing consensus of philosophers of science.[62]

This acknowledgment of decision-making values in scientific theory selection is an important development in the philosophy of science, and it serves to undermine scientism's assertion of the unique and superior rationality of the method used in the natural sciences, for two reasons: (1) it places human subjectivity (in the form of the values and commitments of the scientific community) right in the center of science, and (2) many other disciplines make use of similar criteria to the values listed by Kuhn. Thus, if the growing consensus in the philosophy of science is correct, scientism's claims are clearly in error.

Research Traditions

As pointed out above, the case for a broader conception of rationality than that allowed by scientism can be seen in contemporary discussions of theory assessment. Current models of theory assessment since Kuhn, while criticizing many of his claims, also reinforce the idea that values and commitments play an important role in theory assessment. Larry Laudan, for example, has criticized Kuhn and offered an approach he calls "research traditions" as an alternative.[63] Laudan's methodology views theory evaluation as primarily success in solving problems, and it includes two basic principles. The first is that theory evaluation is always a matter of comparison -- one cannot evaluate a theory in isolation but can only compare two contemporaneous theories. His second principle is that one must distinguish between the term "theory" construed in a specific way (for example, Bohr's theory of the atom), and a broader use of "theory' (as in referring to the atomic theory of matter). Bohr's theory of the atom is one attempt to give specific form to the atomic theory of matter. When Bohr's theory was shown to be incorrect, it was given up, but another form of atomic theory took its place. For the latter, larger kind of theory, Laudan uses the term "research tradition."

Each research tradition will be exemplified by a number of specific theories and will go through various modifications and developments. At any one time, some of the specific theories under the general heading of the research tradition may be mutually contradictory. For example, the research tradition of evolution includes as specific theories incompatible accounts of the exact rates and mechanisms of evolution. What distinguishes one research tradition from another is partly the theories that exemplify it but also the metaphysical and methodological commitments that constitute it.

Laudan views the work of Kuhn and Lakatos as developing accounts of research traditions (though they call theirs "disciplinary matrices" and "research programmes"), but he finds their work unsatisfactory for several reasons. He believes that neither Kuhn nor Lakatos take sufficiently into account the importance of conceptual, as opposed to empirical, problems in evaluating the progress of research traditions. He also disagrees with Kuhn's claims about the extent to which a research tradition is implicit in the practices of the community and with Lakatos's separation of questions of rational acceptability from issues of progress. Laudan views progress as the mark of rationality, and in his evaluation of progress, Laudan stresses there are two factors to be considered: (1) the amount of progress a tradition has made, and (2) the rate at which progress is made. It is always more rational to pursue the research tradition yielding the greatest amount and the highest rate of progress, and these criteria rescue science from the relativism implied by Kuhn's approach by providing a rational manner of theory testing, namely, success (progress) in solving problems.

According to Laudan, there are two kinds of scientific problems: (1) empirical problems, and (2) conceptual problems. Empirical problems are substantive questions about the world that strike us as in need of explanation, as for example, the periodic movement of the planets. There are three kinds of empirical problems: (1) unsolved problems (not explained by a theory), (2) solved problems (explained by one or more theories), and (3) anomalous problems (those that a particular theory has not solved but at least one of its rivals has solved). Anomalies can be removed by either revising the empirical base, adding an auxiliary hypothesis, or by making a significant change in the relevant theory.

Conceptual problems involve the clarity or intelligibility of a scientific theory in its structure or conceptual apparatus. There are two types of conceptual problems: (1) internal, and (2) external. Internal conceptual problems arise when a theory exhibits circularity, vagueness, internal inconsistencies, and so forth. External conceptual problems are often caused by some discipline outside science (such as philosophy or mathematics), and they should be taken seriously provided they are supported by rational argumentation, and the resolution of external conceptual problems can be solved by a revision of methodology or elements within one's world-view.

By including external conceptual problems as legitimate aspects of science itself, Laudan broadens scientific methodology and rationality to include, as part of science itself, metaphysical, philosophical, and theological issues, and any clean line of demarcation between science and non-science will be naive and out of touch with the way science has actually developed throughout its history. Furthermore, Laudan views the development of science as taking place within what he calls a "reticulational model of scientific rationality," which he contrasts with a "justificatory hierarchy model" of scientific development.[64]

Disputes arise in science whenever there is an attempt to solve a problem, and, according to Laudan, the justificatory hierarchy views these disputes as occurring on three levels. The first and lowest level involves factual disputes about laws and theories. These are competing claims about what exists in the world and can be about directly observable facts and unobservable theoretical entities. Disputes occur when there is a disagreement about the significance, existence, or explanation of the relationship between things thought to be found in the world. Disputes at the lowest level are resolved by an appeal to the second level, which involves disputes about methodological rules, such as the principle of "inference to the best explanation" or the limiting-case view of theory replacement which states acceptable theories should retain "significant portions of the theoretical content (or extension) of their successful predecessors."[65] Disputes at the second level are settled at the third, or highest level, which Laudan calls the axiological level. The axiological level is concerned with the aims, goals, and values that science seeks to embody. The axiological level includes different understandings of the nature of science and such differing aims or values as truth, simplicity, predictive success, novel predictions and directions for research, internal clarity and consistency, and so forth.

Laudan rejects this hierarchical model for a number of reasons, the most important being that the justificatory hierarchy leaves unanswered the question of how scientists are to resolve disputes at the axiological level. Laudan suggests that disputes at the axiological level need to be modified by considerations at lower levels in order to fit important episodes in the history of science,[66] and argues "the pecking order implicit in the hierarchical approach must give way to a kind of leveling principle that emphasizes the patterns of mutual dependence between these various levels."[67]

According to Laudan, the hierarchical model should be replaced by a Reticulational Model that does justice to the reciprocal relations between theories and methodological rules, methodological rules and cognitive aims, and cognitive aims and theories. Scientific problem solving involves a complicated interplay among theories, methodological rules, and cognitive aims and values, and proper interpretations of scientific evaluative practice will include a harmonious relationship among the dynamic equilibria of the Reticulational Model's triadic network. Disputes at one level can cause an adjustment at other levels so that the triadic network of facts, rules, and values is returned to a stable harmony that is internally consistent, and Laudan emphasizes that science progresses in solving problems not by progressively giving an increasingly truer picture of the world (as in scientific realism) but by constantly readjusting different parts of the web of theories, methods, and cognitive aims.[68] These successive readjustments keep harmony in our web of beliefs, and scientific problems get solved as we continually adjust the different parts of our conceptual framework until consistency is restored.

Laudan's approach to theory acceptance has won some acceptance, but various aspects of his method have been subjected to substantial criticism. C. A. Hooker has charged that Laudan's case against realism is ineffective and inconclusive for Laudan's presentation of realism is guilty of a "straw man" attack.[69] W. H. Newton-Smith has argued that Laudan's approach to theory acceptance is not workable, for it has no real way to show that more problem-solving effectiveness has taken place, and, more importantly, that Laudan's approach is not neutral in regard to truth or falsity as Laudan claims, and therefore some form of scientific realism is ultimately necessary to explain progress in science.[70] Others have challenged Laudan's treatment of the levels present within science and the justificatory hierarchy.[71] It is important to note, however, that all these critics of Laudan's retain some notion of the importance of the presence of values in scientific theory acceptance and reject the narrow view of scientific rationality which would support the claims of scientism.

The Testing Paradigm of Scientific Inference

Ronald Giere also has challenged Laudan's approach and has offered an alternative which he calls the "testing paradigm of scientific inference."[72] Giere has argued that alternatives such as Laudan's do not provide a norm for scientific judgments despite their claims, and that the best they can do is merely provide descriptions of situations which we now intuitively regard of rational acceptance. Giere, like Kuhn, is critical of attempts to provide an over-arching methodology for theory evaluation, and his testing paradigm of scientific inference is designed to provide and approach to theory testing in which the history of science plays an indispensable role in the philosophy of science and is not simply a convenient source of examples. Giere wants to take his clues about the testing of scientific theories from the practice of actual scientists, and he defends induction as an accurate description of scientific method on what he calls "nonfoundationalist" grounds.[73]

According to Giere, the unit of appraisal in science is a theoretical hypothesis, which is a construct that identifies elements of a theoretical model or defined type of system with elements of real systems of objects and then goes on to claim that such a real system of objects exhibits the structure of the model. The appropriate test of a theoretical hypothesis is a physical process with a high probability of a positive outcome if it is true and a high probability of a negative outcome if it is false. The result of such a test is a simple acceptance of the hypothesis if it is true or rejection of it if it is false. In short, an hypothesis is either accepted because it has passed an appropriate test or rejected because it has not. It is not accepted because it has a high probability of being true relative to its evidence (as in justificationism, which Giere's model superficially resembles); it is accepted because it has passed the test.

Giere calls this simple acceptance the "general decision rule," and the many problems associated with adopting this posture require a general decision principle for its defense. The decision principle Giere offers is the principle that tells decision makers to choose options that have expected values at least as great as some minimum established either by the decision makers or the decision context. The fundamental scientific value is truth, and it is the goal to which the institution of science aspires. The quest for truth is enough to justify the risk of error, and acceptance of an hypothesis if it passes a test within its given context is justified.

Giere is a critical realist; that is, he does think scientific investigation gives us limited but genuine information about physical processes actually present in the world, and these processes put a check on scientific investigation which prevents it from being pure relativism. However, he also includes pragmatic considerations such as the context-dependent nature of scientific claims into his account, and in many ways his approach resembles that of van Fraassen's constructive empiricism with the addition of a realist view concerning the world. As a result, one of the important consequences of Giere's account is that no theoretical hypothesis is regarded as true for all purposes or in any possible context, for the acceptance of a theoretical hypothesis is automatically relativized to a scientific context.

The testing paradigm of scientific inference can be challenged on a number of points. Bas van Fraassen would no doubt argue that the realism Giere adheres to is an unnecessary addition to the method of theory testing and that considerations like truth are irrelevant, for one should accept, not believe, a theory for its empirical adequacy should be enough. Likewise, Larry Laudan would argue that values such as truth are irrelevant to the scientific enterprise if progress if observed. Giere's view of theory confirmation may or may not be correct, but the important point for this discussion is that Giere's conception of theory confirmation, like the others discussed above, will not support scientism's claim that theological statements cannot be rational.

The Confirmation of Scientific Theories: Conclusion

It is clear that no one approach to validating theories has claimed wide enough support to unite the philosophy of science into a generally accepted view,[74] and it is not clear whether or not that more discussion of this topic will yield a consensus in the near future; however, some general areas of agreement have emerged.[75] First, earlier accounts of scientific rationality, with their excessive logicism, are clearly untenable, for it is simply not possible to give an adequate account of scientific explanation which conforms to a rigid logic, eliminates all subjective and pragmatic factors, and has everything rest on the empirical. Second, it is generally recognized that science is a deeply human activity, and what are usually called "subjective" factors do play a role in scientific rationality. Scientific judgments are made within a context of one's background beliefs and commitments; that is, other theories, beliefs, values, or commitments bear on one's acceptance of a theory, interpretation of data, and how one conceives of the relationship between a theory and data. Furthermore, creative acts of the imagination are clearly involved in theory formulation.[76] Third, there is an increasing awareness of the importance the history of science plays in attempts to understand scientific explanation and rationality. The history of science does not merely provide useful examples for the philosopher of science; rather, it provides important clues to the nature of scientific rationality and how theory acceptance has actually taken place within the practice of science.[77] And fourth, there is an increasing emphasis within the philosophy of science on the way scientists themselves actually conduct their work.[78] It is generally conceded that scientific rationality, like other forms of rationality, is context dependent in that it answers specific questions generated within a limited and well-defined context, and philosophers of science are now interested more in the actual practices of working scientists than they are in trying to lay down prescriptive rules of scientific rationality to which any discipline which claims to be a science must conform.

As one can see, each of the four points listed above undermines the claim made by scientism for science's exclusive rationality. First, scientism's claims fit better with the older conceptions of scientific rationality, but, as we have seen, this conception is no longer tenable. Second, science, like other disciplines, does have the presence of what are ordinarily called "subjective" factors within its mode of rationality; it is not purely objective as scientism has claimed. Furthermore, since science shares many elements of its rationality model in common with other disciplines, it cannot be said to be the exclusive standard of rationality as scientism claims. Third, other disciplines, like history, can actually help to improve our understanding of the development and nature of the natural sciences, and this should not be the case if the natural sciences alone set the standard for rationality; rather, the sciences should improve our understanding of history (or any other discipline).[79] And fourth, an examination of how scientists actually do their work shows that scientism's claims simply cannot be substantiated, for the actual practices of scientists reveal science to be a much more complicated task than scientism acknowledges. Thus, scientism's claims about the rationality of science are clearly in error, and it will now be shown that scientism's claims about the nature of scientific theories to reality are in error as well

The Debate Over Scientific Realism

One of scientism's claims is that science alone gives us a true picture of reality. This claim, however, involves what is probably the most controversial issue in the philosophy of science, namely, the nature of scientific theories to reality. Does scientific knowledge give us a true account of the way the world actually is, or are scientific theories purely summaries of data, calculating devices, useful fictions, convenient methods of representation, or mental or social constructs? The way in which one answers this question determines whether he or she is a realist or an anti-realist, and these two positions (which can be divided into a variety of forms) are the leading options in the current debates about the relation of scientific theories to reality.

Defenders of scientism, in order to be consistent with their claims, must (1) be realists, and (2) show that no other discipline reveals true information about the world unless it conforms to the methods of the natural sciences. Arguments for (2) are usually based on a narrow view of scientific rationality which has already been shown to be in error, and (1) is a much more complicated matter than defenders of scientism seem to acknowledge. The question of the relation of scientific theories to reality is a highly controversial issue that is far from settled, and, in this section, I will give a sketch of the leading positions in the debate concerning scientific realism in order to show that scientism's claim that science alone gives true information about the world has not been made.

Naive Realism

The most extreme version of realism is now widely referred to as "naive" realism. In this position, scientific concepts and mechanisms are literal descriptions of the world and reproductions of objective reality. Science discovers (or uncovers) the hidden mechanisms of the world of nature and shows what is actually there. Scientific knowledge is "read off" the world, and every proposition in science, from the most general theoretical principle tot he most particular observational report, simply reports a more or less comprehensive empirical set of facts about nature and aspires to be an accurate, objective mirror of the more or less universal facts about which it speaks.

Naive realism is not generally accepted, for the world described by some areas of modern physics and astrophysics is far removed from simple extrapolations from the world observable by the senses.[80] In addition, scientific knowledge has been subjected to the scrutiny that sociologists have long directed toward other human activities, and advocates of the "weak program" and "strong program" in the sociology of knowledge have raised serious objections to naive realism. In the weak program, the social circumstances in which science is practiced is considered to see how they retard or accelerate scientific development, but it retains the belief that the actual contents of a science are derived primarily from the interaction of an external nature with human rationality.[81] The strong program goes further and examines the mental construction and other aspects of science to see how they are socially influenced in their formation and acceptance.[82] The strong program itself has been challenged, but the objections it raises against naive realism are very effective in undermining that position.[83]

Critical Realism

Naive realism has suffered serious casualties, but critical, or limited, realism is alive and well. Unfortunately, there are almost as many kinds of critical realism as there are critical realists, and Jarrett Leplin has strikingly described realism as being like the Equal Rights Movement in that "scientific realism is a majority position whose advocates are so divided as to make it appear a minority."[84] However, realists do share in common the convictions that scientific change is, on balance, progressive and that science makes possible knowledge of the world beyond its accessible, empirical, manifestations. Realists do not claim that final truth is to be attributed to today's scientific theories, but they do believe some truth is given about the world, for the limited realist does not hold that every part of a theory is to be interpreted realistically; rather, some parts of some theories are. However, there is much disagreement among them about what scientific success consists in, how it is to be explained, and the role realism plays in scientific explanation.

Despite the conflicting positions found under the heading of critical realism, Ernan McMullin has given a formulation of critical realism which can serve as a general expression of the essentials of the position.[85] According to McMullin:

> The basic claim made by scientific realism... is that the long-term success of a scientific theory gives reason to believe that something like the entities and structure postulated in the theory actually exist. There are four important qualifications built into this: (1) the theory must be a successful one over a

significant period; (2) the explanatory success of the theory gives some reason, though not a conclusive warrant, to believe it; (3) what is believed is that the theoretical structures of the real world; (4) no claim is made for a special, more basic, privileged, form of existence for the postulated entities. These qualifications: "significant period," "some reason," "something like," sound very vague, of course, and vagueness is a challenge to the philosopher. Can they not be made more precise? I am not sure that they can; efforts to strengthen the thesis of scientific realism have, as I have shown, left it open to easy refutation.[86]

Thus, critical realism, according to McMullin, is a limited claim which purports to explain why certain ways of proceeding in science have worked out as well as they (contingently) did. McMullin mounts his case for scientific realism based on the fact that in many areas of natural science (geology, cell biology, chemistry) there has been over the last two centuries a progressive and continuous discovery of hidden structures in the entities of the natural world, and these structures account causally for the observed phenomena.

Metaphoric Realism

McMullin's own version of critical realism is a metaphoric realism in which one employs the concepts of one domain in a partially descriptive manner in another domain. When a term from everyday experience like "particle" or "wave" is used in a theoretical context and with reference to something unobservable, something true but not literally descriptive is being said. As with any metaphor, some aspects of the concept used metaphorically will not apply in the metaphorically described situation, and those aspects will suggest areas for further research to see whether in fact they do apply.

McMullin's form of critical realism greatly undermines scientism's claims. McMullin's position, if correct,[87] would mean that all our scientific descriptions are limited to partial descriptions and our theories are unavoidably incomplete in ways that we cannot anticipate. Science may give us a description of the "way the world really is," as scientism claims, but it is at best only a part of the way the world really is and contains some aspects which are clearly not the way the world really is. Furthermore, it is clear that other disciplines besides the natural sciences can give metaphoric descriptions of the world, and, for scientism to be successful, it must make the case that metaphoric descriptions from other disciplines are somehow inferior or inadequate compared to the metaphoric descriptions of the world found in the natural sciences, and this is a case that simply has not been made, and it is difficult to see how it could be made. Thus, scientism is incompatible with metaphoric realism in science.

Verisimilitude

A second form of critical realism has been proposed by W. H. Newton-Smith.[88] He argues for the "verisimilitude," or approximate truth of scientific theories. Theories replace previous theories through a movement toward truth by which our understanding of the physical world becomes increasingly more accurate; however, this understanding is not total and is always capable of further improvement, for, while our theories may increase in the degree to which they are approximately true, they remain adequate descriptions of circumscribed physical regimes which are not adequate for all purposes. Theories never achieve full or complete truth, and future theories will replace those of today just as they will be replaced at a further point in time.

It is apparent that the "verisimilitude" version of critical realism will not support the grandiose claims made for science by the proponents of scientism, and this version of critical realism poses no real threat to religious beliefs.[89] The question of whether this version of realism is correct is another matter. Two key difficulties remain for this approach: (1) it is not clear as to what it means to say one theory more closely approximates truth than another, and (2) it is not clear what conditions would justify our thinking that one theory is more approximately true than another.[90] In addition, the history of science is replete with examples of successful theories that have turned out to be false, and it also contains evidence of theory replacement, not merely theory refinement, as verisimilitude seems to demand. The presence of difficulties such as these have led a number of philosophers of science to abandon realism altogether.

Anti-realism

Anti-realism, like realism, comes in a variety of forms, some of which have already been discussed.[91] It will not be possible to treat all the varieties of anti-realism which have been advanced, but a survey of two of the leading representatives of this position, Bas van Fraassen and Arthur Fine, should be sufficient to illustrate the essential features of anti-realism and how it relates to the debate with scientism.[92]

Constructive Empiricism

Bas van Fraassen is perhaps the most influential anti-realist, and his arguments have generated a considerable response on the part of realists.[93] Van Fraassen holds that all the arguments for realism have been weighed in the balances and found wanting, and he argues that science does not aim at a literally true account of the world and that its success is not to be reckoned by its progress toward achieving this aim; rather, the aim of science is the empirical adequacy of theories. Van Fraassen claims that if two theories are both empirically adequate, then there is no reason to worry about choosing between them. The theories of science give an account only of observable things and events in the world, and van Fraassen offers his position, known as constructive empiricism, as an alternative to scientific realism.

One of the reasons for van Fraassen's rejection of realism is that he views realism as engaging in unnecessary metaphysical speculation. If one argues for realism, one engages in metaphysical speculation that is virtually identical to the argument form medieval philosophers used to prove the existence of God, that is, one postulates unobservable essences, properties, dispositions, causal powers, and so forth that are taken to be features of theoretical entities that are causally responsible for observational evidence. Such postulations go beyond the observational evidence, and that evidence does not select one and only one characterization of the theoretical entities, for several different metaphysical characterizations are empirically equivalent regarding the observational data. This is an error and unnecessary addition, according to van Fraassen, for science is indifferent about whether unobservable theoretical entities such as electrons really exist and cause things, and the proper scientific stance toward unobservable theoretical entities is agnosticism.

In place of realism, van Fraassen proposes constructive empiricism -- "constructive" because van Fraassen views the aim of scientific activity to be the construction of theoretical models, not the discovery of truth concerning unobservables, and "empiricism" because the main goal of science is "to save the phenomena," that is, to develop empirically adequate theories that accurately describe and predict observational phenomena.

For van Fraassen, there is an important difference between accepting a theory and believing it. To believe a theory is to hold it is true, that is, to hold some model or picture accurately represents the world of unobsevable, theoretical entities. In contrast, accepting a theory involves two actions. First, acceptance involves belief that the theory is empirically adequate, that is, the theory is true regarding what it says about what is observable by scientists. An acceptable model or picture of the theory will be isomorphic with the observational world, for it draws a picture of the world and certain aspects of that picture refer to what is observable. Put differently, if a theory is accepted, that means one believes that those aspects of it that describe or predict what can be observed do so in an accurate way. What the theory says we should observe is what we observe. Accepting a theory involves no more belief than that the theory accurately represents observational phenomena. In contrast, the realist believes a true theory is a true description of the observable and unobservable world, and he or she is therefore forced to deal with the problems associated with metaphysical claims.

Second, accepting a theory involves agreeing to act as if the theoretical entities postulated by it are real. One adopts this stance as a pragmatic posture that facilitates the scientific search for new empirically observable correlations in the world. Unobservable theoretical aspects of a theory are pragmatically justifiable if they aid in the search for new observational correlations and become unjustifiable if they fail to yield accurate empirical descriptions and predictions of observational phenomena.

It is precisely at this point that the realist would object to van Fraassen's account, for constructive empiricism, according to the realist, is unable to give a reason as to *why* the pragmatic acceptance of theoretical entities leads to greater accuracy. The realist has an answer, for he or she claims that the theory refers to real entities which are causally responsible for the observational data and describes them in an approximately true way. The constructive empiricist must claim the success of science is a miracle or happy coincidence.

Van Fraassen has three replies to the realist. First, he thinks the argument from the success of science is faulty, for the success of science is no mystery at all. Science is a type of biological phenomenon, and a Darwinian model of theories may be the best view of them. For example, two reasons can be given for why a mouse runs from a cat. Augustine said a mouse perceives a cat as an enemy and therefore runs, that is, the mouse adequately mirrors the world and grasps the relation of enmity and survives. According to Darwinism, the mouse does not survive because it grasps the relation with the cat; rather, mice that don't run die; only mice which run survive. It is thus not surprising our theories get better, for as van Fraassen writes

the success of scientific theories is no miracle. It is not even surprising to the scientific (Darwinist) mind. For any scientific theory is born into a life of

fierce competition, a jungle red in tooth and claw. Only the successful
theories survive – the ones which *in fact* latched on to the
actual regularities in nature.[94]

Second, realism pushes explanation to excess, and van Fraassen claims
there are limits to scientific explanations. The constant demand for hidden
variables leads to an infinite regress of explanations, and this can be
avoided only if some set of regularities are taken as brute givens. The
constructive empiricist would rather accept observable regularities to fill
this role as opposed to the realist, who relies on unobservable regularities
for explanations. An example of an inadequate search for hidden
regularities can be seen in the attempt of those who try to make quantum
physics deterministic, for they think there must be another explanatory
regularity available even though their view is at odds with the predominant
interpretation of quantum mechanics.[95]

Finally, the relativity of explanation runs contrary to realism.
Explanatory inferences do not seem to be able to carry truth if there are
many explanations of the same phenomena, each of which is context
dependent to the nature of the investigation. Accurate empirical
descriptions and predictions of observational phenomena should be
sufficient; the question of which explanation truly mirrors the world is
outside the realm of science and enters into metaphysical speculation.[96]

Van Fraassen's work presents a considerable challenge to those who
defend scientific realism, and the issues he raises are still under debate.
It is important to note that van Fraassen's work provides no support for
those who defend scientism and presents no challenge to theological
statements as such; however, it does provide a challenge to theologians
who take a realist view of science. Realists have responded to each of van
Fraassen's three arguments against realism and to his formulation of
scientific explanation, and, despite his serious challenges, realism, in one
of its chastened forms which will not support the claims of scientism,
remains the leading position in the current philosophy of science.[97]

The Natural Ontological Attitude

However, the debate over scientific realism is far from settled, and van
Fraassen's anti-realism has been challenged by other anti-realists as well.
One of the most important anti-realist critiques of van Fraassen has been
written by Arthur Fine.[98] Fine is dissatisfied with both realist and anti-
realist positions. He finds van Fraassen's position unnatural, depending as
it does on an expectation that science give an unequivocal and non-circular

answer to what is observable but then uniformly suspend belief beyond that point. Fine argues in favor of a "natural ontological attitude" (NOA) toward science, an attitude that eschews both realism and anti-realism. Such an attitude, Fine stipulates, allows science to speak for itself; that is, science should provide its own local interpretations of its own results, rather than be interpreted by either realism or anti-realism, which Fine sees as a metaphysical and dispensable superaddition. The NOA rejects interpretations, whether the purpose be either to give a realist or anti-realist cast to science or to find sharp demarcations between science and pseudo-science. Attention should be paid to the actual practice of science, and if one adopts the natural ontological attitude, realism and anti-realism become idle overlays to science which are not necessary, not warranted, and, in the end, not even intelligible.

Fine's position, if correct, clearly will not support the claims of scientism. The NOA is commendable in many respects, such as its emphasis on the actual practices of scientists, but it seems simply to refuse to address the problems Fine wants to solve rather than offer a solution to them, and in the end he is left with a confusing hybrid position which wants the best of both of both worlds but ultimately fails.[99]

Critical Realism: A New Direction

Despite the powerful attacks of anti-realists, some limited version of realism remains the dominant view, but the issues are far from settled, and the current debate is taking new directions, with an increasing interest in how the actual practice of science should factor into the realism/anti-realism debate. Michael Gardner and Ian Hacking represent two very promising approaches to the realism/anti-realism question which follow this direction and mark a step forward from earlier discussions. Both are critical realists, but each places his emphasis on a different aspect of the issue -- theoretical science for Gardner and experimental science for Hacking.

Interpretation and the Realism/Anti-realism Question

Gardner argues the realism/anti-realism question, as usually conceived, is the question whether scientific theories are correctly interpreted as true (realism) or as merely convenient devices for summarizing facts (instrumentalism).[100] This question requires a single answer applicable to all theories, but a question such as this should be settled through an examination of particular scientific theories rather than in general terms, given the possibility that the question might have different answers for different theories. In fact, the history of science is filled with examples oft a theory being first put forward or accepted merely as a calculational device and then only later coming to be regarded as actually true. Therefore, Gardner suggests a successor question to the realism/anti-realism question – Under what conditions is it reasonable to accept a theory on a realist interpretation rather than on an instrumentalist interpretation?

To answer this question, Gardner examines in detail the debate over the status of Copernican astronomy in the sixteenth century. He finds that Copernican astronomy was accepted on a realistic interpretation or an instrumentalistic interpretation depending on whether or not the theory was thought to satisfy or fail conditions like the following: (1) the theory satisfies the laws of physics; (2) the theory is consistent with all observational data; (3) the theory is consistent with other putative knowledge (like the Scriptures); (4) the theory contains only determinate quantities; (5) the theory is able to predict facts; (6) the theory is a central hypothesis supported by a large variety of evidence; (7) the theory is within the realm of possible human knowledge; (8) the theory explains facts that competing theories postulate; and (9) the theory agrees with some of the nonobservational claims of some previous theories purporting to explain the same observations.[101] If, according to Gardner, it is plausible these conditions which are operative in the case of Copernican astronomy are also found to be operative in a variety of other cases in which the issue of realism/instrumentalism has arisen, one might accept them as good reasons for adopting a realistic interpretation of a theory. The justification for such an answer to the new version of the realism/anti-realism question is that the answer agrees with the judgments of most good scientists of the past and present on most of the relevant occasions.

Entity Realism

Ian Hacking's suggested revision of the realism/anti-realism question takes a different form than Gardner's since the emphasis is different.[102] Hacking argues that experimental work provides the best evidence for scientific realism, and he formulates the question to be asked as: Under what conditions is it reasonable to accept the entities postulated by a theory (and this includes processes, states, fields, etc.) as actually existing, rather than hypothetical entities? Like Gardner's version of the realism/anti-realism question, Hacking's version allows one to form different judgments about the entities postulated by theories at different stages of development; however, unlike Gardner's version, Hacking's position focuses on the reality of the entities postulated by a theory instead of the truth of the theory. Concentration on entities rather than theories is correct, according to Hacking, for: (1) a false theory as well as a true one may postulate real entities, and different, even incompatible, theories indeed have frequently postulated the same entities (for example, many different theories have postulated the existence of atoms); and (2) the existence of entities can be affirmed by discerning causal lines whereas theories are remote and more questionable.

By the time an entity such as an electron can be used to manipulate other parts of nature in a systematic way, the electron has ceased to be theoretical and has become experimental. Experimental physicists are realists about the entities they use, and Hacking thinks they cannot help but be so, for entities are tools or instruments, not merely for thinking, but also for doing. He concludes that engineering, not theorizing, is the best proof of scientific realism, and that "practical ability breeds conviction."[103]

The widespread practice of experimental scientists leads Hacking to answer the question about the existence of entities in the following way – when scientists' understanding of the causal properties of postulated entities allows them to use such entities as tools to investigate other aspects of nature, then it is reasonable to accept such entities are real. Hacking also notes that reality is bigger than human beings and that much of it may remain always beyond our knowing, but the ability to measure entities or to understand their causal powers provide good reasons for thinking them to be real. However, the acceptance of such entities as real does not commit scientists to accepting as true any particular theory in which the entities are postulated.

Hacking does not so much present an argument for realism as give persuasive accounts of how realism is generated as experimenters build particle accelerators or refine microscopes. The details of his accounts carry one toward realism much as the actual experiments did for the scientists performing them. It is the successful experimental doings themselves that "breed conviction" of realism, and they do not produce irrefutable arguments for realism as much as produce conviction in us that the entities described are real.

Neither Gardner or Hacking's version of limited realism will support the claims of scientism, for each incorporates elements which counter the claim that the natural sciences alone can give us reliable information about the world,[104] and each recognizes that the relation of scientific theories to reality is a much more complicated matter than scientism acknowledges. Making a truth-claim for a scientific theory or a part of a scientific theory requires making an assertion that is far from automatic, foolproof, or shaped by the foibles of human activity and subjectivity. The kind of realism scientism claims for science is simply not justified, and, in fact, the difficulties confronting realism presented above are so great that only very limited claims can be made for scientific realism. In the following chapter, I will address the question of the relevance of scientific realism to theology, but first I must conclude the case against scientism.

The Self-Refuting Nature of Scientism

Scientism is self-refuting for in its statement it is susceptible to the same weakness as Logical Positivism in that it includes itself within its field of reference and fails to satisfy its own criteria of acceptability.[105] Scientism's claim that "only what can be known by science or quantified and empirically testable is true and rational" is clearly self-refuting, for this claim cannot be tested empirically nor quantified, and more importantly, is not itself a statement of science, but a second-order philosophical claim about science. Defenders of scientism fail to realize that questions about the definition, aims, and justification of science are second-order philosophical questions about science which cannot be validated by science, and arguments to the contrary will be philosophical, rather than scientific, arguments.[106] The only way for scientism to succeed would be if it was able to show that philosophy can be subsumed under or completely reduced to the natural sciences in some way, but no attempt to do this has thus far been successful,[107] and, due to scientism's inadequate conception of science and of rationality, its self-refuting nature, and the limits of science to be discussed below, I think it safe to predict that this case will not be made.

The Limitations of Natural Science

In order for scientism to be correct, all of reality should be capable of being brought within the scope of the natural sciences. If any part of reality lies outside the boundaries imposed on science by its methods, that part of reality will be beyond the competence of science and reveal a limitation to science which shows the claims of scientism to be false. This section will argue that there are three specific kinds of limits to natural science: (1) the presuppositions on which science depends, (2) the areas of investigation which lie outside the domain of the natural sciences, and (3) the limits within science itself.[108]

The Presuppositions of Natural Science

Science is committed to a number of presuppositions which make it possible. John Kekes has classified these presuppositions as follows: (1) methodological presuppositions, such as intersubjective testability, quantifiability, and the public availability of data; (2) existential presuppositions, such as the belief that nature exists, is uniform, and has a discoverable order; (3) classificatory presuppositions, such as the distinctions between cause and effect, the observer and the observed, real and apparent, and the orderly and the chaotic; and (4) axiological presuppositions, such as the honest reporting of results, the worthwhileness of getting the facts right, and scrupulousness in avoiding observational or experimental error.[109] Abandonment of any of these foundational presuppositions would make it impossible for science to be done, and, despite their common acceptance, each presupposition has been challenged, and philosophers and scientists have been forced to go outside natural science in order to defend science's foundational presuppositions, thus revealing important limitations to natural science.

First, science is susceptible to methodological limits. Science cannot validate scientific methodology itself or the presuppositions of its methodology which rely on existential presuppositions. For example, scientists accept the principles that nature is uniform (that process and patterns observed on only a limited scale hold universally) and intelligible (or understandable). These principles are not the result of science but are presuppositions used to produce results. If regularity and intelligibility were not assumed, there would be no reason to attempt to understand nature or to expect it to behave in an orderly way, for one would not know if causal connections discovered by intersubjective testability in the past will hold true in the future, or if nature is predictable, or if scientific results will be reproducible. Observations and data are interpreted in light of these accepted presuppositions, and that interpretive role is shown by the continuing attempt of scientists to understand nature and the protected status accorded the uniformity principle. When nature does not behave according to currently accepted theories, scientists do not assume nature has changed how it operates; rather, the assumption is that the theories are in error in some way. Thus, the principles are not generated by the scientific method; rather, they are brought to the scientific method and control the interpretation of the results.

In this regard, natural science is similar to geometry in that both of these disciplines require assumptions in order to have a place to start. In geometry, one cannot construct proofs without axioms (or unproven assumptions), and the axioms are not generated by the system; rather, they are the foundations without which the system could not exist, and, as discussed earlier, science also requires methodological presuppositions not generated out of science itself. Sometimes unexpected results do cause scientists to re-examine foundational presuppositions, but those reexaminations are primarily philosophical rather than scientific.[110] Thus, one is left with the conclusion that if accepting the foundational presuppositions of science is rational, then the rationality of science is based on something other than the scientific method, and therefore the defender of scientism, who claims that science is *the* model of rationality, must either claim the acceptance of science is not rational or that at least some beliefs are rational which lie outside the scientific method. Either way, a real limit exists to science and scientism's position is untenable.

Second, there are a number of existential presuppositions which indicate a limit to science. These important presuppositions include: (1) the existence of the world, (2) the uniformity of nature, and (3) the discoverable order of the world, and natural science is unable to answer the fundamental questions associated with each of these foundational principles.

Science takes the existence of the world for granted as a "brute given," and all scientific work proceeds from this assumption.[111] The discussion of scientific explanation showed that the sciences seek to answer specific questions relevant within a specific context, and as such natural science is an internal approach to the universe, for it considers only the internal interactions of one part of the corporeal cosmos with other parts of that same cosmos, and as such it is simply not equipped to answer the question of the cause or ground of existence of the universe as a whole. Science is limited to the study of physical properties and the behavior of material systems, their interactions with one another, and the character of the space-time continuum in which they function; external, nonmaterial influences or interactions, if they exist, are outside the scope of science, and the affirmation or denial of their existence is more properly the subject of philosophical or theological debate.[112] Thus, the existence of the world poses a question to which science does not have the answer.[113]

Science also presupposes the uniformity of nature. Science assumes spatial and temporal invariance; that is, nature behaves according to the same rules everywhere in space and that the rules for material behavior do not change over time. It is the allegiance to the principle of uniformity which allows science to make use of induction in its method; however, as noted earlier, the justification of induction is a serious philosophical problem which is far from solved.[114] Induction has been defended, but attempts to justify induction rely on philosophical, not scientific, arguments. Scientists continue to rely on induction irrespective of the arguments of philosophers, for their acceptance of the presupposition of the uniformity of nature is taken for granted as a fundamental part of scientific method, and, as a presupposition which cannot be justified within science itself, marks another limit to the methods of natural science.

Furthermore, science presupposes the discoverable order of the world. The world exhibits various kinds of order which can be known. This presupposition involves two claims: (1) the world has a mind independent order which we sometimes discover, and (2) the human mind is an adequate instrument to discover the world's order. Included in the latter are the assumptions: (1) the laws of logic are useful to make inferences in forming, testing, and using theories; (2) the human senses are reliable in discovering nature; (3) language is adequate to describe the world; (4) mathematics is true and adequate to describe the physical world; and (5) formal concepts are able to organize and classify phenomena broadly enough to give us a conception of how to approach these phenomena.[115] Each of these presuppositions has been challenged, and the history of philosophy is replete with examples of problems raised by skeptics in asserting the truth-claims of any of the above propositions. Justification of these claims which science takes for granted will rely on philosophical arguments and reveal another limit to science.

Third, science relies on classificatory presuppositions. As George Bealer has argued, certain formal concepts are essential to science and constitute presuppositional limits to science.[116] When scientists classify their objects of study, they make use of formal concepts to describe natural-kind entities (such as water is identical to H_2O). One type of formal concept is the category concept which describes "stuff" and includes: (1) compositional concepts, and (2) functional concepts. The identity conditions for compositional stuff are different from those of functional stuff. Bealer illustrates this point by discussing a chemist who investigates water on Earth and knows it to be H_2O, and finds stuff on Twin Earth which is used exactly as water is used on Earth but is composed of the chemicals XYZ. Since it is composed of different chemicals, the stuff on Twin Earth is not water, even if used as such. Food, however, is a functional stuff, and, if one country only had food composed of mutton stew to eat and another country had a variety of cuisine such as fettucini, both would still be eating food though the composition of the food is different. The ability to use formal concepts appropriately is essential to the kind-identities science makes, but the answer to the question of how one knows how to use formal concepts appropriately is a matter of philosophical debate, and science presupposes solutions to this debate which are not themselves generated by the natural sciences.[117]

And four, science relies on axiological presuppositions which are not themselves generated by science. Scientists rely on certain moral values as necessary for conducting the practice of science, including accuracy in recording data, honesty in reporting results, acknowledgment of indebtedness to another's research, and an openness to refutation. Furthermore, there is the even larger question of whether or not the pursuit of science is a moral good. The justification of these presuppositions are matters for philosophy and theology, not science, though science may provide input necessary to constructing a philosophical argument.

Areas of Investigation Outside the Realm of Natural Science

The natural sciences are not the only disciplines which treat cognitive issues, for other academic disciplines exist which do not clearly interface with natural science and are outside of the domain of the natural sciences yet still are open to rational argumentation and assessment, and are, in principle, capable of yielding knowledge. These areas of investigation are too numerous to give an exhaustive list, but a few examples will be sufficient to make the point. First, professors of English Literature enter into debates which are irrelevant to natural science such as the question as to whether or not Shakespeare wrote all of the plays attributed to him or the meaning of a certain stanza in the poetry of Milton. Second, historians debate cognitive issues irrelevant to the natural sciences such as what factors caused the Civil War or the rise and fall of the Roman Empire. And third, economists make judgments which are largely irrelevant to the natural sciences about the most desirable economic courses of action which should be pursued. In each of these disciplines, rational arguments are offered, evidence is presented, and data is assessed, but the natural sciences need not (though may in some cases) have any bearing on the discussion.

Limits within Science Itself

Some issues arise which mark limits to science from within science itself.

First, scientific research is limited by what its methods and instruments are capable of finding. One can only discover what is discoverable by the technique one uses. Examples of this point are numerous and obvious and include: scales will reveal weight but not height, a telescope will only enable one to see as far as the power of the lens, sonar will only detect sound waves, and other examples far too many to mention.

Second, as Nicholas Rescher points out, an internal limitation derives from the very nature of scientific questions themselves.[118] In order for a question to be meaningful, certain presuppositions of the question must be assumed to make sense. For example, Rescher shows the question "What is the melting point of lead?" makes sense only if one assumes there is such a thing as a melting point, one knows what it is and how to recognize it, lead has a stable melting point, and so forth. The presuppositions constitute the formative background that make the question possible, and this background is dependent on and relative to the current conceptual framework of science. For example, if quantum theory is true, quantum levels existed in Newton's time, but Newton could not have asked questions about them. Thus, some questions are limits for science not because one understands the question and simply does not know the answer; rather, the problem is that one cannot even pose the question. These types of limits may be only temporary, but new limits are always present relative to a current scientific framework.

Third, a limit within science arises from another observation about questions which Rescher calls the "Kantian principle of question propagation;" that is, the answering of our factual questions always leads to further unanswered questions.[119] As various phenomena are explained, other phenomena are discovered which require explanation. The more we learn, the more we discover there is more to learn about any given body of knowledge.[120]

Fourth, limits may arise within the currently accepted theories themselves. For example, Heisenberg's principle of uncertainty states that the more accurately the position of an electron is determined, the less accurately its momentum can be determined and vice-versa. This limit comes from within the scientific theory itself and is unavoidable.[121]

And fifth, one branch of science can limit another. Chemists describe the relationships and processes of the chemicals in a given organism;

biologists may explain the existence of the group by appealing to biological concepts outside the range of chemistry, such as the evolution of the organism, its functional role, and how the organism relates to its ecosystem. This kind of limit will exist within science unless all fields of science are completely reducible to one (biology to chemistry to physics, for example).[122]

Conclusion

This chapter has refuted the claims of scientism and demonstrated the broader conception of scientific rationality now prevalent in the philosophy of science, thus removing one obstacle to viewing the relationship between theology and natural science as one of each of the disciplines as part of an ongoing dialogue of mutual modification which contributes to a coherent world view. However, another issue needs to be addressed, for many who reject scientism claim that natural science and theology are irrelevant to each other. Chapter Two will directly address the issue of the relevance of natural science to theology.

Notes

1.A discussion of these treatments can be found in a number of works. E. L. Mascall, *Christian Theology and Natural Science* (London: Longmans, Green & Co., 1956), pp. 1-16; A. R. Peacocke, *Creation and the World of Science* (Oxford: Clarendon Press, 1979), pp. 7-13; and Harold Nebelsick, *Theology and Science in Mutual Modification* (New York: Oxford University Press, 1981) are representative.
2.A good discussion of scientism can be found in Nicholas Rescher, *The Limits of Science* (New York: Harper & Row, 1984).
3.More sophisticated and nuanced positions than the two discussed here existed, but they were much less influential in shaping the understanding of the relation between theology and science.
4.The actual situation was of course more complicated than the popular view. For a discussion of the trial of Galileo and the error of viewing the trial as a clash between rational science and irrational religion see Diogenes Allen, *Christian Belief in a Postmodern World* (Louisville: Westminster/John Knox Press, 1989), pp. 27-34.
5.See Herbert Butterfield, *The Origins of Modern Science: 1300-1800* (New York: Macmillan, 1957), pp. 7-8, for a discussion of the significance of science's impact on the modern world.

6.The most well-known and most prolific defender of creation science is Henry Morris and his Institute for Creation Research. See his *Scientific Creationism*, 2d ed.(El Cajun, CA: Master Books, 1985) for the essentials of his position. Devastating critiques of the creation science position can be found in Phillip Kitcher, *Abusing Science: The Case Against Creationism* (Cambridge, Mass.: MIT Press, 1982) and Laurie Godfrey, ed., *Scientists Confront Creationism* (New York: W. W. Norton, 1983); and Howard J. Van Till, *The Fourth Day: What the Bible and the Heavens Are Telling Us About the Creation* (Grand Rapids: Eerdmans, 1986). A theological critique can be found in Roland M. Frye, ed., *Is God a Creationist? The Religious Case Against Creation-Science* (New York: Charles Scribner's Sons, 1983). It should be pointed out that the theory of evolution is a theory, not a proven fact, and that a number of criticisms and unanswered questions remain unsolved. See Holmes Rolston, *Science and Religion: A Critical Survey* (Temple University Press, 1987) for a good summary of this point; however, even if neo-Darwinism is vulnerable and may someday be replaced, the case for creation science is so weak that it will not be its successor.
7.John S. Habgood, "The Uneasy Truce between Science and Theology," in *Soundings*, ed. A. R. Vidler (Cambridge: Cambridge University Press, 1962), pp. 21-41.
8.This position is also known as scientific imperialism. See John Kekes, *The Nature of Philosophy* (Totowa, N.J.: Rowan and Littlefield, 1980). It has been said nobody actually espouses scientism, see the article "scientism" in *The Oxford Companion to Philosophy*, ed. Ted Honderich (Oxford: Oxford University Press, 1995), p. 814; however, one can find many examples of scientism in varying degrees, including this robust claim by Frank Tipler: "Either theology is pure nonsense, a subject with no content, or else theology must ultimately become a branch of physics." See *The Physics of Immortality* (New York: Doubleday, 1994), p. 3; pp. 328-339. Many more examples of scientism can be found in Tom Sorell, *Scientism: Philosophy and the Infatuation with Science* (London: Routledge, 1991).
9.Ian Barbour, *Religion in an Age of Science* (San Francisco: Harper & Row, 1990), pp. 4-5. I will limit my critique to scientism and will not directly take up the question of materialism.
10.One of the claims Sagan makes as if it is a scientific fact rather than philosophical claim is "The Cosmos is all that is or ever was or ever will be." *Cosmos* (New York: Random House, 1980), p. 4. Other defenders of scientism mentioned by Barbour are the biologist Jacques Monod and the sociobiologist Edward O. Wilson.
11.The most influential statement of positivism is A. J. Ayer's *Language, Truth, and Logic* (New York: Dover, 1946) and the essays collected in A. J. Ayer, ed., *Logical Positivism* (New York: Free Press, 1959).
12.An example of an analytic statement is "All bachelors are unmarried."The statement of the Verification Principle is from Ayer, *Language, Truth, and Logic*, pp. 35-40. There is more than one formulation of the Verification Principle since it was continuously revised, but Ayer's treatment is sufficient to get the gist of it.

13.One could spend the rest of one's days reading books about the decline of positivism, but the following treatments show the inadequacy of positivism as a philosophy of science: Frederick Suppe, *The Structure of Scientific Theories* (Urbana: University of Illinois Press, 1977); Harold I. Brown, *Perception, Theory, and Commitment* (Chicago: University of Chicago Press, 1977); and Dudley Shapere, "Meaning and Scientific Change," in *Scientific Revolutions*, ed. Ian Hacking (Oxford University Press, 1981), pp. 28-32.

14.A full discussion of this point can be found in Hilary Putnam, *Reason, Truth, and History* (Cambridge: Cambridge University Press, 1981), pp. 124-125.

15.A good discussion of this point can be found in Alvin Plantinga, *God and Other Minds* (Ithaca: Cornell University Press, 1967), pp. 156-168.

16.Discussions of this point with special reference to religious beliefs can be found in Diogenes Allen, *The Reasonableness of Faith* (Washington: Corpus Publications, 1968), chapters one and two; and the essays collected in *The Logic of God: Theology and Verification*, eds. Malcolm Diamond and Thomas Litzenburg, Jr. (Indianapolis: Bobbs-Merrill, 1975).

17.To attempt to treat all the different conceptions of scientific explanation would be an impossible task; however, a treatment of a few of the leading positions held by current philosophers of science should be enough to make the point against scientism.

18.Their position is explicated in "Studies in the Logic of Explanation," *Philosophy of Science*, Vol. 15 (1948), pp. 135-175.

19.In deductive arguments the truth of the conclusion is logically guaranteed by the premises (All men are mortal; Socrates is a man; Therefore, Socrates is mortal). Inductive arguments give strong, but not conclusive, grounds for believing the conclusion provided the premises are true (99% of all seminary students read the Bible regularly; Sue is a seminary student; Therefore, Sue reads the Bible regularly).

20.The original essay dealt only with deductive-nomological explanations, but Hempel came to see that it was inadequate to cover all types of scientific explanation. Hempel expanded on the earlier paper written with Oppenheim to include deductive-statistical and inductive-statistical explanations in *Aspects of Scientific Explanation* (New York: Free Press, 1965), pp. 376-386.

21.Hempel did not defend his position against this charge and conceded in a least one instance the inability of his model to explain certain events. See "Deductive-Nomological vs. Statistical Explanations," *Minnesota Studies in the Philosophy of Science*, Vol. III, (1962), pp. 109-110.

22.Michael Scriven, "Causation as Explanation," *Nous*, Vol. 9 (1975), pp. 3-10; "Explanation and Prediction in Evolutionary Theory," *Science*, Vol. 130, (1959), pp. 477-482; "Explanations, Predictions, and Laws, *Minnesota Studies in the Philosophy of Science*, Vol. III, eds. H. Feigl and G. Maxwell (University of Minnesota Press, 1962), pp. 170-230.

23.Israel Scheffler, *The Anatomy of Inquiry* (New York: Alfred A. Knopf, 1963), p. 63f.

24.For Scriven's position, see note 22. Salmon, who earlier held what he called the statistical-relevance model, modified it considerably to include causal factors when it was argued conclusively against his earlier position that mere indirect statistical correlations explain nothing. He explicates his current view in "Why Ask, 'Why?'?" An Inquiry Concerning Scientific Explanation," reprinted in *Scientific Knowledge: Basic Issues in the Philosophy of Science*, ed. Janet A. Kourany (Belmont, Ca.: Wadsworth, 1987, pp. 51-64.

25.Ibid., pp. 55-56.

26.An excellent summary of the difficulties in overcoming Hume's position is found in the article "Causation," in *The Encyclopedia of Philosophy*, vol. 1, ed. Paul Edwards (New York: Macmillan, 1967), pp. 56-66. Nelson Goodman has raised a new problem concerning causality which he calls the "new riddle of induction," found in *Fact, Fiction, and Forecast* (Cambridge: Harvard University Press, 1955). Hume raised the problem of how one can know that future cases we have not experienced will be like experiences we have had in the past; Goodman thinks this understates the problem. Even if we had an assurance that the future will resemble the past, this will not tell us *how* the future would resemble the past. The problem is the difficulty of knowing how precisely to move from the past to the future.

27.Bas van Fraassen points out a number of objections to Salmon's treatment from a number of sources, including the point that Salmon's account is limited to macroscopic phenomena and that quantum mechanics raises a serious challenge to Salmon's position. See Chapter 5 of *The Scientific Image* (Oxford University Press, 1980). Van Fraassen does view Salmon's conception as helpful for other scientific explanations, but at best it can only be considered as a subspecies of explanations in general.

28.Ibid., Chapter 5.

29.The use of this example and its application to van Fraassen is taken from Janet Kourany, *Scientific Knowledge: Basic Issues in the Philosophy of Science* (Belmont, Ca.: Wadsworth, 1987), pp. 24-25. A discussion of Mendel's work and its importance for the history of science can be found in C. C. Gillispie, *The Edge of Objectivity* (Princeton: Princeton University Press, 1960), pp. 328-337.

30.Clark Glymour, "Explanation and Realism," in *Scientific Realism*, ed. Jarrett Leplin (Berkeley: University of California Press, 1984), pp. 173-192.

31."Realism Versus Constructive Empiricism," in *Images of Science*, eds. Paul Churchland and Clifford Hooker (Chicago: University of Chicago Press, 1985), pp. 197-221. This volume contains a collection of essays written in response to van Fraassen's challenges to scientific realism.

32.An excellent treatment of the development of turning to the actual practices of scientists can be found in John Losee, *Philosophy of Science and Historical Enquiry* (Oxford: Clarendon press, 1987). John Passmore further develops the point that explanation cannot be reduced to formal considerations in "Explanation in Everyday Life, in Science, and in History," *History and Theory 2* (1962), pp. 105-123.

33.Carl Hempel used this model in his work, but it is Rudolf Carnap's account which currently attracts the most interest. Carnap's position is developed at length in his work *Philosophical Foundations of Physics* (New York: Basic Books, 1966), chapters 1-3 and 23-24.

34.Hempel, *Aspects of Scientific Explanation*, pp.14-20.

35.For a discussion of this point and the number of other problems that arose from justificationism in Carnap's and Hempel's positions, see Losee, *Philosophy of Science and Historical Enquiry*, pp. 16-19, 49-53 and 73-77.

36.Karl Popper, *Conjectures and Refutations* (New York: Basic Books, 1963), pp. 33-58; *The Logic of Scientific Discovery* (New York: Basic Books, 1959).

37.Lakatos's criticism of Popper and his exposition of his alternative can be found in "Falsification and the Methodology of Scientific Research Programmes," *Criticism and the Growth of Knowledge*, edited by Lakatos and Alan Musgrave (Cambridge: Cambridge University Press, 1970), pp. 91-195.

38.A notable example would be that in the nineteenth century Newtonian theory gave incorrect positions for the orbits of Mercury and Uranus. Instead of abandoning Newtonian theory Adams and Leverrier calculated (independently) what it would take to preserve the theory and this work led to the discovery of Neptune, which accounted for the irregularities.

39.Duhem's theory is presented in *The Aim and Structure of Physical Theory*, trans. Phillip P. Weiner (Princeton: Princeton University Press, 1982). See especially pages 144-147, 183-190, and 208-218.

40.It is interesting to note that Popper himself admitted that conventionalism was unassailable on logical grounds and that the way to overcome it was simply not to employ its methods, see *The Logic of Scientific Discovery*, pp. 78-82. Popper's work was instrumental in defeating positivism, but as Popper's own narrow view of what could constitute as genuine knowledge came to breakdown, conventionalism emerged as a viable option in the philosophy of science.

41.Duhem's position has been criticized on a number of different grounds than the one offered by Lakatos. One of the features of Duhem's approach is that the theoretical axiom system must be linked to experimentally determined magnitudes, and this linkage can be accomplished in some cases by the use of models. However, models are not part of the logical structure of the theory and can be dispensed with. Rom Harre has argued that models are an indispensable part of scientific theories, and his position has claimed wide support. See Rom Harre, *The Principles of Scientific Thinking* (London: Macmillan, 1970). Mary Hesse has argued a similar view in *Models and Analogies in Science* (South Bend: University of Notre Dame Press, 1966).

42.See Larry Laudan, *Progress and Its Problems* (Berkeley: University of California Press, 1977), p.. 163; Paul Feyerabend, "Consolations for the Specialist,' in *Criticism and the Growth of Knowledge*, pp. 215-223; and Clark Glymour, *Theory and Evidence* (Princeton: Princeton University Press, 1980), pp. 98-99.

43.Ernan McMullin, "The History and Philosophy of Science: A Taxonomy," in *Minnesota Studies in the Philosophy of Science*, vol. 5, ed. Roger Stuewer (Minneapolis: University of Minnesota Press, 1970), pp. 12-67.

44.W. H. Newton-Smith, *The Rationality of Science* (London: Routledge and Kegan Paul, 1981), ch. 4, especially page 92.

45.See Feyerabend's *Against Method* (London: Verso, 1983) for a discussion of this point.

46.Thomas Kuhn, "Objectivity, Value Judgment, and Theory Choice," in *The Essential Tension: Selected Studies in Scientific Tradition and Change* (Chicago: University of Chicago Press, 1977), pp. 320-339.

47.This part of the discussion of Kuhn's work is based on his *The Structure of Scientific Revolutions*, second edition (Chicago: University of Chicago Press, 1970), especially pages 92-110. The first edition of Kuhn's book came out in 1962, and in the second edition Kuhn made an explicit effort to clear up the ambiguities critics found in the first edition and to respond to their objections.

48.Ibid., first edition, pp. 35-42. More about Kuhn's understanding of a paradigm is to come.

49.Ibid., second edition, pp. 152-155.

50.Ibid., p.157.

51.Dudley Shapere, "The Structure of Revolutions," *Philosophical Review*, Vol. 73 (1964), pp. 383-394; and Margaret Masterman, "The Nature of a Paradigm," in *Criticism and the Growth of Knowledge*, pp. 61-65; point out the ambiguity in Kuhn's treatment of paradigm.

52.*Structure of Scientific Revolutions*, first edition, p. 175.

53.Ibid., p. 43.

54.See pages 174-210.

55.Ibid., pp. 180-181.

56.See Donald Davidson, *Inquiries into Truth and Interpretation* (Oxford: Clarendon Press, 1984), p. 185. Davidson's point is that if we could not interpret a conceptual scheme, we would have no basis for calling it a conceptual scheme, and he uses a humorous example of communicating with Martians to illustrate his point. Davidson's argument is similar to the refutation of Protagoras Plato makes in the *Theaetetus*, see Edward N. Lee, "Hoist on His Own Petard," in *Exegesis and Argument; Studies in Greek Philosophy Presented to Gregory Vlastos*, ed. E. N. Lee, A.P.D. Mourelatos, and R.M. Rorty (Assen: Van Gorcum, 1973, pp. 225-261, for a lively discussion of these arguments.

57.*Structure of Scientific Revolutions*, p. 47; "Reflections on My Critics, " pp. 267-268; and Alan Musgrave, "Kuhn's Second Thoughts," in *Paradigms and Revolutions*, ed. Gary Gutting (Notre Dame: University of Notre Dame Press, 1980), pp. 39-53.

58.Kuhn, *Essential Tension*, p. 338; and "Reflections on My Critics," p. 266.

59.*Structure of Scientific Revolutions*, p. 125; also see 111-112, 121-129, 150.

60.A number of problems remain with Kuhn's notion of incommensurability and are discussed in Michael Devitt, *Realism and Truth*, second ed. (Oxford: Blackwell, 1991), pp. 168-172; and W. H. Newton-Smith, *The Rationality of*

Science, pp. 148-182. Newton-Smith argues that Kuhn's views are unable to explain the success of science, and he argues that realism and a return to the categories of "true" and "false' when applied to scientific theories is needed to correct Kuhn's (and other anti-realist's) deficiencies. Newton-Smith's point appears valid, especially in light of Kuhn's desire to posit "something out there" which is independent of one's paradigms and can jointly determine our world even if there is no unmediated access to this "something."

61. A more recent statement of Kuhn's views can be found in Thomas Kuhn, "Theory-Change as Structure-Change," *Erkenntnis*, 10 July 1976), pp. 179-199. Kuhn continues to distance himself from relativism in this article, and attempts to give a notion of justification that is "nonparadigmatic," that is, not simply a creature of the local epistemology and standards of the time. In this article it seems Kuhn is saying that though we cannot interpret the term "phlogiston" in the language used by present-day scientists, and that the meaning and reference of the term "electron' were very different in 1900 and in 1934 after Bohr, the meaning of reasonableness and justification can be equated, or at least partially equated, across changes in our paradigms of justification even when as great as those which occurred between the tenth century and the time of Newton. Thus, incommensurability has come to mean for Kuhn intertheoretic meaning change rather than uninterpretability.

62. A discussion of the growing acknowledgment of the place of values in science can be found in Ernan McMullin, "Values in Science," Presidential Address to the Philosophy of Science Association, *Proceedings of the Philosophy of Science Association*, 2 (1982), pp. 1-25. McMullin is also a defender of the view that adopting some limited form of scientific realism can overcome the difficulties in Kuhn's position, and this does seem to be a step in the right direction.

63. Larry Laudan, *Progress and Its Problems*, pp. 155-170.

64. Laudan develops this model in *Science and Values* (Berkeley: University of California Press, 1984), especially pp. 23-66. The reticulational model represents a modification in Laudan's position from this earlier work, for he came to acknowledge the criticisms of his earlier work by Ronald Giere and others that Laudan's position does not provide a norm for scientific judgments but rather merely provides descriptions of situations which we now intuitively regard as rational acceptance. See Ronald Giere, "Testing Theoretical Hypotheses," in *Minnesota Studies in the Philosophy of Science*, Vol. X (Minneapolis: University of Minnesota Press, 1983), ed. by John Earman, pp. 269-298. In his new model, Laudan has changed the emphasis of his earlier position on an inviolable procedure for assessing rational reconstructions of scientific progress to a descriptive generalization about the way conflicts have been adjudicated within science.

65. *Science and Values*, p. 105.

66. *Science and Values*, p. 57. Laudan lists a number of examples of conflict between the aims of science and the types of theories particular scientists were constructing, focusing on the tension between the goals of Newton's "Experimental Philosophy" and theories which postulated hypothetical entities,

such as Franklin's one-fluid theory of electricity and Lesage's theory of gravitational corpuscles.

67.Ibid., p. 63.

68.For Laudan's criticism of epistemic realism, see *Science and Values*, pp. 105-106, 113-123.

69.C. A. Hooker, *A Realistic Theory of Science* (Albany: SUNY Press, 1987), pp. 178-179, 395. I am unsure of how to use inclusive language for the "straw man" fallacy. Perhaps renaming it the "scarecrow" fallacy would fit the bill?

70.W. H. Newton-Smith, *The Rationality of Science*, pp. 185-198, 245.

71.Stephen Wykstra has defended the justificatory hierarchy against Laudan's Reticulational Model in his Pittsburgh Ph. D. dissertation: *The Interdependence of History of Science and Philosophy of Science: Toward a Meta-theory of Scientific Rationality* (Ph. D. dissertation, University of Pittsburgh, 1978), pp. 126-145. Wykstra argues that "height" and"achievability" can serve as a constraint on scientific aims at the axiological level and thus rationally mediate disagreements about the aims of science.

72.Ronald Giere, "Testing Theoretical Hypotheses," in *Minnesota Studies in the Philosophy of Science*, Vol. X, ed. John Earman (Minneapolis: University of Minnesota Press, 1983), pp. 269-298.

73.He develops this position at length in "The Epistemological Roots of Scientific Knowledge," *Minnesota Studies in the Philosophy of Science*, Vol. VI, ed. G. Maxwell and R. M. Anderson (Minneapolis: University of Minnesota Press, 1975), pp. 212-261.

74.One approach to theory validation which I have not included in this discussion is Bayesianism, which attempts to spell out scientific confirmation by using Bayes' Theorem, named after its discoverer Thomas Bayes (1702-1761). There are many varieties of Bayesianism, but they share the view that a theory has an initial plausibility, and the probability that it is true increases or decreases with the additional evidence. The practical limitation of length requires that not all current positions in the philosophy of science can be included, and Bayesianism is not as widely accepted as other approaches discussed above. In addition, Bayesianism, like the other positions discussed here, includes subjective features regarding human participation in science which broaden the conception of scientific rationality and therefore pose no threat to my argument against scientism. A discussion of the varieties of Bayesianism and its subjective features can be found in John Passmore, *Recent Philosophers* (La Salle: Open Court, 1985), pp. 108-109, 161; and on pp. 21-22 of Richard Boyd's essay "Confirmation, Semantics, and the Interpretation of Scientific Theories" in *The Philosophy of Science*, edited by R. Boyd, Philip Gasper, and J. D. Trout (Cambridge, Mass.: MIT Press, 1991), pp. 3-22. Criticisms of Bayesianism which show why this approach is not more widely accepted in the philosophy of science can be found in Clark Glymour, *Theory and Evidence* (Princeton: Princeton University Press, 1980); R. Miller, *Fact and Method* (Princeton: Princeton University Press, 1987); and J. Pollock, *Contemporary Theories of Knowledge* (Totowa, N.J.: Rowman and Littlefield, 1986).

75.In the philosophy of science, as with any discipline, there are any number of dissenters from each of the emerging mainstream opinions discussed above; however, the various forms of resistance to the general agreements in the contemporary philosophy of science have not yet been able to make a persuasive case to justify abandoning the mainstream views.

76.The best treatment of creativity in scientific discovery remains Michael Polanyi's *Personal Knowledge: Towards a Post-Critical Philosophy* (Chicago: University of Chicago Press, 1962). Treatments of how creative acts operate in both science and literature can be found in Arthur Koestler, *The Act of Creation* (New York: Macmillan, 1964); and Brewster Ghiselin, ed., The *Creative Process* (Berkeley: University of California Press, 1952). Garrett Green's *Imagining God: Theology and the Religious Imagination* (San Francisco: Harper & Row, 1989) discusses how imagination functions in science and theology. These works refute scientism's claim for a unique rationality in the natural sciences by showing the key role creative acts of imagination play in a variety of disciplines.

77.John Losee's *Philosophy of Science and Historical Enquiry* provides a thorough discussion of this point.

78.Paul Feyerabend has gone so far as to say that scientists should go about their work and study the history of science, but the philosophy of science should be ignored for it is irrelevant to their concerns. See "Philosophy of Science: A Subject with a Great Past," *Historical and Philosophical Perspectives on Science*, ed. R. Stuewer (Minneapolis: University of Minnesota Press, 1970), pp. 172-183. The irony of Feyerabend's title is that the philosophy of science has a great past because it has no future. Feyerabend is no doubt right to point out the excessive logicism that once characterized the discipline, and he is pointing to important factors that must be considered by philosophers of science, but, as usual, he goes too far in his claims. A good discussion of the strengths and weaknesses of Feyerabend's work can be found in W. H. Newton-Smith's *The Rationality of Science*, pp. 125-147.

79.I am not suggesting that the sciences cannot improve our understanding of history (or other disciplines) for I think in many cases they can; my point is that if scientism is correct that science alone sets the clear standard for rationality, then our understanding of scientific rationality should not be improved by a use of other disciplines.

80.The incompatibility of naive realism and modern physics is succinctly discussed by Ian Barbour in *Issues in Science and Religion* (Englewood Cliffs: Prentice-Hall, 1966), pp. 284-286.

81.See M. Mulkay, *Science and the Sociology of Knowledge* (London: Allen and Unwin, 1979), pp. 59-60.

82.See David Bloor, *Knowledge and Social Imagery* (London: Routledge and Kegan Paul), 1976), pp. 4-5; and Mulkay, Ibid., pp. 60-62.

83.Ernan McMullin has argued against the strong program that even though science is a social product, there is a crucial difference between it and other social products, namely, that the social and personal influences on theory that are occasionally distortive are limited by the progressive use of the complex methods of testing characteristic of science. Distortions are gradually uncovered and progressively eliminated, and McMullin thus argues that the sociology of knowledge has not weakened the cognitive privilege of science on matters concerning the natural world. See E. McMullin, *The Sciences and Theology in the Twentieth Century*, ed. Arthur Peacocke (University of Notre Dame Press, 1981), pp. 301-302. It is important to note that though McMullin speaks of science's "cognitive privilege," he does not claim science is a unique source of truth or that its theories are culture neutral. Furthermore, it is clear that the sociology of knowledge does not imply that scientific knowledge is merely a social product, for it is not true that *any* theory may be proposed and accepted regardless of the input of the natural world. See Diogenes Allen, *Christian Belief in a Postmodern World*, pp. 132-133.

84.*Scientific Realism*, ed. Jarrett Leplin (Berkeley: University of California Press, 1984), p. 1.

85.One of the leading defenders of critical realism is Hilary Putnam. Putnam has argued that realism is the only theory that can explain the regularities of observed phenomena, the usefulness of scientific theories, and the ongoing success of mature scientific fields. Other positions make the success of science a "miracle." See Hilary Putnam, "What is Scientific Realism," in *Scientific Realism*, pp. 140-153. This argument of Putnam's dominates the literature and is widely quoted and endorsed by realists and argued against by anti-realists. Putnam's own version of critical realism (called convergent realism) has been challenged by Willard Sellars, who argues attention should be paid more to the entities postulated in theories rather than the theories *per se*. See Willard Sellars, *Science, Perception, and Reality* (New York: Humanities Press, 1962). W. H. Newton-Smith's *The Rationality of Science*, pp.164-172, also raises objections to the details of Putnam's position and offers yet another version of critical realism.

86.Found in *Scientific Realism*, ed. Jarrett Leplin, p. 26. The full essay "A Case for Scientific Realism" is found on pages 8-40.

87.Some philosophers of science argue that metaphors and models are dispensable within science and would thus object to McMullin's reliance upon them; however, the majority of philosophers of science find metaphor and model essential to the pursuit of science. For a defense of models and metaphors, see Rom Harre, *The Principles of Scientific Thinking* (London: Macmillan, 1970); Mary Hesse, *Models and Analogies in Science* (Notre Dame, Ind.: University of Notre Dame Press, 1966); and Janet Martin Soskice, *Metaphor and Religious Language* (Oxford: Clarendon Press, 1985). Still others have objected that models and metaphors cannot be reality depicting; Soskice and Harre argue against this claim.

88.See his *The Rationality of Science* cited above.

89.Two theologians who have argued for the compatibility of this version of scientific realism and Christian theology are John Polkinghorne, *One World: The Interaction of Science and Theology* (Princeton: Princeton University Press, 1986); and Michael Banner, *The Justification of Science and the Rationality of Religious Belief* (Oxford: Clarendon Press, 1990).

90.Discussions of these points can be found in Larry Laudan, *Science and Values*, pp. 117-124, and *Progress and Its Problems*, pp. 123-127; and R. Harre, *Varieties of Realism* (Oxford: Basil Blackwell, 1986), pp. 35-51.

91.See the discussions of Laudan and Kuhn in the section on the confirmation of scientific theories.

92.Operationalism, one of the early and influential varieties of anti-realism developed by P. W. Bridgman, has been omitted from the discussion since its influence has waned due to its excessive empiricism and problems with its reduction of scientific terms to purely performable physical operations (for example, the length of an object is not a property of an object but simply the procedure by which the object is measured). For Bridgman's views see *The Nature of Physical Theory* (Princeton: Princeton University Press 1936); *The Logic of Modern Physics* (New York: Macmillan, 1927). Excellent critiques can be found in Carl Hempel, *Philosophy of Natural Science*, pp. 88- 100; and G. Schlesinger, "Operationalism," *The Encyclopedia of Philosophy*, vol. 5, ed. Paul Edwards (New York: Macmillan and Free Press, 1967), pp. 543-547.

93.Bas van Fraassen, *The Scientific Image* (Oxford: Oxford University Press, 1980); "To Save the Phenomena," in *Scientific Realism*, ed. Jarrett Leplin (Berkeley: University of California Press, 1984), pp. 250-259; Paul M. Churchland and Clifford Hooker, eds., *Images of Science: Essays on Realism and Empiricism, with a Reply from Bas C. van Fraassen* (Chicago: University of Chicago Press, 1985). Van Fraassen's reply to his critics is found on pp. 245-305. The discussion of van Fraassen's position which follows is taken largely from Chapter 2 of *The Scientific Image*.

94.*The Scientific Image*, p. 40.

95.*The Scientific Image*, pp. 23-34.

96.*The Scientific Image*, especially pp. 119-134.

97.See *Images of Science*, eds. Paul Churchland and Clifford Hooker for a complete discussion of van Fraassen's work and his reply to his critics.

98."And Not Anti-Realism Either," *Nous*, Vol. 18 (1984), pp. 51-65; "The Natural Ontological Attitude," in *Scientific Realism*, ed. Jarrett Leplin, pp. 83-107. Fine denies he is an anti-realist, but he is by the definition used in this discussion: an anti-realist is one who rejects realism.

99.Ernan McMullin, "A Case for Scientific Realism," in *Scientific Realism*, ed. Jarret Leplin, pp. 25-26, 37, 39.

100.Gardner's position is developed in "Realism and Instrumentalism in Pre-Newtonian Astronomy," in *Minnesota Studies in the Philosophy of Science*, Vol. X, ed. John Earman (Minneapolis: University of Minnesota Press, 1983), pp. 201-265.

101.Ibid., pp. 237ff.

102.Ian Hacking, "Experimentation and Scientific Realism," in *Scientific Realism*, ed. Jarrett Leplin, pp. 154-172. This essay has been printed in a number of anthologies, and it originally appeared in *Philosophical Topics*, Vol. 13, No. 1, (1983), pp. 71-87.

103. Ian Hacking, *Representing and Intervening* (New York: Cambridge University Press, 1983), p. 191. Hacking appears correct to me on this point, for I have found engineers much more likely to be convinced of the truth of science and susceptible to scientism than theoretical scientists, and, while the move toward realism may be correct on their part, their embracement of scientism is not.

104. For example, Stephen Wykstra has developed an argument which shows that Hacking's work actually suggests a parallel for a theory of religious rationality in that in both science and religion experiment breeds conviction. In the religious life, it is by acting on claims about God that one tests the norms for identifying God's disclosures and comes to deep conviction about the beliefs they sanction. See Stephen Wykstra, "Reasons, Redemption, and Realism: The Axiological Roots of Rationality in Science and Religion," *Christian Theism and the Problems of Philosophy*, ed. Michael Beaty (Notre Dame: University of Notre Dame Press, 1990), pp. 119-161.

105. For a fuller treatment of scientism's self-refutation, see J.P. Moreland, *Christianity and the Nature of Science*, pp. 106-108.

106. Discussions of the differences between doing science and doing philosophical thinking about science can be found in John Losee, *A Historical Introduction to the Philosophy of Science*, pp. 1-4; Ernan McMullin, "Alternative Approaches to the Philosophy of Science," in *Scientific Knowledge*, ed. Janet Kourany (Belmont, California: Wadsworth, 1987), pp. 3-19.

107. The best defense of the claim that philosophy can be reduced to the natural sciences has been made by W. V. O. Quine in his discussion of "Epistemology Naturalized" found in *Ontological Relativity and Other Essays* (New York: Columbia University Press, 1969), pp. 69-90. According to Quine, a naturalized epistemology attempts to ground or justify beliefs within the framework of science and does not try to justify the framework as a whole, and he argues that epistemology is simply a chapter of psychology and hence of natural science. What this means is that epistemology uses the resources of science to explain how it is we know what we know and does not first try to justify science before using it to justify other claims. Philosophy, like science, is a descriptive, not prescriptive discipline. It is important to note that Quine uses a *philosophical*, not a scientific, argument to defend science's self-justification, thus contradicting the claims of scientism (and perhaps his own position). Furthermore, Quine's position is considered too extreme even by other philosophers who defend naturalized epistemology, and a number of serious objections to his version of naturalized epistemology have been raised. One of the best responses to Quine has been made by Jaegwon Kim's essay, "What is 'Naturalized Epistemology'?," in *Contemporary Readings in Epistemology*, eds. Michael Goodman and Robert Snyder (Englewood Cliffs, N.J.: Prentice-Hall, 1993), pp. 323-337. Kim argues that Quine's position fails for it does not adequately deal with the question of normativity, which, despite Quine's claims, is unavoidable. Kim points out that psychology is a descriptive discipline that can tell us how we form beliefs, but epistemology is concerned with justification and is a normative endeavor that focuses on how we *ought* to form our beliefs. Psychology, as a descriptive discipline, cannot

ultimately answer questions about which, if any, of our beliefs are more justified than another. Furthermore, Kim argues that normative considerations cannot be purged from psychology or epistemology, for in order to attribute beliefs to people, we must evaluate how beliefs relate to one another and to the evidence that supports their being beliefs of a particular sort. Other objections to various aspects of Quine's thought can be found in Hilary Kornblith, ed., *Naturalizing Epistemology* (Cambridge, Mass.: MIT Press, 1985). Kim and others in the book edited by Kornblith continue to defend naturalized epistemology, but not in the form advocated by Quine. The "psychological turn" in epistemology which highlights the causal relations between beliefs and the evidence which explains why beliefs are justified is at the center of current epistemological debates, and there is an increasing number of philosophers who argue that beliefs are justified insofar as they are produced by reliable belief-forming mechanisms. These philosophers, unlike Quine, do not attempt to get rid of normative considerations or reduce them to natural properties; rather, they are attempting to set up naturalistic criteria that allow us to explain why some beliefs are justified and others are not.

108.Other classifications of the limits of science can be found in Nicholas Rescher, *The Limits of Science* (Berkley: University of California Press, 1984); Peter Medawar, *The Limits of Science* (New York: Harper & Row, 1984); John Kekes, *The Nature of Philosophy* (Totowa, N.J.: Rowman and Littlefield, 1980), pp. 147-163; Del Ratzsch, *Philosophy of Science: The Natural Sciences in Christian Perspective* (Downers Grove, Ill.: Inter-Varsity, 1986, pp. 97-105; and J. P. Moreland, *Christianity and the Nature of Science* (Grand Rapids, Michigan: Baker Book House, 1989), pp. 103-138.

109.Kekes, *Nature of Philosophy*, pp. 156-157. Kekes' classification needs to be corrected in that he does not point out the interrelation of the various presuppositions. For example, some existential presuppositions are intertwined with methodological presuppositions, and classificatory presuppositions such as causation are directly related to questions about the uniformity of the world which is an existential presupposition.

110.See Newton-Smith, *Rationality of Science*, p. 270; Kuhn, *Essential Tension*, p.336; and McMullin, "Values in Science," pp. 20-21.

111.See Nicholas Rescher, *Limits of Science*, pp. 174-218, for a discussion of this point.

112.Van Till, *The Fourth Day*, pp. 98-104.

113.For more on the philosophical issues involved on this point, see Diogenes Allen, *Christian Belief in a Postmodern World*, pp. 64-84; and Del Ratzsch, *Philosophy of Science*, pp. 99-101.

114.See the discussion of Hume and Goodman in the section on the causal account of scientific explanation.

115.J. P. Moreland, *Christianity and the Nature of Science* (Grand Rapids: Baker, 1989), pp. 11-126.

116.George Bealer, "The Philosophical Limits of Scientific Essentialism," in *Philosophical Perspectives, Vol. 1: Metaphysics, 1987*, ed. James E. Tomberlin (Atascadero, Calif.: Ridgeview, 1987), pp. 289-365.

117.Bealer also uses the example of defining life to illustrate his point. If one found living beings on Twin Earth which had a radically different composition than living beings on Earth, one would still count them as alive. The decision to count them as alive would involve the philosophical decision to define life functionally rather than compositionally.

118.Nicholas Rescher, *Limits of Science*, pp. 18-27.

119.Rescher, *Limits of Science*, pp. 27-34.

120.A successful response to this claim would have to make the case that eventually human beings will be able to exhaust all the knowledge to be found within the world and nothing new will be discovered.

121.It must be granted that this limitation may be only a temporary one, for if Heisenberg's theory is ever abandoned this limitation may be capable of being resolved by another theory. For a discussion of differing interpretations of Heisenberg's theory, see Ian Barbour, *Religion in an Age of Science*, pp. 101-104.

122.Paul Oppenheim and Hilary Putnam have argued that higher level explanations in science can be reduced to those on a lower level. See "Unity of Science as a Working Hypothesis," in *Concepts, Theories, and the Mind-body Problem*, edited by Herbert Feigl, Michael Scriven, and Grover Maxwell *Minnesota Studies in the Philosophy of Science, Vol. II* (University of Minnesota Press, 1958), pp. 3-36. Against this position, Patrick Suppes has shown the difficulties present in a reduction of the theories of the different sciences to the theories dealing with elementary particles and has argued it is not possible because: (1) despite all the research that has gone into the question, we still do not know what these theories and their postulated elementary particles are; (2) nor is there reason to believe that we will one day find them out, given the continual revision of our views regarding them and the continual increase of complexity of high-energy physics and elementary particle theory; (3) nor is there reason to believe that the theories of one branch of science will one day be better able to explain the observational data explained by the theories of other branches of science, given that the experimental languages of the different branches of science – the languages in which such observational data are expressed – are diverging rather than converging; and (4) the case for scientific unity through reductionism is based on a belief in a completeness which is really not possible. See Patrick Suppes, "The Plurality of Science," in *Scientific Knowledge*, ed. Janet Kourany, pp. 317-325.

Chapter 2

The Relevance of Natural Science to Theology

Introduction

The question of the relationship between two disciplines can be answered in a number of different ways, and theologians have given a variety of answers to the question of the relevance of natural science to theology. Solutions to the problem have described the disciplines as irrelevant to one another, directly relevant to one another, indirectly relevant to one another, or perhaps relevant to one another in some combination of these answers at different levels.

This chapter will: (1) give a brief sketch of the main ways that science has been thought to be relevant to theology, (2) argue the claim science is completely irrelevant to theology has failed to make its case, and (3) argue theologians have good reasons for viewing science as relevant to theology.

The Ways of Relevance Between Science and Theology

W. H. Austin has provided a helpful sketch of the main ways science has at various times been thought to be relevant to theology. Austin schematizes how science may be thought to be relevant to theology as follows: directly, quasi-directly, or in any of three indirect ways.

Direct relevance occurs when

a set S of scientific statements bears directly on theological doctrine d if d or its negation can be inferred from S.[1]

Scientific statements may either support or contradict theological doctrines. Examples of direct relevance include theologians who reject the theory of evolution for it contradicts a literal reading of Genesis 1-3 and those who claim that the Big Bang theory of the origin of the universe supports the Christian doctrine of creation.

Quasi-direct relevance describes a situation in which theologians and scientists offer alternative and competing explanations of the same data.[2] Austin uses the differing explanations of the phenomena of organic adaptiveness offered by Darwin and Paley as an example of quasi-direct relevance.[3]

The three indirect ways science might be relevant to theology are: (1) metaphysical relevance, (2) methodological relevance, and (3) heuristic relevance. Each of these will be examined in turn.

Metaphysics is defined as "a discipline which attempts to provide a conceptual scheme in terms of which the leading results of every special discipline can be expressed..."[4]and therefore raises the possibility of the relevance of science to theology. Theologians often use metaphysical schemes to aid in systematizing their doctrines, and science may influence theology indirectly by affecting the theologian's choice of possible metaphysical systems. Process theologians serve as an example of this approach, for they recast theological propositions in terms of Whitehead's metaphysics in part because they believe this conceptual scheme fits well with contemporary science.[5]

Theologians also adopt a specific methodology to systematize their work or to impose a formal structure on the doctrinal materials with which they work. If the theologian conceives of his methodology as analogous with the methods of natural science, or if he or she orders doctrinal materials in accordance with a formal or axiomatic structure like that of a science, then we have another form of the indirect relevance of science to theology.[6]

Austin's third form of indirect relevance is heuristic relevance. Heuristic relevance means that science is capable of suggesting fruitful analogies for theology. An example of this is the methodological parallelism mentioned above, but there could be a number of other ways the methods or the contents of natural science may offer useful suggestions for theological reflection.[7]

Austin's discussion of the possible ways science might be relevant to theology provides a good general scheme for determining the issues involved in relating theology and natural science; however, it is futile to attempt to integrate theology and science if the argument that the two disciplines are irrelevant to one another is successful. The next section will address the claim that science is irrelevant to theology because the two disciplines should be understood as totally independent of one another.

The Irrelevance of Natural Science to Theology

Theologians who argue that science is irrelevant to theology do so because they understand the two disciplines to be totally independent and autonomous of one another. Science and theology are understood to be non-interacting, noncompeting, approaches to reality. Each discipline has its own separate domain which must be investigated by asking its own questions using its own methods. Neither discipline has any bearing on the work of the other.

If theology and natural science are indeed related to one another as has been described above, then there is little, if any, reason for theologians to concern themselves with science; however, though the case for irrelevance has been argued in a variety of forms, each of these ultimately fails.

The case against the irrelevance of natural science to theology has been argued successfully, and many of the approaches which attempt to insulate the two disciplines from one another have been refuted by W. H. Austin. Austin takes issue those theologians and philosophers who "have tried to show that natural science is in principle irrelevant to their enterprise,"[8] and he proceeds to show that arguments for the irrelevance of natural science to theology fail on logical grounds. Austin's case against the irrelevance of natural science is theology is forcefully made, but his work has not received the attention it deserves in current discussions of the relationship between theology and natural science, and, unfortunately, his work is now out of print. What follows will present Austin's case in extensive detail in order to show the success of his argument and its ongoing relevance for current debates. I will supplement Austin's arguments with those of my own in the discussion, and I will point out my divergences from Austin in those particular cases.

In order for the case for irrelevance to be made, defenders of this position must be able to show that irrelevance holds for each of the possible ways of relating science to theology. One who holds that science is not directly relevant to theology must show that in cases where a claim for direct relevance is made either the theological doctrine in question is not a genuine theological statement or that it is not legitimately inferable from a scientific statement.[9] Opposition to quasi-direct relevance must show that science is not in the business of offering explanations, or that theology is not, or that they ask and answer radically different kinds of questions.[10] The case against metaphysical relevance must deny the way Austin has defined metaphysics or deny that a theologian should ever formulate his or her community's doctrines in terms of a particular metaphysical scheme.[11] In order to defeat methodological relevance and heuristic relevance, the case must be made that the theologian could never draw useful suggestions from the methods or contents of the natural sciences.[12]

There are two major classes of arguments which attempt to demonstrate the irrelevance position: (1) instrumentalist arguments, which deny that the function of either scientific or theological assertions is to make claims about what is the case, and (2) two-realms arguments, which claim scientific and religious assertions are so different that they can neither support each other nor conflict with each other.[13]

Instrumentalist Arguments

Scientific Instrumentalism

Scientific instrumentalism, which holds that scientific statements are merely devices for the classification and prediction of phenomena, is the first position examined by Austin. Austin initially focuses on Pierre Duhem, a physicist regarded by many as the finest champion of instrumentalism, and then turns his attention to other versions of an instrumentalist interpretation of science.

Duhem's version of the argument fails to demonstrate the irrelevance of science to theology, according to Austin, for two significant reasons: (1) Duhem's position allows statements from all scientific disciplines to bear directly or indirectly on theology except those of theoretical physics,[14] and (2) Duhem's position makes important concessions to realism which allow the statements of theoretical physics to bear on theology indirectly by way of metaphysics.[15] Furthermore, more drastic versions of instrumentalism, which do not make Duhem's concessions to realism, are unable to rule out that scientific statements have at least some indirect bearing on theology.[16] Thus, scientific instrumentalism is unable to establish that science is in principle irrelevant to theology.[17]

Religious Instrumentalism

Instrumentalist accounts of religious doctrines deny that theological assertions refer to a God who exists beyond the world, and the two leading instrumentalist theories of religion hold that religious myths and stories serve one of two functions: (1) as aids which commend the values a religion holds by capturing the imagination and strengthening the will, or (2) as aids to evoke mystical experiences, which on this view, are intrinsically valuable and the main object of the religious quest.[18] Since religious doctrines do not refer to anything which is actually the case, but express, poetically, the ideal of life a religion holds, they cannot conflict with or be supported by scientific statements. Austin associates the view that religions are essentially policies of action with R. B. Braithwaite; the view that religious beliefs are primarily for evoking mystical experiences is the position of W. T. Stace.

Braithwaite holds that the stories of a religion are entertained, not held or asserted as true, in order to help the followers of a religion to behave in a certain way, that is, they serve as psychological aids to strengthen one's resolve to pursue the values commended by the religion.[19] Austin criticizes Braithwaite's view on a number of counts, including the charges that it provides an inadequate account of religious life and is internally inconsistent; however, the most important claim made by Austin is that Braithwaite's view allows an indirect bearing of science on theology, for science could have a role in shaping and selecting the stories used to strengthen the resolve to follow the course of action endorsed by the religion. Furthermore, there is no reason why theologians could not take suggestions from science in developing new stories.[20] Thus, while Braithwaite's position can rule out metaphysical relevance, it cannot insulate religion from all influence by science.

W. T. Stace's version of instrumenatlism argues that the purpose of religious doctrines is to evoke mystical experiences. Science belongs to the natural order and theological statements belong to the eternal order, and serious errors occur whenever one takes a theological statement to tell us something about the natural order.[21] However, even if this account of theological statements is correct, there still remains an important way in which science may have direct bearing on theology, namely, the branch of theology which describes how mystical experiences are to be achieved. For if it is the purpose of religious doctrines to produce certain states of consciousness, then any science which deals with such states (such as physiology) will be relevant to the achievement of such states.[22] At this point Stace does have recourse to some version of the two realms approach, and it is to this way of understanding the relation of science to theology that we now turn.

Stace's mystical account of religion is one form of a more general view that reality consists of two orders or two realms, one of which concerns science and the other which concerns theology. Religion and science belong to entirely different orders, and any interaction between the two is entirely out of the question.[23] In Stace's case, science concerns itself exclusively with the natural order; theology concerns itself exclusively with the eternal order. Any attempt to understand the eternal in terms of the natural or the natural in terms of the eternal is doomed to fail for it marks a confusion of the orders, and each order has its own wholly adequate explanations. It is the mystic in the moment of enlightenment who recognizes the two orders, for, when in the moment of mystical illumination, he or she is in both orders at once as the eternal is experienced in the temporal moment as an actual fact.   Mystical illumination is the *intersection* of the two orders and enables the mystic to know the truth of the eternal beyond the natural.

It is precisely this notion of "intersection" which Austin shows to be the cause of Stace's view being logically incoherent, for: (1) it cannot be reconciled with the view that each order is comprehensive and leaves nothing out, (2) it violates Stace's claim that in the moment of mystical illumination there is no awareness of the natural order, and (3) it leaves ambiguities that would make the mystic unable to interpret his or her experience in any adequate way.[24] Stace's inability to give a coherent account of how the two orders intersect leaves his case for the irrelevance of science to theology a failing effort; however, the possibility of other types of two-realms positions remains open.

Two Realms Arguments

There are a number of possibilities for developing a two-realms approach, but, as Austin points out, all of these suffer from an inability to find a satisfactory definition of the realms which would make a demonstration of their mutual exclusiveness possible.[25] There are two types of two-realms arguments based upon: (1) ontological dualism, or (2) conceptual dualism. Furthermore, there is a special category of conceptual dualism based upon linguistic arguments.

Ontological Dualism

The first and most common type of approach argues for an two-realm ontological dualism which divides reality into two classes, one of which belongs to science and the other theology. Several examples of such dualisms have been proposed, such as: the natural/the supernatural, the spatio-temporal/the eternal, the natural (or physical)/the historical, dead matter/living spirit, and so forth. These dualistic ontologies have failed to insulate theology from science, however, for two reasons. First, ontological dualisms have repeatedly led theologians who relied on them into the "God of the gaps" difficulty as one area after another thought outside the realm of science came to be brought within its domain.[26] And second, ontological dualisms are inconsistent with the Christian doctrine of creation, which is universal in scope and claims God as creator of all things with the consequence that there is no realm independent of God's creative and providential activity.[27] As a result of this doctrine, theological assertions should be capable of being made of every realm, and to restrict God's relation to nature to merely the human spirit (or some other isolated domain within nature)[28] involves a truncation of Christian theism that is clearly unacceptable, for to make all theological statements about the relation between God and the world completely independent of our beliefs about nature itself would be to render either the statements or the relations vacuous.[29] Furthermore, this position generates a contradiction, for it has the peculiar consequence that

> statements about the relation between the two realms belong to the discipline (theology) that deals with one of the realms, and not to the discipline (science) that deals with the other.[30]

Thus, the claim for the complete autonomy of the realms is violated.

Conceptual Dualism

A second approach to the two-realms position is to locate the division not in ontology but in mutually exclusive realms of thought.[31] This approach relies upon the view that science and theology deal either with different aspects or dimensions of things, or different patterns or relations among them in order to obtain a distinction of realms which does not exclude any member of the universe from the purview of science or theology. Examples of this approach include Karl Heim's notion of "spaces" and D. M. MacKay's use of "complementarity."

Heim set forth the theoretical basis for this discussion of the relations between science and theology in *Christian Faith and Natural Science*,[32] and the crucial concept of his discussion is the idea of a "space." Heim adopts from science the idea of a dimension, or way of ordering events, and the idea of a space, or a continuum in one or more dimensions.[33] Human beings live in three spaces: (1) the space of spatio-temporal objectivity, which is public, accessible to science, and marked by "polarity" (which means that the members in the relation are always linked in such a way that they are mutually exclusive yet mutually dependent), (2) the space of ego beings, which is the area of the self and human encounter and is also marked by polarity, and (3) the space of the supra-polar, which is the dimension in which one encounters God. These spaces are "hermetically sealed off from each other" (hence the separation of theology and science), and one can tell one has entered a new space when one encounters a paradox or contradiction within the space one has previously known.[34] The membership of the objective spatio-temporal realm and the subjective realm is the same, and only an abstract distinction can be drawn between the two, for the difference between the two spaces lies in the structural relations by which they order their common membership.[35]

Austin rightly points out that Heim's notion of spaces is too incoherent and too vaguely defined to adequately demonstrate the irrelevance of natural science to theology. One of the incoherences to be found in Heim's position is his use of paradox as the avenue to a new space, for, despite his efforts, Heim's arguments do not establish paradoxicality as either a necessary or sufficient condition for the presence of a new space.[36] Furthermore, Heim's treatment of supra-polar space is so obscure that: (1) it is difficult to see how it could qualify as a space at all, (2) it is unclear how the supra-polar space is to overcome the polarity of the first two spaces, and (3) it is hard to see how one could know the supra-polar space was a genuine space since we are not told how we are able to grasp this space's structural relations.[37] Thus, Heim's argument is too weak to bear the weight of justifying the irrelevance of natural science to theology.

D. M. MacKay's carefully formulated definition of a logical relation he calls "complementarity" provides a much more promising approach to the explication of the "dimensions" metaphor than Heim's "spaces;" however, MacKay's position is unable to give a completely convincing case that science is irrelevant to theology.[38]

MacKay's description of complementarity is:

Two (or more) descriptions may be called logically complementary when (a) They ... have a common reference, (b) Each is in principle exhaustive, (in the sense that none of the entities or events comprising the common reference need be left unaccounted for), yet (c) They make different assertions, because (d) The logical preconditions of definition and/or of use (i.e. context) of concepts or relationships in each use are mutually exclusive, so that significant aspects referred to in one are necessarily omitted from the other.[39]

Thus, if two statements are complementary, they are not about different things, nor is either necessarily incomplete in itself, nor are they synonymous, nor are they necessarily contradictory. The two statements can be in conflict, however, for the complementarity relation offers

an alternative both to the view that makes all divine activity supplementary to the (presumed incomplete) chain mesh of scientifically describable cause and effect ("God in the Gaps") and to the "watertight compartment" theory that religious and scientific statements are logically independent. Complementary statements are not logically independent. By saying that they are about the same situation we mean that there is at least one feature of one of the statements whose alteration would necessitate a change in the other(s).[40]

It would appear that the quote given above would clearly indicate that science is relevant to theology, for a change in one order would necessitate a change in the other; however, MacKay seeks to avoid this by distinguishing between symmetric complementarity and hierarchic complementarity. In hierarchic complementarity, a change in one of the complementarity statements will necessitate a change in the other, but not *vice versa*. Examples of hierarchic complementarity include: (1) a line of print analyzed according to a list of the letters and a physical account of the ink particles, (2) a mathematician's and an engineer's descriptions of what is going on in a computer programmed to solve a mathematical problem, (3) mentalistic and physicalistic descriptions of a person's behavior, and (3) theological and scientific accounts of the same situation or event.[41]

MacKay's complementarity concept fails to demonstrate the irrelevance of natural science for a number of important reasons. First, if theology is hierarchically complementary to science in a way similar to the analogies given by MacKay, then it would seem a theological account could be compatible with any of several scientific accounts (just as the line of print could be compatible with a variety of different quantities of ink particles). If so, theological statements would not have to necessarily change when scientific statements to which they are complementary are modified, but it is not at all clear *how* the former are immunized from the impact of all possible changes in the latter, and whether or not changes in scientific statements would require the modification of theological statements or the rejection of the two accounts as complementary would seem to have to be determined in each particular case, thus leaving the theological claims somewhat susceptible to influence by science.[42]

Second, if theology is hierarchically complementary to science, a change in a theological statement would necessitate a change in its complementary scientific statement, and therefore it would seem any given scientific account could be complementary and compatible with only one account from a given theological standpoint. But this would still leave science relevant to theology in a very important way, for it could help to settle disputes between rival theological accounts, for, if one were certain a scientific account were accurate, one could choose the theological account compatible and complementary with the scientific account since a theological statement not compatible with the scientific account would require a change in the scientific account.[43]

Third, MacKay's usage of complementarity is susceptible to serious criticism. A number of scholars, including Ian Barbour, have pointed out that the use of complementarity as a model for the "science-religion" relation as a whole by MacKay (and some other theologians) results in an over-extension of the analogy, but MacKay does seem to have a satisfactory answer to these objections.[44] However, Peter Alexander has offered a more important objection and has argued MacKay's usage of complementarity can never have useful application as formulated for it is incoherent in the sense that MacKay's four conditions can never be simultaneously satisfied.[45] If two accounts of the same situation take all of the same features into account, then condition (d) is violated; if they do not, condition (b) is not met (see above). MacKay tries to rescue his position by distinguishing between the components of a situation and the aspects of a situation, with the aspects being the pattern or relation among the components,[46] but this distinction still leaves ambiguities that undermine the coherence of his position.[47] Failure to provide an effective way of making his description of the distinction between components and aspects apply to specific cases leaves MacKay's case unsuccessful.

MacKay's attempt to define the relation between theology and science as one of complementarity also runs into a number of other difficulties common to all attempts to formulate the relationship between theology and science in this way.[48] Advocates of complementarity differ on some of the details of their position, but they share the view that science and theology are often concerned with the same objects but that each discipline deals with those objects in different categories of description and different types and levels of explanation. Strict complementarists insist that each discipline can give complete explanations on its own level; limited complementarists do not accept the idea that explanations are complete and limit the common areas of the two disciplines' concerns to certain initial starting points for theology and science.[49] Both views run into serious difficulties, but only strict complementarity is relevant to the present discussion.

Strict complementarists make a number of important mistakes which undermine the position. First, scientific explanations do not appear to be able to offer complete explanations, for they always depend on philosophical presuppositions which are not part of science.[50] Second, the attempt to maintain the independence of the various levels runs into difficulties, for the simple fact that complementary descriptions refer to the same things or events places constraints on the independence of the descriptions and therefore can leave scientific descriptions relevant to theology.[51] Thus, the complementarist position is unsuccessful in its attempt to demonstrate the irrelevance of natural science to theology.

The final category of positions arguing for the irrelevance of natural science to theology is a form of conceptual dualism which Austin calls "linguistic arguments."[52] Advocates of these types of arguments stress the multiple uses of language, the necessity of careful attention to the conditions and contexts in which these uses are learned and practiced, and the problems which result from violating the "grammar" or rules of the language in question. Types of linguistic arguments include: (1) the "language-games" arguments of philosophers of religion influenced by the latter writings of Wittgenstein, such as D. Z. Phillips, W. D. Hudson, and Peter Winch,[53] and (2) the argument that religious language expresses involvement and commitment whereas scientific language requires detachment, objectivity, and logical neutrality, found in the works of Donald Evans and Alasdair MacIntyre.

The "language games" argument has been developed from some remarks made on the nature of religious belief by Ludwig Wittgenstein in his *Lectures and Conversations on Aesthetics, Psychology and Religious Belief.*[54] While it is difficult to give a short summary of this position due to the complexity of the issues involved and the diversity of opinion held by its proponents, advocates of the language games argument share the view that a language is composed of a number of distinct and disjunct bodies of discourse or language games, each of which is given its internal coherence from its being grounded in, and learned and practiced within, a distinct social setting or form of life. Each language game has evolved to express the multiplicity of interests human beings have, and each has its own rules (or grammar) of meaning, use, and truth. Confusion results if one applies within it the rules from another setting, and to further avoid error, one must closely observe how the language is used in its natural setting to discover its rules of use, for the rules are often not explicitly given. One must become a participant, or one who uses the language to express the appropriate interest, to understand properly how the language is to be used.[55]

It is clear even from this brief treatment to see how the argument is to be made for the irrelevance of science to theology. Theological language is one form of life, and scientific language is another. Each has its own rules and is learned within its own context.[56] Conflicts between the two may emerge because some of the same words are used in both, but a proper analysis of the meanings and use of the words in their respective contexts will reveal the conflicts are not genuine problems but mistakes based on the misuse of language. Theology and science, so this argument goes, have logical preconditions which show that one has no bearing on the other.

As Austin rightly points out, the language games argument precludes any form of direct relevance, and indirect forms of relevance such as metaphysical relevance are also excluded, but in arguing against heuristic relevance an important concession will have to be made which undermines the language games argument, for it must rely on supporting reasons other than the autonomy of language games when it moves beyond arguments based on the sheer distinctness of forms of life in order to suggest why some pairs of forms of life are more disparate than others.[57] This becomes especially clear when one examines the fact that Christian theologians throughout history have indeed spent a great deal of time and energy trying to answer the question of how their doctrines are related to the results of scientific inquiry and what knowledge of God can be found in the Two Books of Nature and Scripture.[58] The game of relating science and religion is played as an important sub-game within the field of theology. The proponent of the language game argument would have to say these theologians were confused or in error in attempting to relate theology and science, even though such an effort was an important part of their own religious life, and he or she would have to show just how these efforts were inappropriate. As Austin points out:

But then we are faced with a vast and intricate job of disentanglement. Religious discourse as empirically available to us comprises, we are supposing, a confused intertwining of genuinely religious elements with others. How are we to extract and reconstruct from this the genuine religious language game? It seems that we would need at least a partial theory of what religion is and what it is about – enough of a theory, at least, to show why it has nothing to do with science. And we would need some justification for the theory. *But to develop and defend such a theory is also to develop an argument, independent of the notion of language-games, for the irrelevance of science to theology.* The games being once entangled, we cannot separate them unless we have an independent basis on which to make the separation; and if we have that basis, we don't need the language games argument.[59]

Thus, the argument based on the autonomy of language games is simply not enough to support the irrelevance of natural science to theology.[60]

The second type of linguistic argument is based upon the contrast between the personal involvement and commitment of religion with the objectivity and logical neutrality of scientific activity. Donald Evans's essay "Differences between Scientific and Religious Assertions" is probably the most influential statement of this position.[61] In this essay, Evans makes three important claims about the differences between science and religion which are pertinent to this discussion.

First, Evans claims religious assertions are "self-involving" and scientific assertions are not for they are logically neutral. By "self-involving" Evans means that a statement implies that those who make them are committed to certain courses of action or possess certain attitudes for or against the assertion made.[62] Even if Evans is correct about religious assertions being self-involving and scientific assertions as not, science still can be directly relevant to theology, for, according to Evans, religious assertions do have factual presuppositions, and therefore scientific findings are relevant to them.[63] Furthermore, Evans's claim that religion is self-involving and science is logically neutral is exaggerated and over-simplified. Some religious statements are logically neutral (in Evans's use of the term) such as theological or second-order statements about religious assertions and theological debates in which self-involving elements are set aside to pursue purely intellectual considerations.[64] In addition, it is now widely acknowledged that personal involvement and commitment play an important role in the process of scientific discovery.[65] Thus, Evans's contrast between "logically neutral" science and "self-involving" religion is over-drawn and a matter of *degree*, not *kind*, though one can freely acknowledge that religious beliefs do encompass all of one's life in a way scientific beliefs do not.

Evans's second contrast makes the claim that there are personal conditions (such as attitude or character) for understanding religious assertions which do not apply to science. However, Evans is forced to concede that science does involve attitudinal training and does require the development of certain moral virtues, thus leaving personal conditions present in understanding science.[66] Once again, it appears at best that Evans could argue that this contrast is a matter of *degree*, not *kind*, though he does finally ground the contrast in "depth-experiences" such as I-Thou encounters which are not found in science and require certain attitudes and qualities of character.[67] But, even if Evans is correct on this point, it remains clear that whatever personal conditions there are do nothing to prohibit the relevance of science to theology.[68]

Evans's third contrast between science and religion states that religious assertions are unlike scientific assertions for they are not testable by observations. This point could be argued in a number of different ways, but the important contrast here is that adherence to religious doctrines must be decisive, that is, religious faith must be unconditional and held irrespective of any evidence, thus leaving no bearing of science (or virtually any other discipline) on theology. Indeed, to hold beliefs any other way is faithless, to have no faith. Alasdair MacIntyre, in objecting to an argument of Ian Crombie's about the verification of religious beliefs, protests a view which makes of

> religious belief...a hypothesis which will be confirmed or overthrown after death. But, if this is correct, in this present life religious beliefs could never be anything more than as yet unconfirmed hypotheses, warranting nothing more than a provisional and tentative adherence. But such an adherence is completely uncharacteristic of religious belief. A God who could be believed in in this way would not be the God of Christian theism. For part of the content of Christian belief is that a decisive adherence has to be given to God. So that to hold Christian belief as a hypothesis would be to render it no longer Christian belief.[69]

MacIntyre's view, if correct, would rule out any direct relevance of science to theology, and it appears indirect relevance would be ruled out as well, but it is inadequate as a description of both scientific hypotheses and faith. As Austin points out, Imre Lakatos has shown that many scientists hold their hypotheses much more tenaciously than philosophers of science (such as Karl Popper for example) who emphasize the tentativeness of hypotheses have thought,[70] and Thomas Kuhn has offered a number of historical examples which demonstrate the tenacity of scientists' loyalty to their theories.[71] In addition, MacIntyre's description of faith as unconditional in the sense of decisive adherence is incorrect. Basil Mitchell has pointed out that this MacIntyrean sense of faith stems from a confusion, for faith has the meaning of trust, and to be faithless means to have failed someone by not giving them the trust that they expect. One must admit God's existence in order to have a duty to believe in God, as Mitchell writes:

> although there is a Christian duty to trust in God, this does not imply a duty, let alone an unconditional duty, to go on believing that there is a God. Indeed, once it is admitted to be a genuine possibility that there is no God and that the case against his existence might become cumulatively overwhelming, it is pointless to maintain that one ought to go on believing nevertheless that there is a God, even when the belief could be seen to be false. It could not, in these circumstances be a duty owed to God, and there could be no other conceivable reason why it should be a duty. This is to say that the requirement of unconditional faith is one which has its place within the system of theistic belief and cannot properly be interpreted as an obligation to continue to embrace the system itself.[72]

As one can see, a duty to believe in God first requires that one embraces the system, and within that system one can have unconditional faith in God; however, unconditional faith should not be interpreted in a MacIntyrean fashion, for, to quote Mitchell again:

> The faith that *is* unconditional is the believer's trust in God; it is this which forbids him to despair in the face of doubts and difficulties This trust is the corollary of God's nature as he believes it to be. The God 'in whom is no variableness and shadow of turning' is a faithful and merciful God who will not abandon his creature.[73]

A true faith is unconditional in that it pursues wholeheartedly the obligations and actions appropriate to one who believes in God, but one can be open to the revision of one's particular theological ideas or system.[74] Religious beliefs do involve a much greater degree of commitment than science in that they influence one's entire life and take precedence over all other areas of life, but they are neither as rigid nor as inflexible as MacIntyre has claimed. Thus, once again the strong contrast between scientific and theological statements turns out to be a difference more of degree than kind, and the case for the irrelevance of science to theology has not been made.

None of the several arguments considered are able to establish in principle the irrelevance of natural science to theology, but Austin does not attempt to argue that science is relevant to theology or to show how science might be relevant to theology. He advises theologians:

> *For the moment*, theologians *may* be tactically wise to ignore science, while working to recapture a firmer grasp of what their discipline essentially aims to do; and critics of theology might be wise to build their case on other grounds. But only, if I am right, for the moment. If science is relevant, it cannot be ignored indefinitely.[75]

Austin is correct; science cannot be ignored indefinitely. In the next section, arguments for the relevance of science to theology will be explored.

Why Science is Relevant to Theology

As noted earlier, theology is a much broader discipline than is natural science in that it makes claims on every aspect of a person's life. Because of this, science can be thought to be relevant to theology for a number of important reasons. This section will argue why and how science is relevant to theology by examining: (1) the consensus among the majority of Christian theologians about the nature of truth, (2) the relationship between noetic structures and the categories of relevance described by Austin, and (3) the theological reasons science is relevant to theology.

The Consensus among Theologians about the Nature of Truth

The statement, "There is a consensus among the majority of Christian theologians about the nature of truth" probably appears at first sight to be an obvious absurdity. Theologians throughout the history of the church have proposed a multitude of explanations of how one knows something to be true and of related issues such as the relationship between faith and reason. In addition, theologians differ as to whether truth should be understood as correspondence, coherence, pragmatic, or any number of variations on these basic positions. The understanding of truth I have in mind, however, is a characteristic of truth which transcends debates about these issues, for theologians of all persuasions, whether "liberal" or "conservative," agree on one basic principle – the unity of truth or the necessity of coherence among individual beliefs in one's world-view.

What is meant by the phrase "unity of truth" can be best explained by looking at the controversy between Thomas Aquinas and the followers of

Averroes, for it is illustrative of the understanding of truth prevalent among contemporary theologians.[76] The Averroists defended the idea that there were two different bodies of truth: (1) the truths of faith, and (2) the truths of reason. These two bodies of truth existed in what might be called "logic tight compartments," and no question ever arose or had to be confronted about their coherence with one another for there was no possible conflict between philosophy and religion. Truths of reason belonged to the sphere of the intellect and were definitely superior to the truths of faith which belonged to the sphere of the imagination. This theory of "double truth" included the claim that a proposition could be simultaneously factually true in philosophy or science and factually false in religious faith and vice-versa, thus making it possible to hold incompatible and contradictory propositions within one's world-view.[77]

Aquinas rejected the claim that a proposition could be factually true in philosophy or science and at the same time factually false in religious faith. Aquinas argued that there is only one all-embracing sphere of logical or factual truth, in which all the parts, regardless of how diverse they may be in other respects, must be coherent and compatible with one another. Truths of faith and truths of reason are the same kind of truth and are subject to logic, for they both try to match up with reality, or the way things really are.[78]

Aquinas' position did not rule out the possibility of more than one kind of truth. Following Aristotle, he acknowledged the difference between truths of reason and poetical truths which are appropriate to narratives. Poetry gives delight but also instruction; that is, poetry gives instruction derived from the insights and the understanding that result from the imaginative exploration of possibilities and probabilities, and these imaginative explorations can enrich one's understanding of the actual, about which we receive instruction from, for example, history, science, and philosophy.[79] The insights provided by poetry do not contradict the truths of reason, but rather are consonant with them, for they are of a different kind and all the details of a poem are not to be treated as literally true since they emerge in an imaginative context. No contradictions emerge within one's noetic structure for one understands that it is the insights from a poetic narrative rather than whether or not it coincides with actual historical details that is important.

Aquinas rejected the idea that religious truths were merely poetic truths or that they were inferior to the truths of reason in any way, but that is less important for this discussion than the idea that all the beliefs of one's noetic structure must be coherent with one another. Aquinas could acknowledge a unity of truth that contained both truths of reason and poetical truths, but he simply could not accept any view of truth which allowed for one to hold simultaneously contradictory ideas both of which could claim to be factually true.

The basic belief of Aquinas' in the unity of truth is one shared by contemporary theologians regardless of the differences that may exist among them. The majority of theologians would no doubt reject or at least question the following features of Aquinas' theology: (1) the "Aristotelian leaven,"[80] (2) the correspondence theory of truth, (3) the assertion that religious claims are factual statements, and (4) the understanding of the relationship between faith and reason; however, the need for coherence in one's world-view which constitutes a unity of truth is widely accepted.[81] This point is clearer if one translates Aquinas' principle into the language of contemporary debates within the philosophy of science and discusses scientific or religious statements as realist or instrumentalist in nature. Two contradictory statements cannot both be taken realistically; the only valid options are to take one as realist and one as instrumental or to take both as instrumental.

Like Aquinas, many theologians feel it incumbent upon them to try to resolve contradictions in their world-view by treating either theological statements or scientific statements instrumentally[82] or by denying the proposed truth of the findings of one or both of the disciplines altogether,[83] but the desire to achieve coherence remains constant regardless of the strategy employed, and it is this commitment to the unity of truth and coherence in world-view on the part of theologians which will always leave the natural sciences relevant to theology in at least some limited fashion. For this reason, the claim that science is in principle irrelevant to theology is doomed to failure not only in specific cases such as those discussed above but in a general sense as well since indirect relevance will always be present.

Noetic Structures and Categories of Relevance Re-examined

A commitment to the unity of truth places a number of constraints on the options available to the theologian seeking to relate theology and science within his or her noetic structure. This section will first briefly discuss the nature of a person's noetic structure and world-view and then demonstrate the place of theology and science within it by the use of Austin's categories of the possible relevance of science to theology.

Noetic Structures and World-views

Noetic Structures

Everyone has a noetic structure or a "set of propositions he believes, together with certain epistemic relations that hold among him and these basic propositions."[84] A person's noetic structure may include true and false beliefs as well as probably true and probably false beliefs, and all noetic structures have at least four identifiable features.

First, a noetic structure is the sum total of everything a person believes. Since the objects of beliefs are propositions (statements which are either true or false), a complete inventory of any person's noetic structure will include all the propositions one believes, including those which may not be present at the current moment to one's consciousness. In addition, the beliefs which make up our noetic structures vary greatly in their significance or importance, and the importance of any particular belief is often relative to the person who holds it,[85] and the content of each person's noetic structure will be different.

Second, a noetic structure is characterized by the way its beliefs are related. Many of a person's beliefs may be totally unrelated to other beliefs. Others, however, are related logically, such as one may hold two beliefs which contradict one another thus forcing one to accept one and reject the other (or perhaps reject them both) or hold two propositions related by the entailment of one from the other. In addition, beliefs can often be related in ways which have little to do with logic as, for example, on the basis of psychology or training or habit. The most important distinction between beliefs, however, is the division between basic and nonbasic beliefs. A nonbasic belief is derived from or inferred from or based upon beliefs that are more fundamental, or basic. A basic belief does not depend on any other belief.

Third, a person's noetic structure includes different degrees of certainty, firmness, and conviction with which the person holds his or her beliefs. Every person is more committed to some beliefs than others and feels more confidence or assurance in asserting some beliefs more than others. For example, I am more certain two plus two equals four than I am about the amount of the current available RAM on my computer.

And fourth, the beliefs which constitute a noetic structure will differ with regard to the kind of influence or control they have over the rest of the beliefs within that structure. For example, one basic, unproven, belief is the belief that other people have minds.[86] The belief in other minds exercises a controlling influence on the way one relates to other human beings, and to abandon this belief would profoundly influence other elements in one's noetic structure. The analogy often used for this aspect of a noetic struture is that of a spider's web.[87] Some beliefs lie at the outer edge of our noetic structures and a change in them will have little or no impact on the rest of our particular stucture; however, changes in regard to central and truly important beliefs will have a major effect on the structure. The degree of influence or control a particular belief has within any noetic structure will be relative to the person, as, for example, the belief that God exists occupies a central place in some noetic structures, is rejected by others entirely, and still others may have the proposition as a very minor part of their noetic structure. A change in the status of this belief would effect each of these positions differently.

World-views

Within noetic structures one can also find a smaller set of related beliefs that constitute each person's world-view, or "a conceptual scheme by which we consciously or unconsciously place or fit everything we believe and by which we interpret and judge reality."[88] Every person has a world-view whether he or she is aware of it or not, and world-views are important for:

> It can be argued on the basis of facts concerning the nature of man and the conditions of human life that human beings have a deep-seated need to form some general picture of the total universe in which they live, in order to be able to relate their own fragmentary activities to the universe as a whole in a way meaningful to them; and that a life in which this is not carried through is a life impoverished in a most significant aspect.[89]

Philosophers and theologians can help others to understand their world-view by helping them to realize what a world-view is, by assisting them to a better understanding of their world-view, and by aiding them in improving their world-view by helping them to eliminate inconsistencies and providing new information which can challenge or strengthen the world-view held.

Christian theologians should see Christianity as a conceptual system or a total world-view or life-view rather than just a collection of theological bits and pieces. As William Abraham has put it:

> Religious belief should be assessed as a rounded whole rather than taken in

stark isolation. Christianity, for example, like other world faiths, is a complex, large-scale system of belief which must be seen as a whole before it can be assessed. To break it up into disconnected parts is to mutilate and distort its true character. We can, of course, distinguish certain elements in the Christian faith, but we must stand back and see it as a complex interaction of these elements. We need to see it as a metaphysical system, as a world view, that is total in its scope and range.[90]

Abraham's statement must be qualified, however, for I disagree with the quote on two points: (1) Christianity should not be called a metaphysical system, for I think it is mistaken to reduce a religion to a metaphysical system since a religion seems to meet more diverse kinds of needs and answer more diverse kinds of concerns than purely metaphysical ones; and (2) I do not think a metaphysical system is identical with a world-view but is only part or one component of a world-view.[91]

In every noetic structure, certain beliefs are contained which are presupposed or accepted without support from other beliefs or arguments or evidence. For example, the discussion of the presuppositions of natural science pointed out that scientists make important epistemological, metaphysical, and ethical assumptions. These presuppositions are indispensable to noetic structures, and constitute the basic beliefs of the structure. Theologians are no exception to this rule, nor are they unique in this regard.[92] It is also possible for one to come to doubt one's basic beliefs, and an abandonment or modification of basic beliefs will result in a change in a person's world-view.

Two other observations about the nature of world-views are important. First, Ronald Nash has pointed out that every well-rounded world-view will discuss at least five topics: (1) God, or it will have a theology or atheology, (2) metaphysics, or some beliefs about ultimate reality, (3) epistemology, or a theory of knowledge, (4) ethics, or a way of making moral judgments, and (5) anthropology, or an understanding of the nature of human beings.[93] And second, world-views have "touchstone presuppositions." As William Halverson puts it:

> At the center of every world-view is what might be called the "touchstone proposition" of that world-view, a proposition that is held to be *the* fundamental truth about reality and serves as a criterion to determine which other propositions may or may not count as candidates for belief. If a given proposition P is seen to be inconsistent with the touch-stone proposition of one's world-view, proposition P must be regarded as false.[94]

Halverson's notion of "touchstone proposition" needs to be modified, however, for he leaves out another option. One could reject the "touchstone proposition" and the world-view it entails and embrace a new world-view. In addition, a world-view may have more than one proposition which qualifies as a touchstone proposition.

This brings us to the important question of how to choose a world-view. What initial factors go into the formation of our world-views and when does counter-evidence to our world-view become sufficient to require us to reject or modify our world-view? Because of the complex nature of our noetic structures these questions are difficult to answer, and it may very well be that a single set of necessary conditions that precipitate the need for a world-view change cannot be defined precisely. I will return to these questions when I discuss the epistemological relevance of science to theology, but for now it is important to note that theology is a much broader and all-inclusive discipline than that of the natural sciences, and, due to the acceptance of the unity of truth discussed above, the beliefs we hold from the natural sciences as a legitimate part of our noetic structures need to be able to fit within our theological world-view. It is to the possible ways science may be relevant to theology that we now turn.

Austin's Categories of Relevance Re-examined

Direct Relevance

As mentioned earlier, direct relevance occurs when a set of scientific statements either support or contradict theological statements. A scientific statement which supports a theological statement poses no problem for a theological statement, but a word of caution needs to be given to theologians who use scientific statements to support their theological claims. First, theologians should be clear that they really understand the claims made by a scientific statement so they are not guilty of drawing support for a theological statement based on only a superficial resemblance between a theological and scientific claim. A good example of this error can be seen among those theologians and scientists who tried to identify the "Big Bang" theory of cosmology with the Christian doctrine of creation.[95] And second, theologians should be aware of the difficulties present in the realism/anti-realism debate for any claims that a scientific statement is true. If an accepted theory which supports a theological statement is later shown to be false or in need of serious modification, the theologian must realize his or her theological statement loses any support gained from the scientific statement, and the theological statement should have other grounds for accepting it or it too will need to be abandoned or seriously modified. The theologian should exercise caution and adopt a "wait and see" attitude in re-casting theological statements in terms of currently accepted scientific theories or in fitting them into one's world-view, but there may be some scientific statements which are acceptable to use in this manner.[96]

Scientific statements which contradict theological statements pose different problems for theologians. The commitment to the "unity of truth" demands that the contradiction be resolved, but there a number of ways this can be accomplished. The theologian can take the scientific statement instrumentally rather than realistically and thus solve the problem of direct relevance. However, in order for the theologian to do this, he or she must have good reasons that show that it is appropriate to treat the scientific statement in this way. In order to do this in a general sense which will apply to all scientific statements a complete theory of anti-realism which is successful is required, but the problems with this position have already been discussed and it is unlikely that this effort will succeed. Another option would be to take the "wait and see" approach on a given scientific statement, and in many cases this is appropriate, but this will only postpone the difficulty if the theory becomes accepted in a realist manner, since there are good reasons to accept some form of limited realism for enduring scientific statements.

The other option, which has a noble ancestry in Christian theology, is to take the theological statement in a instrumentalist manner. Augustine, in his commentary on Genesis, formulated principles for the interpretation of Scripture which are relevant to this debate.[97] His two precepts were: (1) hold to the truth of Scripture without wavering, for it is revealed truth and we must not abandon our belief in its truth, and (2)since Scripture can be interpreted in a multiplicity of senses, one should adhere to a particular interpretation only in such measure as to be ready to abandon it if it should prove to be false, lest Holy Scripture be exposed to the ridicule of nonbelievers and obstacles be placed in the way of their believing. When conflict arises between a literal reading of the biblical text and the truth about the nature of things which has been demonstrated by reliable argument, the Christian must strive to reinterpret the Bible in a metaphorical way. Since real conflict is impossible between the two sources of truth, revelation and our tested knowledge of the world, the presumption will be that when we are *sure* of our natural knowledge, the apparent conflict between the Bible and natural knowledge must be resolved by reading the Bible in such a way as to eliminate the conflict.[98]

Augustine's principle is a good starting point, but it must be modified to be of practical use to guide theologians today. There is very little in all fields of natural knowledge, based upon empirical belief and rational reflection, that we know with certainty or demonstration, and so there is really very little that could possibly conflict with Scripture, articles of faith, or theological propositions. However, if we modify the standard to include those scientific statements which should be taken realistically, we have a valuable guide for contemporary theologians.[99] When an apparent conflict emerges between a scientific statement which should be interpreted realistically and some theological statement, the theologian ought to examine the theological statement very carefully in order to see whether the scientific statement will enable the theological statement to be reformulated in a more adequate way; that is, a way which will remove the conflict and restore the unity of truth. In addition, the scientific statement should be analyzed carefully to see if there is a genuine conflict with the theological statement or interpretation of Scripture, for more sophisticated hermeneutical approaches to Scripture are used today than in the time of Augustine. Augustine's insights, updated to incorporate contemporary understandings of Scripture, theology, and the philosophy of science, can still be of use as a general principle in the approach to relating theology and natural science, for: (1) they are compatible with a number of different theories of both the interpretation of texts and of the philosophy of science, (2) his insistence that the Christian theologian needs to hold to the normative authority of Scripture, while open to a number of different understandings, is indeed a necessary requirement or touchstone proposition of the Christian world-view, and (3) the potential of problems of direct relevance should be rare and careful analysis should be capable of resolving the difficulties.

Quasi-direct Relevance

Quasi-direct relevance, or the offering of competing explanations, poses yet another problem for the theologian, for if one is committed to the unity of truth, rival explanations should never occur except at some surface level. Some theologians do run into this problem, especially those who reject scientific statements which contradict their theological views, as, for example, those theologians who reject the explanations of the existence and dispersion of fossils offered by evolutionary theorists. However, in such cases either philosophical, scientific, or theological errors are present (and perhaps combined), and the unity of truth can be restored.[100] Attempts to resolve the difficulties by simply claiming that theology and science answer different types of questions or are not in the business of offering explanations have, as Austin and others have shown, proven to be unsuccessful, and the theologian need not rely on these strategies nor fear occasional difficulties with quasi-direct relevance, for the Christian theologian should have confidence that all these problems are ultimately resolvable with his or her noetic structure. If they are not, then his or her noetic structure is in need of modification, and, depending on the seriousness of the conflict, may call for modification in one's world-view. Quasi-direct relevance, then, should be understood as a problem the theologian need solve, not necessarily as a permanently existing difficulty for the Christian world-view.

Indirect Relevance

The three indirect forms of relevance formulated by Austin pose the most serious questions in the relationship between theology and science. The three indirect ways science might bear on theology are: (1) heuristically, (2) by way of metaphysics, and (3) by way of methodology.

Heuristic relevance, or the belief that science may suggest fruitful analogies for theology, is probably the least likely of the forms of relevance to be disputed by even defenders of irrelevance. It is hard to see how anyone could make a case in general that theologians could never draw useful suggestions from the methods or the contents of natural science, and perhaps the best one could do would be to argue the analogies derived from science are inadequate for they fail to exhibit enough similarities for fruitful formulations of theological ideas; however, even this claim is suspect, for each analogy needs to be judged on its own and not just by its source since theologians have derived analogies to develop theological concepts from a wide variety of natural sources. There is no reason to single out the natural sciences as incapable of yielding potential useful analogies. Furthermore, some contemporary theologians have actually used analogies derived from the sciences in ways that help to communicate theological statements to our contemporary setting.[101] Although all analogies are limited and will contain dissimilarities with what they are used to describe, analogies from the natural sciences should be explored on a case-by case basis for their fruitfulness in contemporary theological formulations. It may even be the case that a reciprocal relationship exists, and theology may suggest useful analogies for use to the natural sciences.[102]

Metaphysical relevance poses an ever more complicated set of problems for the theologian. Metaphysical beliefs will be part of a developed world-view, but the problem of the relationship of metaphysics to theology and science is a complicated one. Despite the many difficulties involved, some general guidelines for relating the three disciplines are capable of formulation. This section will discuss these difficulties and their place in the relationship between theology and science.

First, there is a real problem in defining metaphysics and giving a satisfactory description of just what this discipline is. George Schlesinger has surveyed the leading definitions of metaphysics and has shown the ways in which each definition is lacking.[103] First, some philosophers take metaphysics to be more general than science as the "overall framework of reality" or a "comprehensive theory of reality," but this definition fails because greater generality is not a universal characteristic of metaphysics. For example, the problem of the nature of minds is much narrower than the physicist's attempt to explain the constituents of matter, for the former deals with only a tiny proportion of reality while the latter deals with a much higher percentage of it. Second, some philosophers see metaphysics as a discipline which attempts to gain access to what transcends observation, but this definition fails for science does deal with unobservables and the realist metaphysician's claim that material objects actually exist and are not mere sense impressions is less removed from immediate experience than the physicist's claim that these objects are assemblies of imperceptible particles. Third, some philosopher's define metaphysics as the presuppositions of all other disciplines and the fundamental assumptions of a world-view, but this definition fails because some metaphysical assertions such as the claim that universals are real or not or that time does or does not flow are not fundamental to a world-view and are often completely irrelevant to other beliefs one may hold. And fifth, there is a whole class of definitions of metaphysics which are so obscure or simplistic as to be meaningless. For example, some philosophers define metaphysics as the science of the non-material, but this ignores the fact that there is a metaphysical theory (materialism) which is based on the belief that ultimate reality is material. Thus, any philosopher or theologian who attempts to rely on these definitions of metaphysics to fit theology and science into his or her world-view has serious difficulties.

The central characteristic of metaphysical statements, according to Schlesinger, is the unique way in which they are related to experience. He describes this relationship as follows:

> The aim of both science and metaphysics is to account for experience, but the roots in observation and experience of metaphysical statements are palpably more tenuous than those of scientific statements. One of the implications of this basic difference is that in science we can always rely on the accumulation of evidence to adjudicate between rival hypotheses, while in metaphysics the controversy may go on forever. A given scientific hypothesis may have looked plausible in the context of the knowledge available a hundred years ago but may appear absurd in the context of the greater knowledge we have today. On the other hand, a metaphysical hypothesis that could reasonably have been held in light of experience a hundred years ago would appear basically just as reasonable today in the context of a much richer experience. The great increase in our empirical knowledge does not have an appreciable impact on its status.[104]

Metaphysics, unlike science, proceeds by arguments and counter-arguments rather than empirical observations, and there is a constancy to metaphysical theories which is not found in science. In addition, scientific hypotheses are much more tightly interconnected than metaphysical hypotheses. Science holds to the interconnectedness of all natural phenomena, and inadequate hypotheses will end up clashing with a large number of observations. In contrast metaphysical hypotheses do not form a tightly knit system, for example, one's position on the existence of universals does not determine the position one will take on whether or not time flows.[105] Some metaphysical problems are independent of one another, and therefore conceiving metaphysics as a general scheme or system for all of reality is mistaken, and a theologian who attempts this has an inadequate conception of metaphysics.

Schlesinger's insightful treatment of metaphysics has important implications for theology. The theologian should not attempt to construct a metaphysical system to integrate theology and science, for such an effort appears to be misplaced. What is required is the harmonization of theology and science into a coherent world-view of which metaphysics is but a part. Metaphysics may or may not be helpful to accomplish some sort of integration, but it is unlikely that a metaphysical system will be due to the relative independence of metaphysical hypotheses from one another and from scientific theories. Furthermore, theological statements are somewhat independent of metaphysical questions, for answering metaphysical questions is not a primary concern of religious beliefs but only arise in the broader context of one who has responded to God's satisfaction of one's need for redemption and who desires to praise God by referring all things to God.[106] What the theologian needs to address are specific metaphysical problems in order to maintain coherence in his or her world-view and to turn back challenges to his or her religious beliefs, but the integration of the findings of natural science into one's world-view can be independent of a systematic metaphysical system.

A second difficulty for adopting a metaphysical system to accomplish the integration of theology and science is the fact that no metaphysical system commands wide enough support to justify its adoption. Even process philosophy, which has been adopted or adapted by a number of contemporary theologians, presents a number of problems which hinder its effectiveness as a tool for integration.[107] Contemporary philosophers are highly skeptical of system building, and the current dominant position in philosophy avoids metaphysics as a general conceptual scheme and instead focuses on attention to specific metaphysical problems.[108] The theologian would be wise to follow this approach in incorporating the findings of natural science into his or her world-view.

The third difficulty for adopting a metaphysical system to integrate theology and natural science concerns the understanding of metaphysical problems in the current philosophy of science. For the philosopher of science, the metaphysical question is not the question of how to build a metaphysical system but rather the question of whether or not to be a realist or an anti-realist about scientific theories. As previous discussion of this topic has shown, there are a tremendous number of difficulties for taking a blanket realist or anti-realist position for all scientific theories; however, limited realism can give some guidance to the theologian concerned about developing consonance between theology and science within his or her world-view.

The theologian must be capable of harmonizing any scientific theory which must be interpreted realistically into his or her world-view in order to preserve the unity of truth and coherence of his or her noetic structure, but the question remains as to whether or not a given scientific theory should be interpreted realistically. It is here that defenders of limited realism have important contributions to make to the concern for consonance, for critical realism does remain the dominant position in the philosophy of science, and answering the question of when to take a theory realistically has been an important part of refining critical realism to meet the challenges of anti-realism. The theologian can benefit by drawing upon insights developed by Gardner, Penrose, Hacking, and McMullin.

First, the theologian need not interpret every scientific theory as realistic but some theories should be. As noted in chapter one, Michael Gardner has argued that scientific theories should be evaluated on a case-by-case basis as to whether or not they should be interpreted realistically, and he listed nine conditions for taking a theory realistically rather than instrumentally. Gardner's position can be valuable for the theologian, and he or she should apply Gardner's criteria to a given theory in order to see if it merits consideration for a realistic interpretation and thus require incorporation as a true statement about reality within one's world-view. If a theory does not merit a realistic interpretation, then the theologian need not worry about any contradiction between the theory and a theological statement; however, he or she may still wish to explore the theory for possible heuristic relevance.

Second, scientific theories will vary in importance for the theologian's concern. Roger Penrose has developed three categories for ranking the importance of scientific theories which can be beneficial to the theologian in consideration of how a physical theory should fit into his or her theological world-view.[109] The categories are: (1) Superb, (2) Useful, and (3) Tentative. Superb theories exhibit a phenomenal amount of range, accuracy, and mathematical elegance, and only a handful of theories can claim to fall into this category.[110] Superb theories, as the most important theories, will demand the most attention from the theologian. Useful theories have some scientific experimental support but have not as yet achieved or may never achieve the observational accuracy and predictive power of Superb theories. Tentative theories lack any significant scientific experimental support and may contain some good ideas or be simply misguided.[111] Useful and Tentative theories can be raised to a higher category over time if they are successful, or they may be subsumed by other theories which later became Superb, or they can fade away like the Ptolemaic system of planetary motion. The theologian will have to deal with Useful and Tentative theories on a case-by-case basis, with some theories requiring attention as they raise in status over time and others meriting little, if any, attention except perhaps for occasional heuristic relevance or challenges which will die with the theory. Furthermore, Penrose's categories reinforce the position that very few scientific theories will actually be of direct relevance to theology, thus preserving theology's and natural science's relative, not total, independence of one another.

Third, even if absolute demonstration of a given theory's realism cannot be given, the entities postulated within a theory may be taken realistically and thus be worthy of the theologian's attention. Ian Hacking provides useful principles for the theologian on the realism/anti-realism question, for he offers sound suggestions about when and how a scientific statement should be taken realistically. As mentioned earlier, Hacking emphasizes "entity" realism; that is, some entities postulated within a theory may be taken realistically even if the theory is false (for example, atoms may be real even if a certain theoretical explanation of the atom is false), and conviction of the reality of these entities comes about from their use in scientific experimentation. What is required is a fit of these entities into the theologian's world-view, but it is highly unlikely that any of these entities will pose any direct relevance to the theologian though the possibility of heuristic relevance should at least be explored.

And fourth, critical realism as a metaphysical position reveals the tentative and limited nature of natural science's ability to grasp reality and thus defeats rivals to the Christian world-view such as scientism and shows the need for the interaction between theology and natural science to take place in an ongoing dialogue rather than in a fixed system. As Ernan McMullin, writing about cosmology in a way that is relevant to the general question of the relationship between theology and a scientific theory, puts it:

> The Christian cannot separate his science from his theology as though they were in principle incapable of interrelation. On the other hand, he has learned to distrust the simpler pathways from one to the other. He has to aim at some sort of coherence of world-view, a coherence to which science and theology, and indeed many other sorts of human construction like history, politics, and literature, must contribute. He may, indeed, *must* strive to make his theology and cosmology consonant in the contributions they make to this world-view. But this consonance (as history shows) is a tentative relation, constantly under scrutiny, in constant slight shift.[112]

McMullin's statement describes very well what is demanded of the theologian in attempting to relate theology and natural science. I would only add that the relationship between theology and science and attention to metaphysical problems need be held in the same relation. It is as a fit into a total world-view that science becomes at least indirectly relevant to theology, and it is to the possible ways of epistemological relevance within that world-view to which we turn.

Methodological relevance is the third form of indirect relevance of natural science to theology and involves issues usually raised by philosophers in debates about epistemology. Often a theologian adopts a specific methodology to systematize his or her work or to impose a formal structure on the doctrinal materials on which he or she works. If the theologian conceives of his or her methodology as analogous with the methods of natural science, or if he or she orders doctrinal materials in accordance with a formal or axiomatic structure like that of a science, then science may be said to be indirectly relevant to theology. A growing number of theologians are attempting to cast theological method in this manner, and some interesting work has been done, but there is not sufficient space to examine each of these attempts.[113] What will be proposed here are two guidelines for methodological and epistemological concerns in developing a coherence between the methods of theology and science.

First, the methods of the natural sciences should not be understood as *dictating* the terms of rationality for theology. There are a number of important reasons for this. First, the belief that all knowledge (including theology) must conform to the methods of the natural sciences is scientism, which is a philosophical claim shown to be in error in Chapter One. Second, there are modes of investigation in the natural sciences, not a single method, and since theology is its own discipline which examines its own unique object, there is no real reason to expect that the mode of examination can or will be exactly the same as the modes of examination in the natural sciences. Third, any understanding of the nature of science should be held tentatively, for there is no consensus on what exactly the scientific method is, and the theologian who chooses to cast his theological statements in a way analogous to the natural sciences will have to choose a particular philosopher of science's description of the nature of science and be prepared to acknowledge the objections that can be raised against that particular description. Fourth, one should not automatically assume a contradiction between a theological and scientific statement requires the theological statement to be taken instrumentalistically, for the question of whether or not a scientific statement should be taken realistically is an open question which requires careful analysis. And fifth, attempts such as evidentialism and foundationalism which claim theology's methods must be dictated to it from other disciplines have failed. This fifth point is at the heart of epistemological debates about the cognitive claims of theology, and so it will be discussed in further detail.

The classic statement of evidentialism can be found in the work of W. K. Clifford. Clifford's claim is: "It is wrong always, everywhere, and for anyone, to believe anything upon insufficient evidence."[114] According to Clifford, people have duties and responsibilities with respect to their epistemological activities, one of which is that is immoral to believe anything without proof or evidence, and religious beliefs should never be accepted for thee is never sufficient evidence or proof for them. Alvin Plantinga has directly responded to the evidentialist challenge by arguing the Christian need not accept the evidentialist thesis because the rationality of religious beliefs does not depend on supporting arguments or evidence.[115] Plantinga points out two fatal flaws in evidentialism: (1) acceptance of the evidentialist thesis would undercut all epistemic activity, and (2) the evidentialist thesis is self-defeating for it is accepted without offering any proof or evidence for it. Furthermore, it is important to note that some human beliefs, such as scientific beliefs, are evidence essential, but not all human beliefs are evidence essential, including very important beliefs like the belief other people have minds.[116] Evidentialism, according to Plantinga, makes the mistake of classifying belief in God with those beliefs which are evidence essential, and the appropriate response for the theist is to reject the evidentialist thesis for it is irrelevant to belief in God.

The collapse of foundationalism also undermines the attempt to let other disciplines dictate the conditions for theology's cognitive claims. Foundationalism is a model of human knowledge which holds

> that some of our beliefs are based upon others. According to the foundationalist a rational noetic structure will *have a foundation* -- a set of beliefs not accepted on the basis of others; in a rational noetic structure some beliefs will be basic. Nonbasic beliefs, of course, will be accepted on the basis of other beliefs, which may be accepted on the basis of still other beliefs, and so on until the foundations are reached. In a rational noetic structure, therefore, every nonbasic belief is ultimately accepted on the basis of basic beliefs.[117]

There are two types of foundationalism: (1) narrow foundationalism, and (2) broad foundationalism. Narrow foundationalism adds to the description above three criteria that a belief must possess in order to be basic: (1) it must be evident to the senses, or its truth or falsity must be based on human experience;[118] (2) it must be self-evident, or necessarily true or false simply by understanding it; and (3) it must be incorrigible, or incapable of being doubted even if it lacks logical necessity.[119] Broad foundationalism does not impose these criteria on basic beliefs.

The collapse of foundationalism has been well-documented in a number of contemporary philosophical works,[120] but Plantinga's two objections to narrow foundationalism will serve to illustrate this point. First, narrow foundationalism is much too restrictive and is incompatible with a great deal of what everyone knows, such as whether or not one has had lunch this noon. Memory-beliefs and other kinds of beliefs, such as the existence of the external world, cannot pass the strict criteria of narrow foundationalism. And second, narrow foundationalism fails its own test of rationality and is self-referentially incoherent, for its criteria are neither self-evident, evident to the senses, or incorrigible.[121] Thus, the foundationalist, like the evidentialist or follower of scientism, is in no position to dictate the terms of rationality to the theist or theologian.

And second, though the methods of the sciences should not dictate either the method or the criteria for rationality to theology, philosophical reflection on the methods and rationality of science may provide helpful clues for the theologian into the nature of rationality and how to resolve methodological problems, especially since the collapse of scientism and the broadening of the conception of scientific rationality. The Christian faith is not opposed to reason, for reasoning is involved in faith itself, and faith is reasonable for it is the appropriate way to respond to revelation because God has freely chosen to make God's intentions known.[122] Faith and reason are both important features which contribute to the unity of truth within a noetic structure, and the proper attitude toward faith and reason within the Christian world-view is expressed accurately by Robert Sokolowski, who states: "Christian faith is said to be in accordance with reason and yet to go beyond reason."[123] Since faith goes beyond, but does not violate, reason, one can expect to find some consonance between faith and reason and some differences between the two as well. The broader conception of rationality found in the current philosophy of science is congenial to the Christian world-view's understanding of faith and reason, and it may provide helpful clues to some methodological problems within theology, but the theologian should not tie his or her theology too closely to any one conception of the philosophy of science, for there are many unsettled issues and each position advocated by the leading philosophers of science has some flaws. Some features of the emerging consensus in the philosophy of science may be helpful, however. For example, it was pointed out earlier that precise logical criteria to make the decision of whether or not to switch world-views cannot be spelled out, but it may be that the informal criteria for switching from one scientific theory to another like those developed by Kuhn, Lakatos, or Laudan could yield fruitful suggestions for theology.

The theologian should explore these possibilities, but two important caveats need to be followed: (1) the theologian should approach methodological problems like metaphysical problems on a case-by-case basis paying close attention to the specific problems and possible solutions involved rather than adopting some general scheme (such as one particular philosopher of science's philosophy of science) for all methodological problems, and (2) the theologian must clearly spell out the *similarities* and the *differences* between the methods of theology and science and not make his or her case on purely superficial resemblances between the two. If these two warnings are heeded, the theologian can proceed with confidence in viewing theology and science as part of a common quest for understanding within his or her world-view.

The Theological Reasons Science is Relevant to Theology

Theology is much more inclusive than natural science in that it involves every aspect of a person's life and serves as one of the fundamental features of a person's world-view. This section will explore the specifically theological reasons why a theologian should see the natural sciences as relevant to theology.

First, theologians need to develop a theology of nature; that is, the theologian understands nature to be God's creation and to bear witness to the glory of God.[124] Since the creation bears witness to its Creator, by studying nature the theologian may find marks of this witness, and the natural sciences enable us to understand the natural world in order to look for the marks. Nature understood this way has traditionally been described by theologians as part of the "Two Books" which reveal God – the Book of Scripture and the Book of Nature.[125] A theology of nature is an important part of the Christian spiritual life, for it enables one to understand all of reality as dependent on God.[126]

Second, there are important ethical reasons for theologians to see science as relevant to theology. Christians are to be stewards of God's creation,[127] and responsible stewardship requires knowledge of how the things under our care work and can best flourish, and science is a means to acquiring this knowledge. In addition, Christians have been explicitly commanded to help the sick, hungry, and poor,[128] and science can help us understand the causes and prevention of disease, how to grow better crops, and so forth. The natural sciences can be of great help to the Christian trying to live out the Christian life. Furthermore, certain scientific advances have led to destructive elements in society such as pollution, and the theologian needs to be aware of environmental sciences in order to assess the moral use of certain technological options.

Third, as John Polkinghorne has pointed out, there are certain points of interaction between theology and science such as areas of possible conflict between the two disciplines.[129] One example of possible conflict concerns God's interaction with the world, especially for those who believe in miracles. The theologian will want to avoid a "God of the gaps" view of God's interaction with the world, but some theological account of how God causally interacts with the world that is in consonance with the findings of science is necessary.

And fourth, the theologian may see science as relevant to theology in the activity of apologetics for the Christian faith. Christianity is an evangelistic religion which seeks to carry its good news to others, and rebutting arguments against the Christian faith and advancing arguments which show Christianity's reasonableness or plausibility may be helpful in articulating Christianity in such a way as to make its message more acceptable to those who reject it. The philosophy of science can be helpful in this way, as for example, in the refutation of scientism which can lead to a new openness for faith.[130]

Conclusion

This chapter has explored the ways science might be relevant to theology, argued science is relevant to theology, and has suggested some guidelines for incorporating theology and science within one's noetic structure. A number of theologians have attempted to move beyond the "wait and see"attitude by exploring the relevance between theology and science and attempting to harmonize the two into a coherent whole. Two of the pioneers in this attempt are Ian Barbour and Thomas Torrance and their influence on the discussion of science and theology has been deservedly significant, and their continuing relevance for current debate should be explored. Chapter Three will examine Ian Barbour's attempt to integrate theology and science and Chapter Four will examine the approach of Thomas Torrance .

Notes

1.W. H. Austin, *The Relevance of Natural Science to Theology* (London: Macmillan, 1976), p. 6.
2.Ibid., p. 7.
3.Another example, not mentioned by Austin, would be the rival explanations of the existence and dispersion of fossils offered by evolutionary theorists and creation scientists.
4.Ibid., p. 7. This definition of metaphysics is highly controversial, for, as W. H. Walsh points out in his article "Nature of Metaphysics," *Encyclopedia of*

Philosophy, vol. 5, ed., Paul Edwards (New York: Macmillan, 1967), pp. 300-307, "there is little agreement among those who call themselves metaphysicians about precisely what it is that they are attempting (p. 300)." I do not agree with Austin's definition, nor do I think a theologian needs to construe metaphysics in this way; however, any theologian who argues for the irrelevance of science to theology and understands metaphysics as a comprehensive conceptual scheme is vulnerable to Austin's criticisms of this position. Theologians who deny the viability of metaphysics as defined here or deny that there are any good reasons to formulate religious doctrines in a particular metaphysical scheme will be treated later.

5.W. H. Austin, *The Relevance of Natural Science to Theology*, pp. 7-8.

6.Ibid., p. 8. Attempts to cast theological method in a way analogous to that of the natural sciences make up a growing genre of books on the contemporary scene. For examples, see Michael Banner, *The Justification of Science and the Rationality of Religious Belief* (Oxford: Clarendon Press, 1990), Phillip Clayton, *Explanation from Physics to Theology: An Essay in Rationality and Religion* (New Haven: Yale University Press, 1989), E. L. Schoen, *Religious Explanations: A Model from the Sciences* (Durham: Duke University Press, 1985), Nancey Murphy, *Theology in the Age of Scientific Reasoning* (Ithaca: Cornell University Press, 1990), and Wentzel van Huyssteen, *Theology and the Justification of Faith: Constructing Theories in Systematic Theology* (Grand Rapids: Eerdmans, 1989).

7.W. H. Austin, *The Relevance of Natural Science to Theology*, pp. 7-8. Austin does not discuss any of these other possible analogies, but I will examine other examples of possible heuristic relevance later.

8.William H. Austin, *The Relevance of Natural Science to Theology* (London: Macmillan, 1976), p. 6.

9.W. H. Austin, *The Relevance of Natural Science to Theology*, p. 7.

10.Ibid., p. 7.

11.Ibid., p. 7.

12.Ibid., p. 8.

13.Ibid., pp. 8-9.

14.Ibid., pp. 19-22. For example, Duhem's position on empirical facts (which physics, like any other science, can turn up) and "common-sense" laws (laws which can be stated without the use of the technical vocabulary of theoretical physics) would allow for geology or evolutionary biology to contradict certain theological claims. Another example would be the claim, not mentioned here by Austin, that the Big Bang theory of the origin of the universe supports the Christian doctrine of creation. Critical discussions of this issue can be found in Willem B. Drees, *Beyond the Big Bang; Quantum Cosmologies and God* (La Salle, Illinois: Open Court, 1990); Ernan Mcmullin, "How Should Cosmology Relate to Theology?" in *The Sciences and Theology in the Twentieth Century*, ed. A. R. Peacocke (Notre Dame, Ind.: University of Notre Dame Press, 1981, pp. 17-57; and the essays collected in *Cosmos as Creation*, ed. Ted Peters (Nashville: Abingdon Press, 1989). It would, of course, be possible to deny that the Big Bang theory supports the Christian doctrine of creation, as McMullin and Drees, I think rightly, do; however, it is important to note that neither Drees nor McMullin see cosmology as irrelevant to theology and seem to favor some form of indirect relevance in the theologian's quest for consonance in his or her world-view.

15. Ibid., pp. 22-23. Austin targets Duhem's doctrine of "natural classification" as the weak link in his argument, for it allows physics to provide support for the choice of one metaphysical system over another. Natural classification, for Duhem, is the view that the classifications provided by theories reflect (not describe, for theories are simply ordered sets of mathematical signs) the real order inherent in whatever real things there are, that is, physical theories establish an order isomorphic to a real order in things, thus enabling physics to play a role in the choice between rival metaphysical systems.

16. Austin, *The Relevance of Natural Science to Theology*, pp. 27-30. The more radical versions Austin has in mind are able at best to rule out only theories of the microscopic domain, and, as I shall argue later, even instrumentalist interpretations of unobservables may still have some indirect relevance for theology.

17. It is important to note that other versions of anti-realism have emerged since the publication of Austin's work that have bearing on this discussion. I will discuss these contemporary positions in the section that makes the argument that science is relevant to theology.

18. Ibid., pp. 31-32. A number of sophisticated anti-realisms concerning theological statements have developed not treated by Austin. One example is Don Cupitt's *Only Human* (London: SCM Press, 1985), *Taking Leave of God* (London: SCM Press, 1980), and *The World to Come* (London: SCM Press, 1982). One could also place (if I understand him correctly) Gordon Kaufman's *An Essay on Theological Method*, rev. ed. (Missoula, Montana: Scholars Press, 1979), *Systematic Theology: A Historicist Prespective* (New York: Scribners, 1968), and *God the Problem* (Harvard University Press, 1972) within this camp. However, these anti-realisms do not claim that science is irrelevant to theology; rather, they claim that theological statements must be instrumental because of scientific and philosophical challenges to theological claims or because theological statements do not meet the proper epistemological requirements of a "scientific method" (universality, in Kaufman's case). Positions like Cupitt's and Kaufman's fail, however, for they based on outmoded views of both science and philosophy. I will discuss allowing philosophy or science to dictate to theology in the third section of this chapter.

19. Braithwaite's position is developed in his essay "An Empiricist's View of the Nature of Religious Belief" reprinted in John Hick, ed., *Classical and Contemporary Reading in the Philosophy of Religion*, 2nd ed. (Englewood-Cliffs, N.J.: Prentice Hall, 1970), pp. 394-405.

20. Austin, *The Relevance of Natural Science to Theology* pp. 32-47.

21. Stace's position is developed in *Time and Eternity* (Princeton University Press, 1952), and *Religion and the Modern Mind* (Philadelphia: J.B. Lippincott, 1960).

22. Austin, *The Relevance of Natural Science to Theology*, pp. 47-50.

23. Stace uses the term order for he thinks each discipline deals with the *whole* of what it claims. He, unlike some other proponents of the two realms approach,

rejects metaphors like "classes" or "territories." See *Time and Eternity*, pp.88f.
24.Austin, *The Relevance of Natural Science to Theology*, pp. 51-54.
25.Ibid., p. 55.
26.Ibid., p. 56. This argument is not conclusive, however, for one could argue that the proper separation of realms simply has not yet been found. Austin's second argument is much more effective and would seem to apply to any two-realms argument.
27.Ibid., pp. 56-57. However, as Arthur Peacocke points out, there is one theologically defensible dualism – between God and the world, or God and everything else which is not God. This is different than speaking of a dualism within that which is not God. See A. R. Peacocke, *Creation and the World of Science* (Oxford: Clarendon Press, 1979), p. 24. I will return to the doctrine of God's uniqueness later.
28.Rudolf Bultmann is one example of this type of approach, and one statement of his position, along with important criticisms by other theologians, can be found in *Kerygma and Myth*, ed. H. W. Bartsch, trans. R. H. Fuller (London: Billing & Sons, 1964). Just how untenable a position like Bultmann's is can be seen in Brian Hebblethwaite's article "Providence and Divine Action," *Religious Studies*, 14 (1978), pp. 223-236.
29.W. H. Austin, *The Relevance of Natural Science to Theology*, p. 56-57. This argument could be further strengthened by a point that Austin fails to mention – that human beings themselves are a part of nature.
30.Ibid., p. 57.
31.Arthur Peacocke mistakenly conflates Austin's treatment of conceptual dualism with his treatment of ontological dualism in *Creation and the World of Science*, see pp. 24-25.
32.(New York: Harper Torchbooks, 1953). Heim applied his idea of spaces to specific problems in relating science and theology in *The Transformation of the Scientific World View* (New York: Harper, 1957) and *The World: Its Creation and Consummation* (Philadelphia; Muhlenberg Press, 1962).
33.For example, time, distance, and temperature are different dimensions, and an event can be arranged according to temporal order, location, or temperature. The range of all possible temperatures would be a one dimensional space, and a plane would be an example of a two-dimensional space.
34.*Christian Faith and Natural Science*, pp. 170, 143-146.
35.Ibid., p. 114.
36.W. H. Austin, *The Relevance of Natural Science to Theology*, pp. 68-69. Austin targets Heim's examples of paradoxicality as unable to demonstrate paradox is a necessary condition for a new space. Furthermore, in order to demonstrate paradox is a sufficient condition for a new space, Heim would have to rule out the possibility of encountering paradoxes *within* a space. And, while Austin does not make this point, it is a fact that paradoxes do emerge within systems that do not seem resolvable by appeals to other "dimensions." For an account of paradoxes in logic and mathematics, see Roger Penrose, *The Emperor's New Mind* (Oxford University Press, 1989), and for a treatment which includes art

and music, see Douglas Hofstadter, *Godel, Escher, Bach: An Eternal Golden Braid* (New York: Vantage, 1979).

37.Austin, *The Relevance of Natural Science to Theology*, pp. 71-72.

38.MacKay's position is stated in a number of works, including "Complementary Descriptions," *Mind*, LXVI (1957), pp. 390-4; "Complementarity II," *Proceedings of the Aristotelian Society*, Supp. vol. XXXII (1958), pp. 105-22; "Complementarity in Scientific and Theological Thinking," *Zygon*, 9 (1974), pp. 225-44; and *The Clockwork Image* (Downers Grove, Ill.: InterVarsity Press, 1974).

39."Complementarity II," pp. 114f., cited in Austin, *Relevance*, p. 74.

40."Complementarity in Scientific and Theological Thinking," p. 226.

41.Ibid., pp. 226-235.

42.W. H. Austin, *The Relevance of Natural Science to Theology*, p. 76. Austin also attacks MacKay's example of the line of print and the ink particles by arguing that it does not illustrate a true hierarchical relation. Austin argues that a Gestalt figure (such as the duck-rabbit) could have a modification of the ink particles and still yield two "higher-order" descriptions (that is, it could be taken as a duck or a rabbit) thus rendering the relation non-hierarchic. I do not find this argument persuasive; however, for MacKay could simply point out that the "higher order" description is not really a choice between a duck or rabbit at all but simply an ambiguous line drawing designed to produce alternative pictures.

43.Ibid., pp. 76-77. Austin points out that the implication of MacKay's notion of complementary is to leave only one theological account compatible with a scientific account; however, he fails to point out the way in which this leaves science relevant to theology.

44.Ian Barbour, *Issues in Science and Religion* Englewood Cliffs, New Jersey: Prentice-Hall, 1966), pp. 290-294; *Myths, Models, and Paradigms* (New York: Harper & Row, 1974), pp. 77-78; and *Religion in an Age of Science* (New York: Harper & Row, 1990), pp. 100-101. Barbour is dubious about MacKay's use of complementarity as an epistemological generalization, for in physics complementarity refers to the analysis of a single entity (an electron) of the same logical type in a single situation (a two-slit experiment) within a single discipline, and he argues that two disciplines can be said to be complementary in an analogical (not inferential) sense only if they analyze the same set of events and if there are independent grounds for justifying using alternative sets of constructs in a new context. The methodological assumptions of physics should not simply be imposed on or transferred to other fields (this would be a new form of the mistake of the early mechanists) unless the use of physical principles is supported by evidence from other fields. Other criticisms of the usage of complementarity to refer to the religion-science relation which hold MacKay's position is an illegitimate departure from Bohr's usage can be found in Hugo Beadau, "Complementarity and the Relation Between Science and Religion," *Zygon* 9 (1974), pp. 202-224; James L. Park, "Complementarity Without Paradox," *Zygon* 2 (1967), pp. 382-8); and Richard Schlegel, "Quantum Physics and the Divine Postulate," *Zygon* 14 (1979), pp. 163-185. However, in fairness to MacKay, it should be pointed out that his usage of the term complementarity does not seem to depend on the features of the wave-particle duality in physics, and therefore whether or not MacKay's usage is consistent with Bohr's does not appear to be a decisive argument against MacKay's position.

45.Peter Alexander, "Complementary Descriptions," *Mind*, LXV (1956), pp. 145-165.

46."Complementary Descriptions," pp. 390-94.

47.W. H. Austin, *The Relevance of Natural Science to Theology*, pp. 79-80. Austin illustrates the force of this point by showing that MacKay's treatment of the parting of Red Sea (Exodus 14:21) as an example of complementarity fails to clear up the ambiguities involved, for, if God is taken to be a component of the event, the criteria for complementarity are violated since God cannot be a component in the scientific description; furthermore, if God is taken to be an aspect of the event, then statements about God become identified with statements about patterns of relations among things in the world, and, for a theologian like MacKay who wishes to retain a strong sense of God's transcendence, this is no doubt too high a price to pay.

48.Examples of other thinkers who use the complementarity model not mentioned by Austin include Richard Bube, *The Human Quest* (Waco, Tex.:Word, 1971); C.A. Coulson, *Science and Christian Belief* (Chapel Hill: University of North Carolina Press, 1955); and William G. Pollard, *Chance and Providence* (New York: Charles Scribner's Sons, 1958).

49.This distinction is taken from Del Ratzsch, *Philosophy of Science: The Natural Sciences in Christian Perspective* (Downers Grove, Ill.: InterVarsity Press, 1986), pp. 133-134, 139-141. Since limited complementarity leaves science relevant to theology, it will not be considered further.

50.I will develop this argument further in the next section. Del Ratzsch offers this objection as well, but I think Ratzsch's claim that these presuppostions may find their justification in religious belief is in need of an argument which he does not supply (see pp. 134-35); however, I agree with him that the philosophical presuppostions upon which science is based do raise theological questions beyond what science is capable of answering. Furthermore, I endorse Ratzsch's second point that the intial conditions of physical theories leave the question of how to account for those conditions between a belief in "brute givens" or a theological principle remains open. For a discussion of how the order and existence of the world as a whole raises this question, see Diogenes Allen, *Christian Belief in a Postmodern World* (Louisville: Westminster/John Knox Press, 1989), Chapters 3, 4, and 5.

51.Ratzsch mentions the attempts to reconcile scientific determinism and human freedom as a clear error illustrating the weakness of this position (obviously MacKay is in mind, and Ratzsch, like Austin, points out the many unresolved questions left by MacKay's approach, see pp. 159-160). Ratzsch's point is that regardless of how we attempt to describe events, the inevitability of those events is still assured, thus leaving no normative force of our descriptions on reality and the independence of the levels merely mistaken, see pp. 136-137.

52.*The Relevance of Natural Science to Theology*, pp. 81-82. Austin acknowledges that the use of the term "linguistic arguments" is not entirely satisfactory as a description of the positions he discusses under this heading, but it does highlight the concerns about language and its proper use which are common to the positions grouped under this heading.

53.Represenative works include: D. Z. Phillips, *The Concept of Prayer* (London: Routledge & Kegan Paul, 1965), *Death and Immortality* (London: Macmillan, 1970), *Faith and Philosophical Inquiry* (New York: Schocken Books, 1971), and *Religion without Explanation* (Oxford: Basil Blackwell, 1976); and Peter Winch, *The Idea of a Social Science* (London: Routledge & Kegan Paul, 1958), and "Understanding a Primitive Society," in *Ethics and Action* (London: Routledge & Kegan Paul, 1972), pp. 8-49. Hudson's work is mentioned in the following note.

54.Ludwig Wittgenstein, *Lectures and Conversations on Aesthetics, Psychology, and Religious Belief*, ed. C. Barrett (Oxford: Blackwell, 1966), see especially pp. 53-59. These remarks appear to be developments of Wittgenstein's discussion of the role beliefs play in our "form of life" and his treatment of language games in *On Certainty*, eds. G. E.M. Anscombe and G. H. von Wright, trans. Denis Paul and G. E. M. Anscombe (New York: Harper & Row, 1972, paragraphs 1, 111, 250; and *Philosophical Investigations*, trans. G. E. M. Anscombe (New York: Macmillan, 1968), paragraphs 19, 23, 123, 241, 249, 630. It is not at all clear that writers like Phillips use the terms "language game" and "form of life" in a way that Wittgenstein would endorse. It is very difficult to interpret Wittgenstein's brief remarks on religion, and an extended discussion of the problems of interpreting Wittgenstein's position regarding the nature of religious belief can be found in W.D. Hudson's *Wittgenstein and Religious Belief* (London: Macmillan, 1975) and "Some Remarks on Wittgenstein's Account of Religious Belief," in G. N. A. Vessey, ed., *Talk of God* (London: Macmillan, 1969), pp. 36-51. Kai Nielsen, in his article "Wittgensteinian Fideism," *Philosophy*, XLII, (1967), pp. 191-209, argues that the use of the language games argument to describe religious life is not true to Wittgenstein's thought; however, whether or not the language games argument is true to Wittgenstien is unimportant, what is important is whether or not Phillip's position is an accurate description of the linguistic facts of science and religion.

55.Winch's essay on Azande witchcraft, "Understanding a Primitive Society," (see note 54) provides an excellent illustration of this position.

56.Phillips argues that true religion is not like science in *Faith and Philosophical Inquiry*, see especially his essay "Philosophy, Theology, and the Reality of God." His main points are: (1) science is public in a way religion is not, p. 9, (2) science answers questions of fact with acceptable tests and theology does not, pp. 1-5, (3) science gives causal explanations and religion does not, pp. 38-40, and (4) science is concerned with contingent things and religion is not, pp. 85-86. The question of the differences between science and theology is an important one that will be addressed later, for now I will restrict the discussion to the claim for the irrelevance of science to theology.

57.W. H. Austin, *The Relevance of Natural Science to Theology*, pp. 85-87. For example, the pair "religion and science" is more disparate than "religion and morality." Austin refers to Phillips' treatment of this topic in *Faith and Philosophical Inquiry*, pp. 77-110, as an example of this point.

58.Ibid., p. 89. It should also be pointed out that "simple believers," not just "theological sophisticates," try to reconcile their religious beliefs with science. See pages 91-93.

59.Ibid., p. 90.

60.Other arguments could be offered against particular features of thinkers such as Phillips represented in this category, but I have tried to restrict my argument to the question of relevance as it pertains to the language games argument. In passing I would mention that Phillips' analysis of prayer seems to be a distortion, rather than description, of actual religious practices. See Gary Gutting, *Religious Belief and Religious Skepticism* (Notre Dame, Indiana: University of Notre Dame Press, 1982), pp. 34-42, for a discussion of this point.

61.The essay can be found in Ian Barbour, ed., *Science and Religion* (New York: Harper & Row, 1968), pp. 101-33. It is important to note that Evans does not explicitly assert that science is irrelevant to theology; however, the stress on the differences between the two disciplines often leads to claims of this type. See Ian Barbour, *Issues in Science and Religion* (Englewood Cliffs, N.J.: Prentice-Hall, 1966), pp. 115-125; and *Religion in An Age of Science* (New York: Harper & Row, 1990), pp. 10-16.

62.Evans, "Differences between Scientific and Religious Assertions", pp. 112.

63.Austin, *The Relevance of Natural Science to Theology*, pp. 95-96. An example of a factual presupposition is "Jesus was crucified for my sins," which presupposes Jesus lived and was crucified.

64.Austin, *The Relevance of Natural Science to Theology*, pp. 98-100. Evans concedes there are these two exceptions to self-involving religious assertions in "Differences between Scientific and Religious Assertions," p. 126.

65.The literature on this subject is far too voluminous to cite; however, important represenative treatments which have influenced much of contemporary philosophy of science can be found in Michael Polanyi, *Personal Knowledge* (University of Chicago Press, 1962); and Thomas Kuhn, "Objectivity, Value Judgment, and Theory Choice," in *The Essential Tension: Selected Studies in Scientific Tradition and Change* (University of Chicago Press, 1977), pp. 320-339 and *The Structure of Scientific Revolutions*, second edition (University of Chicago Press, 1970). A good overview of these developments can be found in John Losee, *A Historical Introduction to the Philosophy of Science* (Oxford University Press, 1980) and *Philosophy of Science and Historical Enquiry* (Oxford University Press, 1987). Austin fails to mention any of these developments in the philosophy of science, and thus his case is not as strong as it could be on this point.

66."Differences between Scientific and Religious Assertions," p. 116.

67.It would be interesting to see Evans attempt to explain the many characters of dubious moral distinction in the Old Testament who encounter Yahweh or Paul's encounter on the Damascus Road in the New Testament. Scripture often seems terribly inconvenient for our theological constructions.

68.Austin, *The Relevance of Natural Science to Theology*, p.103.
69.Alasdair MacIntyre, "The Logical Status of Religious Belief," in *Metaphysical Beliefs*, eds. S. E. Toulmin, R. W. Hepburn and A. MacIntyre, second edition (London: SCM 1970), p. 171.
70.Austin, *The Relevance of Natural Science to Theology*, pp. 111-112. Austin cites Lakatos's landmark essay "Falsification and the Methodology of Scientific Research Programmes, in *Criticism and the Growth of Knowledge*, eds. Imre Lakatos and Alan Musgrave (Cambridge: Cambridge University Press, 1970) to make his point. In this essay, Lakatos developed his now well-known distinction between the "hard core" and the "auxillary hypotheses" of a scientific research program. The hard core is a set of theoretical assumptions held exempt from falsification (in the case of Newtonian physics, for example, the hard core is the Laws of Motion), and the auxillary hypotheses are a revisable protective belt designed to deal with negative experimental results which challenge the hard core. Lakatos gives a number of historical examples which show the tenacity with which theories are held, and one need not share Lakatos's total view of the confirmation of theories to grant that hypotheses are not held as tentatively as Popper thought.
71.Historical examples can be found throughout the text of *The Structure of Scientific Revolutions*, and it is surprising that Austin does not make use of these to strenghten his case.
72.Basil Mitchell, *The Justification of ReligiousBelief* (London: Macmillan, 1973), pp. 139-140. I agree with Mitchell's critique of MacIntyre on the nature of faith and the revisability of theological statements, but I find his notion of a "cumulative case" argument for theism highly problematic for a number of reasons. To cite three examples: (1) though Mitchell defends the use of a cumulative case argument to show theism is rational he does not provide such a case, (2) he does not provide an adequate way of judging exactly at what point a cumulative case argument accumulates enough evidence for it to justifify it or against it to reject it, and (3) it is not at all clear that religious believers need to establish that they provide the best explanation of physical or metaphysical problems in order to be reasonable, for religious beliefs can have other kinds of grounds. On this third point, see Diogenes Allen, *The Reasonableness of Faith* (Washington: Corpus Books, 1968).
73."Faith and Reason: A False Antithesis?", *Religious Studies*, 16 (1980), pp. 131-144. The quote is from page 141.
74.See *The Justification of Religious Belief*, especially chapters 5-8, and also Diogenes Allen, *The Reasonableness of Faith*, especially chapter 5.
75.Austin, *The Relevance of Natural Science to Theology*, p. 11.
76.Averroes' view is developed in "The Decisive Treatise Determining the Nature of the Connection between Religion and Philosophy" reprinted in *Philosophy in the Middle Ages*, eds. Arthur Hyman and James Walsh (Indianapolis: Hackett Publishing Co., 1973), pp. 297-316.
77.Averroes did not actually hold this position, and it is uncertain whether some interpreters of his actually did. See A. Ivry, "Toward a Unified View of Averroes' Philosophy," *Philosophical Forum*, IV (1972). pp. 87-113, and Etienne Gilson,

Reason and Revelation in the Middle Ages (New York:, 1938), pp. 35-58. The position need not have actually been theirs in order for it to be advanced and refuted, however.

78. See Thomas Aquinas, *The Trinity and Unicity of the Intellect*, trans. Sister R. E. Brennan (London: Herder Book Co., 1946).

79. See Aristotle's *Poetics,* Chapter 9.

80. This descriptive phrase of the need to purge the outdated notions of Aristotle's philosophy from theology comes from the work of Austin Farrer, *Faith and Speculation* (London: A. & C. Black, 1967), p. v.

81. Even theologians and philosophers considered to be "fideists" or rejecters of the importance of reason in the Christian faith share the position of the need for a coherent world-view. Two prominent examples come to mind. First, Soren Kierkegaard is often held as a champion of irrationalism and subjectivism, but Kierkegaard was not a defender of arbitrary individualism in the sense of Sartre and Nietzsche as a number of important interpretations of his work clearly show. See the essays collected in *A Kierkegaard Critique*, ed. by Howard Johnson and Niels Thulstrup (Chicago: Henry Regency Co., 1967). John Wild's comment is typical of many of the essays in this collection: "... far from being a lapse into subjective bias and irrationalism, [S. K.'s] philosophical work is a triumph of rational description and analysis, an original penetration of reason into depths of experience long languishing in the dark obscurity of the obvious" (p. 25). Wild's essay, as well as the ones by James Collins, Cornelio Fabro, Valter Lindstrom, Gregor Malantschuk, explore the ways Kierkegaard's work preserves a place for both objectivity and reflection in all stages of human life. Careful reading of Kierkegaard reveals he does create a coherent world-view. The mistake made by those who accuse Kierkegaard of arbitrary individualism is that they take Kierkegaard to be like Nietzsche and Sartre in that the individual's choice *creates* what is good for the individual; in Kierkegaard choice does not create the good but *discovers* it by moving into a context appropriate for grasping the reality in question.

Second, Karl Barth is often taken to be an irrationalist who saw no relevance of philosophy or science to theology due to Barth's ambivalent discussion of theology as a science and his rejection of Henrich Scholz's minimum criteria of a science. See *Church Dogmatics*, vol. 1, part 1 (Edinburgh: T. & T. Clark, 1975), pp. 3-11. It is true that Barth wanted to assert theology's independence from all other disciplines, but Barth is arguing for a coherent world-view in the sense that theology is a valid discipline for it is the appropriate starting-point for reflection whether it can justify itself by the criteria of other disciplines or not. To put it another way, theology as a discipline or "science" is valid as the basic or first principle of any world-view's noetic structure; one does not construct a world-view and then see if it is appropriate to fit theology into it. Barth's primary concern is that no other discipline dictate theology's method or contents to it. It is also important to note that Barth saw a limited value to philosophy and frequently used philosophical concepts to explicate his theology. For a discussion see Karl Barth, "Philosophie und Theologie" in *Philosophie und Christliche Existenz:*

Festschrift fur Heinrich Barth, ed. Gerhard Huber (Basel and Stuttgart: Verlag, Helbing & Lichtenhahn, 1960), pp. 93-106. While it is true Barth's view tends toward an isolation of theology from other disciplines and that he did not see the possibilities present in his theology for developing a world-view which could include a dialogue with the findings of natural science, a number of his disciples, including most importantly Thomas Torrance, have built upon some of Barth's remarks in order to do just that. For a full discussion of how mathematician Gunter Howe, who saw fruitful possibilities for a dialogue between Barth's theology and natural science, tried in vain to get Barth to participate in the "Gottingen Conversations" between physicists and theologians, see Harold Nebelsick, *Theology and Science in Mutual Modification* (New York: Oxford, 1981), pp. 159-172.

82. I give examples of theologians who take theological statements in an anti-realist manner in the discussion of instrumentalism above. Conservative theologians who encourage Christians to take science in an instrumentalist or anti-realist manner include Gordan H. Clark, *The Philosophy of Science and Belief in God* (Nutley, N.J.: Craig, 1964); John Bly, "Instrumentalism: A Third Option," *Journal of the American Scientific Affiliation* 37 (March 1985), pp. 11-18.

83. Scientific Creationism is an example of an attempt to deny the truth of the claims of modern science in regard to evolution.

84. My treatment of noetic structure is derived from Alvin Plantinga's essay "Reason and Belief in God" found in *Faith and Rationality*, ed. Alvin Plantinga and Nicholas Wolterstorff (Notre Dame, Ind.: University Of Notre Dame, 1983), pp. 16-93. The quote is from page 48.

85. For example, remembering the date of my wedding anniversary is much more important to me than someone not married to my wife. Other propositions may be of much greater importance to a large number of people, and there are some propositions that ought to be important to everyone needing to function in society.

86. Plantinga argues this at length in *God and Other Minds* (Ithaca, New York: Cornell University Press, 1968).

87. See W.V.O. Quine and J.S.Ullian, *The Web of Belief* (New York: Random House, 1970).

88. Ronald H. Nash, *Faith and Reason: Searching for a Rational Faith* (Grand Rapids, Michigan: Zondervan, 1988), p. 24. The following discussion of a world-view is indebted to Nash's fine treatment.

89. W. P. Alston, "Problems of Philosophy of Religion," in *The Encyclopedia of Philosophy*, reprinted edition (New York: Macmillan, 1972), vol. 6, p. 286.

90. William J. Abraham, *An Introduction to the Philosophy of Religion* (Englewood Cliffs, N.J.: Prentice-Hall, 1985), p. 104.

91. I will elaborate on this point in the next section.

92. Further discussion of this point will be treated under the indirect relevance of science to theology.

93. Ronald Nash, *Faith and Reason: A Search for a Rational Faith* (Grand Rapids, Michigan: Zondervan, 1988), pp. 30-32.

94. William H. Halverson, *A Concise Introduction to Philosophy*, 3d. ed. (New

York: Random House, 1976), p. 384, cited in Nash, *Faith and Reason*, p. 46.

95.See the works listed earlier by Ernan McMullin and Willem Drees for full discussions of this mistake.

96.I will discuss this more fully when examining the question of metaphysics.

97.Augustine, *The Literal Meaning of Genesis*, 2 vols., translated by J. H. Taylor, S.J. (New York: Newman, 1982), especially Book I, Chapter 21.

98.A full discussion of Augustine's view on this matter can be found in Ernan Mcmullin, "Introduction: Evolution and Creation" in E. McMullin, ed., *Evolution and Creation* (Notre Dame, Indiana: University of Notre Dame Press, 1985), pp. 1-56; and "How Should Cosmology Relate to Theology" in A. Peacocke, ed., *The Sciences and Theology in the Twentieth Century* (Notre Dame, Indiana: University of Notre Dame Press, 1981), pp. 17-57.

99.I will discuss the question of when to take a scientific statement realistically in the discussion of metaphysics.

100.An excellent point-by-point refutation of the "scientific" claims of Scientific Creationism, including its interpretation of fossils, can be found in Howard J. Van Till, Davis A. Young, and Clarence Menninga, *Science Held Hostage: What's Wrong with Creation Science and Evolutionism* (Downers Grove, Illinois: InterVarsity Press, 1988). The book is equally good at critiquing the claims of those who try to use evolution to discount the Christian doctrine of creation.

101.For an example, see Thomas F. Torrance's sermon, "The Theology of Light," in *The Christian Frame of Mind: Reason, Order, and Openness in Theology and Natural Science* (Colorado Springs: Helmers & Howard, 1989), pp. 146-155.

102.Torrance argues that James Clerk Maxwell's theological views did suggest such analogies for his scientific theories in "Christian Faith and Physical Science in the Thought of James Clerk Maxwell," in *Transformation and Convergence in the Frame of Knowledge* (Grand Rapids: Eerdmans, 1984), pp. 215-242.

103.George Schlesinger, *Metaphysics: Methods and Problems* (Oxford: Basil Blackwell, 1983), especially pages 9-13.

104.Schlesinger, *Metaphysics*, p. 1. Schlesinger does not hold an understanding of science marred by scientism, for he holds that the empirical situation is dynamic and it may only gradually cause us to accept or reject a given hypothesis through a scienitific revolution (Kuhn). He also concedes that empircial observations can have some affect on metaphysical claims, see p. 20.

105.Schlesinger, pp. 13-26.

106.A helpful discussion of the religious believer's attitude toward metaphysics can be found in Diogenes Allen, *The Reasonableness of Faith* (Washington: Corpus Publications, 1968), chapters 1-3. I will address the question of the grounds of religious beliefs in the section on epistemology.

107.I will discuss the specific difficulties of process thought in the chapter dealing with the thought of Ian Barbour.

108.This is the approach adopted by Schlesinger in his book. A good survey of the current scene can be found in John Passmore, *Recent Philosophers* (La Salle, Illinois: Open Court, 1985), pp. 87-122.

109.Roger Penrose, *The Emperors New Mind: Concerning Computers, Minds,*

and the Laws of Physics (Oxford: Oxford University Press, 1989), pp. 152-155.
110.The only examples of these theories come from physics and include Einstein's theories of special and general relativity and quantum theory. *Emperor's New Mind*, pp. 152-153.
111.Ibid., pp. 154-155. Examples of Useful theories include the big bang origin of the universe and the quark model of subatomic particles; Tenative theories make up the largest number of scientific theories.
112.E. McMullin, "How Should Cosmology Relate to Theology?", p. 52.
113.See note 6 of this chapter for a list of theologians who try to cast theological method in a way analogous to the natural sciences.
114.W. K. Clifford, "The Ethics of Belief," in *Readings in the Philosophy of Religion*, ed. Baruch Brody (Englewood Cliffs, N. J.: Prentice-Hall, 1974), p. 246. This essay has been reprinted in numerous anthologies.
115.Alvin Plantinga, "Reason and Belief in God," in *Faith and Rationality: Reason and Belief in God*, ed. A. Plantinga and N. Wolterstorff (Notre Dame, Ind.: University of Notre Dame Press, 1983), pp. 16-93.
116.By evidence Plantinga means: (1) propositional evidence, or an argument in which a conclusion is inferred from premises, and (2) evidence from direct experience, in which a belief is produced by experiences without inferring it from premises such as "I am currently typing this sentence on my computer." It is (1) Plantinga means when he says belief in God does not need evidence.
117.Plantinga, "Reason and Belief in God," p. 52.
118.Many narrow foundationalists reject this criteria due to the problems associated basing a belief on sense experience. See *Contemporary Readings in Epistemology*, ed. Michael Goodman and Robert Snyder (Englewood Cliffs, N.J.: Prentice-Hall, 1993) for a good selection of essays on the latest epistemological debates on this and other issues.
119.An icorrigible belief can be illustrated by looking at the following two sentences: (1) I see a red cardinal out my window, and (2) I seem to see a red cardinal out my window. The first statement is not incorrigible, for I am making a statement about the external world and I could be mistaken due to, say, color-blindness or ignorance about types of birds. The second is incorrigible, for it is a statement about what is present to my consciousness and reports about how things appear to me cannot be mistaken.
120.See, for example, Richard Rorty, *Philosophy and the Mirror of Nature* (Princeton: Princeton University Press, 1979) and the collection of essays in *Contemporary Readings in Epistemology*.
121.Plantinga, "Reason and Belief in God," pp. 59-60.
122.For a full discussion see Diogenes Allen, *Christian Belief in a Postmodern World*, chapters 7 and 8.
123.Robert Sokolowski, *The God of Faith and Reason: Foundations of Christian Theology* (Notre Dame, Ind.: University of Notre Dame Press, 1982), p. xi.
124.See Psalm 19:1-4.
125.A full discussion of the history of the "Two Books" can be found in A. R. Peacocke, *Creation and the World of Science*, Chapter One.

126.See also George Hendry, *Theology of Nature* (Philadelphia: Westminster Press, 1980).

127.Genesis 1:26-31; 2:15.

128.Matthew 25:31-46.

129.John Polkinghorne, *One World: The Interaction of Science and Theology* (Princeton: Princeton University Press, 1986), pp. 65-77.

130.Granted some theologians object to any attempt at apologetics or natural theology, but Alvin Plantinga has a convincing defense of the usefulness of apologetics in his essay "Reason and Belief in God," especially pp. 63-73, in which he discusses Calvin and Barth and concludes with a defense of natural theology if it is modified from the traditional view of it.

Chapter 3

Myths, Models, Paradigms, and Process Metaphysics

Introduction

Ian Barbour is arguably the most influential writer on the subject of the relationship between science and religion. His early work *Issues in Science and Religion*[1] became the standard textbook on the subject, and his study *Myths, Models, and Paradigms*[2] has influenced such a wide range of philosophers, theologians, and scientists interested in this area that one reviewer has said of Barbour: "Everyone in the field is indebted to him."[3]

However, Barbour's significance for any discussion of the relationship between theology and science is not derived primarily from his influence, for his real importance lies in the development of one of the most consistent themes running throughout his works – theology and science should be integrated into a coherent world-view by the use of metaphysics, and process philosophy provides the best conceptual scheme to accomplish this integration.[4] Barbour calls this position a *theology of nature*, which views science and religion as contributing to one another indirectly in the search for a consistent metaphysics, in contrast to a *natural theology*, which tries to draw theological conclusions directly from science.[5] Barbour defends this approach against attempts to isolate theology and science into two completely independent spheres, but his claims to achieve an integrated system are modest:

we must not expect to achieve a total integrated system of thought of the kind developed during the Middle Ages. Any conceptual synthesis will be partial and tentative. Human experience is diverse and varied, and each field of inquiry must have its own autonomy; any limited synthesis will have to allow for considerable pluralism. The connection of both science or [sic] religion with any metaphysical system must be a loose one, and the integrity of both fields must be respected.[6]

And, even though Barbour finds metaphysical categories inescapable and process philosophy to provide the best conceptual scheme, the theologian needs "to adapt, not adopt, a metaphysics..."[7]in is or her work.

Barbour's comprehensive survey and treatment of the methodological issues involved in the relationship between religion and science left many of his readers eager to see how he would further develop his position on the integration of the two disciplines, and in *Myths, Models, and Paradigms* Barbour promised his readers a move beyond his discussion of preliminary issues and a future exploration of the way the insights of process philosophy could lead to the modification of classical religious models so that they could more accurately reflect the experiences of the Christian community.[8]

Barbour delivered on his promise with the publication of his 1989-1990 Gifford Lectures *Religion in an Age of Science*.[9] In this work, Barbour gives his most recent and thorough statement of his position by providing a systematic and theoretical overview of the relationship between religion and science. In addition, he draws more heavily on process theology and philosophy than in his previous works in order to demonstrate how process thought can achieve a fruitful integration of theology and science.

The integration Barbour proposes is impressive indeed, and his treatment of the issues involved in relating science and theology contains many valuable insights for those exploring this area; however, Barbour's way of conceiving the integration of theology and science is ultimately unsuccessful. This chapter will make the case for this claim by critiquing both the method which underpins his integration of science and theology and the results of the application of his method to specific areas in which scientific theories may be of theological concern. The order of discussion of Barbour's position will essentially follow the structure of *Religion in an Age of Science*, and Barbour's earlier works will be drawn upon as needed to supplement his treatment of particular issues.

The Integration of Science and Religion: Method

Barbour's exposition of the integration of science and religion begins with a discussion of methodological issues and includes: (1) the possible ways of relating science and religion, (2) the role of models and paradigms in science and religion, and (3) the similarities and differences in science and religion.

Ways of Relating Science and Religion

In his recent work,[10] Barbour articulates his position on the relationship between theology and science within the context of his discussion of four possible stances religion may take *vis-a-vis* natural science: (1) Conflict, (2) Independence, (3) Dialogue, and (4) Integration.[11] Each of these stances includes philosophical assumptions and draws upon three disciplines: (1) science (defined as the "empirical study of the order of nature"), (2) theology (defined as the "critical reflection on the life and thought of the religious community"), and (3) two branches of philosophy, epistemology (defined as the "analysis of the characteristics of inquiry and knowledge"), and metaphysics (defined as the "analysis of the most general characteristics of reality").[12] In addition, each stance has a number of variants, with the Conflict, Independence, and Dialogue models having two variants each; the Integration model has three.[13]

The first major option used to describe the relationship between religion and science discussed by Barbour is Conflict. The Conflict option's two variants are: (1) Scientific Materialism, which holds that the scientific method is the only reliable path to knowledge and that matter (or matter and energy) is the fundamental reality in the universe; and (2) Biblical Literalism, which Barbour identifies with the "Creation Science" movement. Though it may seem strange to put two such opposite ends of the theological spectrum together, Barbour insists the two have a number of common features: (1) both believe there is a conflict between contemporary science and religious beliefs, (2) both seek a sure foundation for knowledge, and (3) both claim science and theology make rival literal statements about the history of nature so that one must choose between them.[14] Barbour rejects the positions taken by both variants for two reasons: first, both positions misuse science by not respecting science's proper boundaries, and second, neither variant respects the differences between the disciplines of religion and science.[15]

The second major option is Independence. The Independence option seeks to overcome the weaknesses of the Conflict option by viewing religion and science as completely independent and autonomous enterprises. Each discipline has its own distinctive domain and its own characteristic methods which can be justified on its own terms; in addition, each mode of inquiry is selective and has its limitations. The motivation for this separation into watertight compartments is the desire to be faithful to the true nature of each field, that is, to preserve the distinctive character of the life and thought of both disciplines.[16]

The Independence option has two variants: (1) Contrasting Methods, which Barbour associates with Protestant neo-orthodoxy and existentialism, and (2) Differing Languages, which Barbour associates with philosophers and theologians influenced by Ludwig Wittgenstein and linguistic analysis. Each of these positions divides the territories of theology and science in its own way. Neo-orthodoxy separates the two by arguing that theology is based on divine revelation and science on human observation and reason.[17] Existentialism views religion as belonging to the realm of personal selfhood and subjective involvement and science as belonging to the realm of impersonal objects and objective detachment.[18] Linguistic analysis understands the two disciplines to be differing language games, with scientific language used primarily for summarizing data, correlating regularities in observable phenomena, and producing technological applications; religious language functions to recommend a way of life, to elicit a set of attitudes, and to encourage allegiance to particular moral principles.[19]

Each of these positions has its own strengths and makes a contribution to the proper understanding of the relationship between religion and science: neo-orthodoxy rightly stresses the centrality of Christ and the prominence of scripture in the Christian tradition, existentialism rightly puts personal commitment at the center of religious faith, and linguistic analysis rightly shows the diversity of functions of religious language; however, each position also has serious difficulties which renders it inadequate as a model for the relationship between theology and science. Neo-orthodoxy emphasizes divine transcendence to the point that it fails to deal adequately with immanence, treats nature as the unredeemed setting for human redemption, and is ineffective in dealing with religious pluralism. Existentialism privatizes and interiorizes religion to such an extent that it neglects religion's communal aspects and leaves everything outside the self devoid of religious significance. Linguistic analysis fails for it cannot develop a coherent interpretation of experience into a unified world view.[20] Thus, Barbour contends the Independence model and its variants leave out the possibility of a constructive dialogue between and a mutual enrichment of theology and science, and, while the Independence model may be valid as a good starting point or first approximation, theologians need to go further in their explorations of the relationship between religion and science.

The third major option for modeling the relationship between theology and science is Dialogue. Advocates of the Dialogue model devote themselves to exploring indirect interactions between religion and science.[21] The two variants of the Dialogue model stem from their respective areas of exploration and involve examining boundary questions and methodological parallels. Those who pursue boundary questions most often concern themselves with the basic presuppositions of the scientific enterprise or certain possible points of contact such as contingency or questions occurring at the limits of the two disciplines.[22] Those who pursue methodological parallels look for common features in scientific and theological method.[23]

Barbour considers the Dialogue model a clear advance over the other models, but he finds it to be inadequate, for he contends that the points of contact between theology and science involve more than just basic presuppositions and boundary questions, and therefore classical theological doctrines need to be reformulated, not merely correlated with science.[24] Furthermore, the consideration of methodology is illuminating for both fields, but it will not serve as the most adequate model for relating theology and science for two reasons: (1) it runs the danger of minimizing the actual differences that exist between science and religion, and (2) it should be viewed as merely a preliminary task to the new insights that theology may gain on substantive issues as a result of the interaction with the theories of science.[25]

The fourth major option is Integration. Defenders of this model hold that some form of integration is possible between the content of the two disciplines. The Integration model has three variants: (1) natural theology, (2) theology of nature, and (3) systematic synthesis.[26]

Natural theology seeks to base arguments for the existence of God on reason rather than revelation or religious experience, and a number of theologians and philosophers have reformulated the teleological argument, claiming that the existence of God can be inferred from evidences of design in nature which are more apparent in light of current developments in science such as the Anthropic Principle.[27] Other defenders of natural theology are at work, such as Richard Swinburne, who has developed an argument for the existence of God based upon Bayes's Theorem.

Barbour has stated that he has little interest in revivals of natural theology such as reformulated versions of the teleological argument,[28] and he gives a number of reasons why he thinks natural theology is of little value. First, debates about the validity of these arguments continue, and the issues are far from resolved. Second, Barbour agrees with Hume that even if these arguments are accepted, they leave one only with an intelligent designer and not the personal God of the Bible. And third, even if natural theology can show the existence of God is a plausible hypothesis, few if any persons have come to faith by argument, and these arguments remain far removed from the life of an actual religious community.[29]

A theology of nature appears much more promising to Barbour than a natural theology. The theology of nature position has a more adequate starting point than natural theology, for the theology of nature position begins within a religious tradition as critical reflection based upon that tradition's religious experience and historical revelation takes place. This reflection results in the theologian seeing the need to reformulate traditional doctrines in the light of current science. Science and religion remain considered as relatively independent sources of ideas, but they do have areas of overlapping concerns, for certain areas, such as the doctrines of creation, providence, and human nature, are affected by the findings of science. Barbour cautions the theologian not to adapt to limited or speculative theories which are likely to be abandoned in the future; rather, he or she should draw mainly from broad features of science that are widely accepted.[30]

Systematic synthesis is the third variant of the integration option and attempts a more complete integration of religion and science than the theology of nature position. In the systematic synthesis approach, science and religion contribute to a coherent world-view which is elaborated into a comprehensive metaphysics. Metaphysics, defined as "the search for a set of general categories in terms of which diverse types of experience can be interpreted,"[31] provides an inclusive conceptual scheme capable of representing the fundamental characteristics of all events and serves as the arena of common reflection between theology and science. Process philosophy, which was formulated under the influence of scientific and religious thought, is the most promising candidate to serve the mediating role between theology and science.[32]

Barbour concludes his discussion of the possible stances religion may take concerning the natural sciences with a statement of his position:

> I am in basic agreement with the "Theology of Nature" position, coupled with a cautious use of process philosophy. Too much reliance on science (in natural theology) or on science and process philosophy (as in Birch and Cobb) can lead to the neglect of the areas of experience that I consider most important religiously. As I see it, the center of the Christian life is an experience of reorientation, the healing of our brokenness in new

wholeness, and the expression of a new relationship to God and to the neighbor. Existentialists and linguistic analysts rightly point to the primacy of personal and social life in religion, and neo-orthodoxy rightly says that for the Christian community it is in response to the person of Christ that our lives can be changed. But the centrality of redemption need not lead us to belittle creation, for our personal and social lives are intimately bound to the rest of the created order. We are redeemed in and with the world, not from the world. Part of our task, then, is to articulate a theology of nature, for which we will have to draw from both religious and scientific sources.... In articulating a theology of nature, a systematic metaphysics can help us toward a coherent vision. But Christianity should never be equated with any metaphysical system. There are dangers if either scientific or religious ideas are distorted to fit a preconceived synthesis that claims to encompass all reality.... I will try to do justice to what is valid in the Independence position, though I will be mainly developing the Dialogue position concerning methodology and the Integration thesis with respect to the doctrines of creation and human nature.[33]

Models and Paradigms

Barbour treats the parallels between the methods of science and the methods of religion in his discussion of models and paradigms. In his discussion, he treats the general structures of science and religion, the role of conceptual models in both fields, the place of paradigms in both disciplines, and closes with a treatment of tentativeness and commitment in each field.

The structures of science and religion

Science has two fundamental components: (1) particular observations and experimental data, and (2) general concepts and theories. Barbour stresses that the relationship between theory and data is a complex one. First, the relationship involves acts of creative imagination since theories involve novel concepts not found in the data and refer to entities and relationships which are not directly observable. New concepts and relationships are often first thought of by analogy with a more familiar concept or relationship coupled with a new modification or adaption. The analogy is then systematically developed as a conceptual model of a postulated entity which cannot be directly observed, and the model leads to the formulation of a generalized and abstract theory.[34] Second, theories must be tested to scientifically useful, and Barbour claims, like the majority of philosophers of science, that theories cannot be tested in isolation but only as part of a network of theories. Third, all data are theory-laden; that is, there is no theory-free observation and theories do influence observations in many ways. And fourth, the process of observation may alter the object observed itself.[35]

Barbour relies on Thomas Kuhn's idea of a paradigm as his description of how theory and data are related. Following Kuhn, he rejects Popper's formalism and empiricism and emphasizes the contextual, historical, and relative nature of science. Theories are to be assessed by Kuhn's criteria of agreement with data, coherence, scope, and fertility. Truth is said to mean correspondence with reality, and thus Barbour defends a version of critical realism, but since one never has direct access to reality, the criteria of truth will include Kuhn's four criteria and use some of the insights of the coherence and pragmatic theories of truth as well. Scientific knowledge does not lead to certainty and is incomplete, tentative, and subject to revision, but it does have reliable procedures for testing and evaluating theories.[36]

Religion also has two fundamental components: (1) religious experience, which forms the data for reflection, and (2) religious beliefs and concepts, which are systematically formalized as doctrines. Religious experience is of six types: (1) numinous experience of the holy, (2) mystical experience of unity, (3) transformative experience of restoration, (4) courage in facing suffering and death, (5) moral experience of obligation, and (6) experience of order and creativity in the world. Religious experiences, like the data in science, are theory-laden, for there are no uninterpreted experiences, and theology is understood by Barbour as critical reflection on religious experience. In addition, religious experiences are not merely solitary but always take place within a community. Differences of degree do exist between the data in science and religion, however, for: (1) religious beliefs exercise an even greater influence on the data than theories do in science, and (2) the experiential testing of religious beliefs is problematic (though not totally dissimilar, for there are adequate criteria for assessing the adequacy of religious beliefs -- they can be evaluated by theologians within a paradigm community using the criteria of fruitfulness, scope, coherence and agreement with data).[37]

The second kind of data for religious reflection is a particular religion's stories and rituals. Religious stories were initially the products of experiences or events interpreted imaginatively which were later recorded in scriptures and became part of the religious experiences of subsequent generations.[38] The three central stories of Christianity are the creation of the world, the covenant with Israel, and the life of Christ. These primary stories are recalled in liturgy and acted out in ritual, and past events thus become present in symbolic reenactment. Subsequent generations respond to these initial stories and add to them new layers of experience and ritual, and systematic concepts, beliefs, and doctrines are elaborated and reformulated to interpret the primary religious phenomena.[39]

The role of models in science and religion

Science and religion have similar structures, and the role of models within science and religion suggest significant parallels as well.

Science uses a variety of models (such as experimental or scale models constructed in laboratories or mathematical models), but the most important for Barbour are "theoretical models" which "take the form of imagined mechanisms or processes postulated in a new domain by analogy with familiar mechanisms or processes."[40] Models have three general characteristics: (1) they are analogical and contain both similarities with familiar situations (the positive analogy) and dissimilarities (the negative analogy), (2) they contribute to the extension of theories and their suggestiveness and open-endedness provide a continuing source of possible applications and modifications, and (3) they are intelligible as units and provide mental pictures whose unity can be understood more readily than a set of abstract equations. Barbour illustrates these features of models with his description of the "billiard-ball model" of a gas in which the behavior of a gas is imagined as analogous to elastic balls colliding within a box.[41]

In discussing the ontological status of models, Barbour rejects classical realism and instrumentalism and advocates what he calls "critical realism." Barbour's version of critical realism views models and theories as

abstract symbol systems, which inadequately and selectively represent particular aspects of the world for specific purposes. This view preserves the scientist's realistic intent while recognizing that models and theories are imaginative human constructs. Models, on this reading, are to be taken seriously but not literally: they are neither literal pictures nor useful fictions but limited and inadequate ways of imagining what is not observable. They make tentative ontological claims that there are entities in the world something like those postulated in the models.[42]

Barbour also defends critical realism for religious models, for they are to be taken "seriously, not literally," since they are human constructs which help us interpret experience by imagining what cannot be observed.[43] Religious models correlate patterns in human experience and are not as conceptually articulated and systematically developed as beliefs or doctrines, which take the form of propositions. Religious models are like scientific models in that both are analogical, extensible, and unitary, yet they are unlike models in science in that they evoke distinctive attitudes which contain life-orienting and emotional power which result in personal transformation and reorientation. In addition, religious models are just as important as conceptual beliefs in a religion; however, in science models are always ancillary to theories.[44] Furthermore, complementary models are used in both science and religion due to conceptual limitations, as, for example, religion's use of personal and impersonal models of the divine reality which parallels the use of wave and particle models in quantum physics.[45]

The role of paradigms in science and religion

Parallels between the structures of science and religion and the use of models in science and religion exist, and there a number of important similarities in the function of paradigms in science and religion as well.

Barbour draws upon Kuhn's work in the philosophy of science and defines paradigms as "standard examples of scientific work that embody a set of conceptual and methodological assumptions"[46] and includes: (1) a research tradition, (2) the key historical examples through which the tradition is transmitted, and (3) the metaphysical assumptions implicit in the fundamental concepts of the tradition. Acceptance of the "paradigm-view" of scientific change leads to three important conclusions about the nature of science, each of which demonstrates a subjective and historically relative feature of science as well as an objective, empirical, and rational feature of science. First, all data are paradigm-dependent, but there are data on which adherents of rival paradigms can agree. Just as all data is theory-laden, all theories are paradigm-laden, for there is no pure observation language and the distinction between theory and observation is relative, pragmatic, and context dependent; nevertheless, adherents of rival paradigms can share some common assumptions. Second, paradigms are resistant to falsification by data, but data does cumulatively affect the acceptability of a paradigm. Contrary data cannot be accommodated indefinitely, and the accumulation of anomalies can undermine a paradigm and cause it to need to be replaced. And third, there are no rules for paradigm choice, but there are shared criteria for judgment in evaluating paradigms. Formal logical rules do not exist to tell one when to abandon a paradigm, but certain values, such as simplicity, coherence, and supporting evidence are agreed upon by the scientific community, and these shared criteria, though matters of personal judgment, keep paradigm choice from being merely arbitrary.[47]

Like science, a religious tradition transmits a broad set of methodological and metaphysical assumptions which Barbour calls a paradigm. Religious paradigms have the historically relative and subjective features of scientific paradigms, but the objective, empirical, and rational features of a religious paradigm is more problematic; however, Barbour comes to three conclusions about religious paradigms. First, religious experience is paradigm-dependent, and, though religious experience is not as public as scientific data, there are common features of a religious community which exert some control on the subjectivity of individual beliefs. Second, religious paradigms are highly resistant to falsification, but people may modify or abandon their most fundamental religious beliefs in light of their experiences, especially if they see a promising alternative framework. And third, there are no rules for paradigm choice in religion, but there are some shared criteria which Barbour suggests for evaluating beliefs within and between paradigm communities.[48] One problem which remains for Barbour's treatment of religions as paradigm communities is the question of how large a group is a paradigm community and how does one determine its boundaries? He concludes that the concept of paradigm shift is most helpful in understanding historical change if the term is used for rare comprehensive conceptual changes such as the emergence of early Christianity from Judaism and, to a lesser degree, the Protestant Reformation. He also raises the related question whether or not Christianity should be considered one paradigm and other religious communities alternative paradigms, and, though he does not explain how to reconcile these usages, he does treat entire religious traditions as single paradigms later.[49]

Barbour closes his discussion of models and paradigms by rejecting the stereotype that science uses tentative hypotheses which are continually revised while religious beliefs are held as unchanging dogmas, and he forcefully argues that scientists often hold their theories with great tenacity and religious believers frequently revise their doctrines. The supposed absolute dichotomies between science and religion are mistaken.[50]

Thus, Barbour concludes that science and religion have a number of parallels and many of the differences between the two are frequently more a difference of degree rather than kind, but he does see some features of religion which are without parallel in science, and it is to these important distinctions he turns before drawing his final conclusions about the methods of religion and science.

Similarities and Differences between Science and Religion

Differences without parallel do exist between science and religion and include: (1) the role of story and ritual, (2) the noncognitive functions of religious models in evoking attitudes and encouraging personal transformation, (3) the type of personal involvement characteristic of religious faith, and (4) the idea of revelation in historical events.[51] Three other important areas of similarities and differences emerge in exploring: (1) the character of historical inquiry in science and religion, (2) the question of objectivity and relativism in science and religion, and (3) the challenges posed by religious pluralism for the integration of science and religion.

History in science and religion

The role of history is important for science and religion for there is an increasing interest in history within the philosophy of science and religious stories are related to historical events.

Barbour compares the nature of scientific explanation with the five distinctive features proposed for historical explanation. First, the interpretive viewpoint is present in both history and science. The interests and commitments of the historian influence the construction of historical accounts, but objectivity (understood as intersubjective testability which requires openness, self-criticism, and fidelity to evidence) is also present. Subjectivity and cultural relativism are more evident in history than in science, but this is a matter of degree not kind, and objective controls decrease and interpretive elements increase across the disciplinary spectrum from the natural sciences, through the social sciences and history, to religion.[52] Second, Barbour contends that those who propose history as the intentions of agents and exclude a history of nature are mistaken, for many diverse factors, such as unconscious motives and social and economic forces, are at work in human history, and he does believe one can develop a history of nature.[53] Third, both science and history must deal with the issues of particularity and lawfulness. Barbour rejects those who see science as purely about general laws and history as purely about singular statements about particulars, for every event in science is unique in that it can never be duplicated in exhaustible detail (though regular and repeatable features are present), and no event in history is absolutely unique for the language used by historians presupposes common characteristics (such as revolution, for example). In addition, historians, while not using universal laws, do use law-like generalizations of limited temporal and geographic scope (for example, the structures of feudalism in medieval France and generalizations about human motives for acting).[54] Fourth, unpredictability is present in both science and history.[55] And fifth, there are a variety of types of explanation within the disciplines of science and history. Explanation makes some area of existence comprehensible either in terms of its components or details or by placing it in a broader context which makes its meaning and significance clear, and thus different types of rationality operate in the natural sciences, social sciences, and theology. Each of these disciplines is rational, however, for each discipline has criteria of judgment accepted by all working within the discipline and standards of intersubjective criticism make possible the discussion and revision of claims.[56]

Stories are central in the life of a religious community, and questions of the historicity of the stories is inevitable for theology. Christian theologians have outlined three features of stories: (1) canonical stories, which are indispensable for theology and reveal God as a character who cannot be exhausted by theological concepts; (2) community stories, which give a religious community its interpretive categories and call forth actions in ways unlike stories in academic historical accounts and are vindicated by patterns of living, not philosophical arguments; and (3) personal stories, which are related to the larger stories in which we see ourselves and shape our character and vision in ways concepts or principles do not. Unlike some narrative theologians, however, Barbour insists that the question of the historical veracity of the stories must be faced, for even though confessing Jesus is the Christ is beyond what is historically provable, Jesus of Nazareth was a historical person and the theologian cannot ignore investigating the events the Bible narrates.[57] In addition, the theologian must examine the validity of the ontological claims implicit in the biblical story, for the God of the Bible is a God who acts in nature, history, and human lives, and we must ask how we are to conceive of God's action. The biblical stories serve as the starting point of philosophical and religious reflection, and the theologian must consider the coherence and validity of belief as well as the transformative power of the stories. Furthermore, Barbour holds the stories must be communicated across communities in order to avoid total relativism, and this can be accomplished if one imaginatively shares in the outlook of other communities. Thus, dialogue becomes possible in way not allowed if one stays within an individual story.[58]

Objectivity and relativism

It is fair to say that Barbour tries to steer the middle course between extremes on most positions, and his treatment of objectivity and relativism is no exception. Barbour rejects both the extreme relativism of "externalist" accounts of science and the extreme objectivism of "internalist" accounts of science. Internalist accounts go too far, for science does have a relative and social structure, but proponents of externalist views underestimate the constraints placed on theories by the data arising from the interaction with nature. Many Third World critiques of science and religion, such as some liberation theology, are guilty of a similar flaw, for they reduce theology and science to simply economic and political interests and fail to do justice to the other factors at work in the two disciplines. Against radical feminist critiques of science, Barbour defends two meanings of objectivity: (1) data should be intersubjectively reproducible even though theory-laden, and (2) criteria should be impartial and shared by the community of inquiry even though they are difficult to apply. In addition, Barbour rejects notions of objectivity which understand theories to be determined only by the object or are reductionistic in the sense that descriptions of the higher-level activities of integrated wholes are less valid than the physicochemical laws of component parts. And finally, radical feminists also go to far in their critique of religion, for they run the risk of eliminating what is valid within a religious tradition by perpetuating dualistic thinking through inverting dualisms to purge a religion's invalid elements.[59]

Religious pluralism

Differing interpretations of religious experience pose a special problem for the rationality of religion for there is much less of a consensus in religion than in science. Barbour examines the nature of the interpretation of religious experience and the diversity of religious communities, and he develops criteria for the assessment of religious claims.

Barbour holds that the distinction between experience and interpretation in religion, like the relationship between data and theory in science, is never absolute; rather, in both disciplines the distinction is relative and can be drawn at different points at different times for particular purposes.

From this point, Barbour concludes:

> If there is no uninterpreted experience, there can be *no immediate religious knowledge*, no "self-authenticating" awareness of God, no incorrigible intuition for which finality may be claimed. For when interpretation is present there is always the possibility of misinterpretation .... The key question is whether religious experience exercises any control on interpretation .... In my view, God is known through *interpreted experience*. Our knowledge of God is like knowledge of another self in being neither an immediate datum nor an inference. Another self is not immediately experienced; it must express itself through various media of language and action, which we interpret.... I conclude that beliefs are both brought to religious experience and derived from it.[60]

Differing religious experiences and their interpretation have produced different religious communities, and these communities take different attitudes toward one another. Barbour again wishes to steer between absolutism and relativism, and he examines five attitudes religious communities may take toward one another: (1) Absolutism, which claims there is only one true religion and all others are false; (2) Approximations of Truth, which claims other religions hold elements of truth more fully present in one's own tradition; (3) Identity of Essence, which claims all religions are the same though expressed in different cultural forms; (4) Cultural Relativism, which claims religion is an expression of a particular culture; and (5) Pluralistic Dialogue, which claims the presence of ultimate reality is present in the faith of persons in all traditions and that we may all learn from one another.[61] Barbour endorses Pluralistic Dialogue as the most adequate attitude toward other religions, even though it is closer to relativism than absolutism, for he sees it as the most promising for religious cooperation in our global age.[62]

Even though Barbour asserts religion cannot claim to be scientific or able to conform to the standards of science, he does hold that some of the same spirit of inquiry found in science can be exemplified in religion.[63] Four criteria can be used to assess religious beliefs within a paradigm community. First, religious beliefs should agree with data. The interpretation of initiating events, formative experiences, and subsequent experiences goes through a process of testing, filtering, and public validation in the history of the community, with some experiences becoming accepted as normative and some rejected. This testing process is far less rigorous than science, however, and does not produce the same intercultural consensus as science.[64] Second, religious beliefs should be coherent. Theology, as critical reflection on the life and thought of the community, is concerned with the coherence and systematic interconnection of beliefs with the core of a religious tradition.[65] Third, religious beliefs should be broad in scope. They should be coherent in offering an account of diverse kinds of experience, consistent with the well-supported findings of science, and capable of contributing to a comprehensive metaphysics.[66] And fourth, religious beliefs should be fertile. They should be able to stimulate creative theological reflection, to nourish religious experience and promote personal transformation, to sustain ethical action, to provide desirable implications for the most pressing problems of our time.[67]

These criteria can also be used to make comparative judgments between religious traditions, for, Barbour argues, if religious language does make implicit and explicit claims about reality, one cannot abandon the use of criteria to evaluate concepts and beliefs. However, in keeping with his commitment to Pluralistic Dialogue, Barbour insists critical reflection upon religious beliefs must be primarily motivated by the search for truth rather than any desire to prove superiority over others.[68]

It is the methodology discussed above which Barbour uses to lay the foundation for his discussion of the relationship between religion and the content of particular scientific theories. Before examining the application of Barbour's method, I will first discuss a number of specific problems with Barbour's methodology, many of which will emerge to cause further difficulties later in his attempt to integrate theology and science.

Barbour's Method of Integration: Critical Evaluation

Barbour's attempt to integrate theology and science on the level of method has much to commend – an awareness of the broader conception of scientific rationality prevalent in the current philosophy of science, a careful examination of the similarities and differences between religion and science, a rejection of claims for the irrelevancy of natural science to theology, and a thoughtful avoidance of extreme positions which may be the current fad. However, despite these strengths, Barbour's method of integration contains important weaknesses which undermine his position. Included among these weaknesses are difficulties with Barbour's: (1) use of the term "paradigm," (2) treatment of religious experience, (3) definition of theology and inattention to revelation, and (4) conception of metaphysics.

Paradigms

Barbour's use of the term "paradigm" runs into two difficulties which greatly undermine its usefulness for integrating science and religion: (1) the use is equivocal, and (2) there is a crucial disanalogy between Kuhn's use of "paradigm" in science and Barbour's use of "paradigm" in religion. Barbour's use of "paradigm" in science is consistent with Kuhn, but when he applies the term to religion problems emerge, for the paradigm concept is too broad to make an adequate description of religion. The difficulty becomes most apparent in Barbour's discussion of the question of how large a group constitutes a paradigm community and how one determines its boundaries.[69] Barbour holds the concept of a paradigm shift is most helpful for relatively rare comprehensive conceptual changes, but he then proceeds to treat large and small historical changes, communities and subcommunities, and even entire religious traditions in a paradigm-like manner.[70] With this move, any specific understanding of what a paradigm is begins to slip into obscurity or else is too vague to be of much use for the integration of science and the beliefs of a specific religious community.

Barbour incorporates Imre Lakatos's distinction of a "hard core" and "auxiliary hypotheses" and Nancey Murphy's notion of a "theological research program" to try to bring more precision to his treatment of religious beliefs,[71] but this leaves problems unanswered and creates new ones, for he now needs to determine how broad a set of ideas should be thought of as a research program as well as specify a theological "hard core."[72] Barbour suggests treating a school of thought as a research program, and he commends process theology as a research program with a hard core taken to be the belief in God as

> creative love, revealed in Christ, while divine omnipotence is treated as an auxiliary hypothesis" that can be modified to allow for the data of human freedom, evil and suffering, and evolutionary history.[73]

But this only reveals the confusion present in Barbour's treatment, for if process theology is a research program one cannot put the process conception of divine omnipotence as an auxiliary hypothesis since it is an integral part of process thought which contrasts it to traditional theism. An auxiliary hypothesis for process thought would be a competing description of *how* God's omnipotence is limited rather than the assertion God's omnipotence is limited. Furthermore, the idea of God "as creative love revealed in Christ" could not function as the hard core of a specifically process research program for there is nothing in this statement distinctive to process thought or exclusive of traditional or some nontraditional varieties of Christian theism. A non-process theologian could take the same hard core proposed by Barbour without any reservations. Barbour's problem here is that treating a school of thought as a research program, like his use of paradigm, is too broad or perhaps confused to be fruitful for application to religious beliefs.[74]

The reason Barbour's treatment of paradigm in religion is too broad to be useful for religious beliefs is not simply a lack of clarity on his part; the problem comes from the existence of a crucial disanalogy between paradigms as understood by Kuhn and Barbour's application of the paradigm concept to religion. As Gary Gutting has put it:

> ...scientific authority is necessarily based on the fact that scientific communities do reach a common judgment about which theories should be used as a basis for exploring a given scientific domain; the mark of a scientific community is consensus about a paradigm. Without such consensus, there would be no unified judgment of the scientific community that could be put forward as authoritative. Because of this, the Kuhnian account of scientific cognitive authority cannot be extended to religion, where there are a wide variety of competing paradigms, without the consensus needed for a cognitively authoritive judgment.[75]

Gutting acknowledges that consensus does occur within specific religious groups, but to take the authority of any one group over another is arbitrary and unlike science where judgments are shared by almost all who are competent in the subject matter. Kuhn disavowed that his theory could apply to social science since there is no agreed-upon paradigm, and religion exhibits even less consensus than social science. Treating a religious tradition as a whole does not help, for if one broadens the discussion from specific sects to general religious communities (such as Christian or Hindu), one observes that there is even less consensus present.[76] And finally, in addition to the difficulties pointed out by Gutting, there is also the problem of defining a paradigm narrowly enough that specific religious sects may qualify as a paradigm community.

As one can see, this crucial disanalogy undermines the treatment of religious communities as paradigms in the sense suggested by Kuhn, for religious beliefs are more like metaphysical beliefs as discussed in Chapter 2 than like scientific theories, and it would be best to drop the term or at the very least modify it by seriously furthering the distance between claims of parallels between religious and scientific paradigms. It is significant that

Barbour concedes that religion cannot claim to be scientific nor does it conform to the standards of science, though he does think that religion can exemplify the same spirit of inquiry found in science and that religion can, in limited ways, use some of the criteria of science in evaluating beliefs. This is indeed the case, but the use of "paradigm" need not be embraced in order to observe adequate rationality parallels between science and religion, and treating religious communities as paradigms suffers from a serious defect, for if the crucial feature of scientific authority is the judgment of the paradigm community, and religion is unable to duplicate this crucial feature, then it appears dubious at best to talk about paradigms in religion. However, all need not be lost for Barbour, for one can accept a broader conception of scientific and religious rationality which incorporates Kuhn's idea of values present in scientific explanation without necessarily accepting his controversial ideas about paradigms,[77] so it makes little difference to the theologian attempting to integrate theology and science whether religion can be considered a paradigm or not. Whether it makes any difference to the success of Barbour's methodology is, of course, another matter.

Treatment of religious experience

Barbour understands knowledge of God to come through "interpreted experience," and he argues that there can be no immediate knowledge or self-authenticating awareness of God due to the presence of interpretation through models in every religious experience and the possibility of error in interpreting religious experience. Barbour's case for these claims is faulty, for he fails to rule out direct religious experience and to show that interpretation takes place in the moment of religious experience. These weakness require careful examination, for Barbour's treatment of religious experience will have direct bearing on his discussion of theology and lack of attention to the concept of revelation.

Barbour rules out direct religious experience because it presupposes a giveness which he thinks is untenable since all experience is theory-laden; however, William Rottschaefer has pointed out some key weaknesses in Barbour's case to rule out direct religious experience.[78] First, the possibility of error is not sufficient to rule out direct or inferential religious experience, for Barbour has confused questions of the mode of cognition (experiential and inferential) with questions of justification (confirmation and falsification). Second, the fact that our beliefs are used to interpret experiences is not enough to warrant the claim that religion is interpreted experience, for cognitive adaptiveness (the ability to bring large interpretative elements to bear on our experiences at one time and at other times to pare down the use of interpretative elements and allow the experiential input to be determinative) leaves open the possibility of direct and inferential modes of cognition.[79] And third, the use of models does not rule out direct or inferential modes of religious cognition, for in a religious experience, such as the feeling of awe and reverence, the experience itself has some religious content regardless of the model used to interpret what the object of this feeling is.[80] Thus, Rottschaefer concludes that Barbour's account of religious experience leaves the question of inferential and direct religious cognition open.

A second difficulty for Barbour's understanding of religious experience is his claim that interpretation is present in the moment of religious experience. Barbour illustrates his understanding of religious experience with the "duck-rabbit" line drawing discussed by Wittgenstein in his *Philosophical Investigations*.[81] Wittgenstein called attention to the fact that seeing something means seeing it *as* a particular object. John Hick developed the idea into "experiencing as" to emphasize the total person's involvement in interpretation, and Barbour contends that "interpreting as" is even better.[82] However, the claim that what is taking place in our "seeing as" is interpretation is highly controversial. Garrett Green, for example, has argued these translations to Wittgenstein's view miss the main point, for "what is striking about the shifting-gestalt figures is that we merely *see* them, quite apart from any deliberative cognitive effort,"[83] and, drawing upon the work of N. R. Hanson, argues that differences of visual aspect are not different interpretations, for if one describes such experiences in this way, one is driven to the absurdity of positing instantaneous and unconscious interpretation.[84] Green concludes something *like* interpretation is part of perception, but, as he points out, interpretation is normally thought of as a deliberative, intentional, activity and is therefore unlike our experiences of gestalt figures.[85] The act of interpretation does not occur when one sees a rabbit (or duck) but only when one thinks about the experience in light of further investigation and becomes aware of other possibilities.[86] I am not so sure that instantaneous interpretation cannot take place, but I think Green and Hanson raise valid questions about what is the exact nature of what is taking place in perception, and it is not clear that interpretation, in the normal sense of the term, is taking place. In addition, I think it important to point out that the difficulty with the duck-rabbit figure can be resolved on a higher level; that is, the drawing is really neither a picture of a duck or a rabbit but a carefully drawn figure *intended* to give rise to a number of possible perceptions and therefore should not be taken as a suitable description for all our perceptions, many of which have little ambiguity.[87] Thus, it is not clear whether interpretation, in the usual sense of the term, necessarily has to be present in religious experience, and, though Barbour is correct to emphasize the importance of context in shaping our experiences, there is perhaps still room for more "givenness" than he is willing to allow.

Theology and revelation

Barbour defines theology as "critical reflection on the life and thought of the religious community,"[88] and, in an extended definition which enjoys current support, as

> ... the systematic and self-critical reflection of a paradigm community concerning its beliefs. The theologian traces the ways in which the memory of historical exemplars has shaped the life and thought of the community. He explores the relationships among its central models and doctrines and the implications of its views of nature, man and God.[89]

This understanding of theology is highly problematic for: (1) it does not adequately describe how mainstream or classical Christianity has viewed its understanding of theology and the relationship of theology to revelation, (2) it is too broad and does not fit well with Barbour's realism, and (3) it is undermined by Barbour's treatment of parallels between science and religion.

First, Barbour's definition of theology does not adequately describe how mainstream or classical Christianity has understood the task of theology and the relation of theology to revelation. The dominant Christian understanding of theology is rooted in the reflections of Anselm, who thought of theology as "faith seeking understanding."[90] Anselm includes, as did many of his predecessors (Augustine a prime example), a prayer to God as part of his attempt to think theologically, which includes requests for direction in his thought and forgiveness for his inability to express the truth of God's reality adequately. Anselm and his predecessors clearly see the attempt to do theology as more than "reflection on the life and thought of the religious community," for they understand their efforts to do theology as *contact* with God, the one who has made prior initiatives toward and communicated with them and will in some way aid and evaluate their efforts. This way of understanding theology is not confined to the past, and a number of contemporary theologians see their task in this way as well.[91] Theology, in this dominant stream of Christianity, is not just reflection upon religious experience; it is itself a form of religious experience, though most contemporary theologians do not begin and end in prayer (at least in their writings). Theology, for the Christian, cannot be limited to reflection on the life and thought of the community, for theology is part of the life and thought of the community and the community's encounter with God. Thus, Barbour's definition of theology does not fit well with how many Christian theologians understand their task, for it skirts the issue of whether or not theology really does speak genuinely of and interacts with God, and it omits what many Christian theologians see as the actual subject matter of theology – God.

Second, Barbour's definition of theology is too broad, for there is nothing in his definition of theology which indicates his own critical realism. Barbour's definition is so broad it is compatible with any number of forms of anti-realism or even atheism. A definition this flexible seems odd for a thinker advocating realism, and one would think a realist understanding of theology would have some acknowledgment of the reality to which it refers (God) in its definition. To his credit, Barbour is a critical realist and would no doubt argue we are having experiences with reality, but his definition of theology does not require this. Perhaps some of this lack of precision is due to Barbour's treatment of critical realism which is in need of more clarification. Barbour does advocate a critical realist view of models in religion, but the strongest claim he makes is to say that models of God should be taken "seriously, not literally," since they are not mere "useful fictions." His description of what it means to take models seriously is unclear and fails to due justice to the fact that taking a model seriously in science means treating at least some of its aspects as *identical* with what is being modeled.[92] A fuller treatment of what it means to take theological models seriously is needed in Barbour's approach, and perhaps this would sharpen his critical realism and his definition of theology.

And third, Barbour's treatment of theology is also undermined by his attempt to draw parallels between science and religion, for his treatment of the relationship between theology and religious experience does not fit well with the parallel of theory and data in science. The theologian seems to have no real parallel role to anyone working within the scientific community, for Barbour clearly would not be willing to define scientific theories, which are the parallel to theological formulations, as "critical reflection on the life and thought of the scientific community." In addition, theology appears to be capable of being separated out from religious experience as a second-order activity, but this is hard to reconcile with Barbour's claim that no sharp distinction between experience and interpretation can be drawn.[93] This last point obfuscates Barbour's position even further, for he sees one of the key problems with drawing parallels between religion and science as whether or not the data (experience) in religion exercises any control over the theory (beliefs or theology). Barbour is clear that religion is simply not capable of achieving the level of agreement (and thus rationality) available to science, and his parallel between science and religion significantly breaks down. The way out of Barbour's dilemma and a stronger case for realism could be made if one started with a recognition that a paradigm or the presence of interpretation need not preclude allowing for some "givenness" or authoritative revelation present in the data of religious experience as Barbour seems to think. One could make the revelation obtained from an interaction with God the parallel to data, for the revelation would still need to be interpreted in light of one's background beliefs such as prior encounters with God in the community's history. Thus, Barbour's description of theology falls short of being as effective as it could be due to flawed analogies of the parallels that can be drawn between science and religion and inattention as to what the data for theology has actually been understood to be within the Christian community.

As noted earlier, theology as practiced in the Christian community has traditionally been thought to begin with a God who has made God's self known in some way through revelation to an individual and/or community. The obvious question to be asked, then, is how does God make God's self known? Barbour consistently holds that it is through certain historical events interpreted by key models, and he rejects any direct revelation from God to human beings for these models arise from "man's analogical imagination."[94] In discussing the work of Austin Farrer, a pioneer in the work on biblical images, Barbour agrees with Farrer that events in the biblical tradition are interpreted through dominant images, but he rejects Farrer's claim that God has revealed the images used to interpret the events in the Bible. The reasons Barbour rejects Farrer's treatment will need to be discussed in some detail, for they reveal some key weaknesses in Barbour's approach.

Barbour contends images are to be rejected as God-given for: (1) there are no directly revealed images, (2) authorized images are immune to criticism and leave the question of on what basis one should accept the claim that images are revealed open, (3) imagination should not be isolated as a separate faculty which God uses, and (4) Farrer detaches images from the human experience in which they occur and thus minimizes the influence of psychological forces and cultural images (literature, mythology, art, etc.).[95] Since these images are products of religious experience as interpreted by the imagination of human beings capable of error, Barbour consistently rejects any God-givenness in the images used of God.

Barbour is consistent but mistaken, for he does not rule out the revelation of the images, and I think Farrer's account makes a convincing case for the God-giveness of inspired images which serves as a much better starting point for theology than Barbour's account. In what follows, I will defend Farrer's treatment against Barbour's objections and show why it provides a better way of understanding theological reflection.

Farrer rejected revelation understood as dictated propositions,[96] for he argued that Christ's thought was expressed in the form of dominant images, such as the Kingdom of God, the Son of Man, the Israel of God, and the "infinitely complex and fertile image of sacrifice and communion, of expiation and covenant."[97] Farrer concluded that "divine truth is supernaturally communicated to men in an act of inspired thinking which falls into the shape of certain images."[98] For Farrer, these images came from the imperceptible operations of God on the natural structures of the human mind. Scriptural revelation operated not by suspending the normal operation of the poetic imagination, but by heightening it so that it became in the highest degree expressive of human capacities.[99] The images are God-given and exert tremendous creative force, interpret the events recorded in scripture, and of themselves signify and reveal.[100] Theology is the analysis and criticism of the revealed images; theology requires the images in order to do its task.

A careful analysis of Farrer's position shows that Barbour's criticisms have little force. First, Barbour's claim there can be no directly revealed images because interpretation precludes any "self-authenticating revelation" is suspect. Farrer does believe the images are both God-given and authoritative, but he holds interpretive activity accompanies the images, and indeed they are interpretations and part of their role is to facilitate more interpretation. As finite creatures who do not have direct access to the divine reality the images are needed and are the best way for God to communicate with us.[101] For Farrer, interpretation and givenness are not mutually exclusive categories. It is Barbour's own confused opposition between "God-given" and "interpretation" which is the problem. Barbour rejects that images can be directly God-given because interpretation is always present and therefore images must arise from the human analogical imagination, and he presents us with a stark "either-or" which is guilty of what Basil Mitchell has called "theological ping-pong."[102] In theological ping-pong, one assumes the question under consideration has two and only two answers which between them exhaust all the possible alternatives and are mutually exclusive. Once this "either-or" is set up the arguer then proceeds to show that one of the alternatives is absurd and by doing this justify the other position. In Barbour's case, the presence of interpretation precludes the givenness of revelation. Farrer's position is much more subtle than this, for it allows for human reception of God-given images without denying the place of human agency in the moment of revelation, and allows for a "both-and" approach to revelation. Furthermore, as the earlier discussion of religious experience pointed out, there is room for more "givenness" in religious experience than Barbour acknowledges, and Farrer's approach avoids the questionable features of Barbour's treatment of religious experience raised by Garrett Green.[103]

Second, Barbour is mistaken in claiming that Farrer believes images to be immune to criticism. As pointed out earlier, Farrer understands the work of theology to be the criticism of images, and he devotes a good bit of effort into developing a rule to criticize the revealed images.[104] Furthermore, Farrer believes religious belief must fit with other knowledge, for the mysteries of faith "must fit into one universe of sense with our natural knowledge of human personality, of history, of the form of nature, of the first principles of being: if they did not, they would not continue to be believed."[105] Granted, Farrer does accept by faith the revealed images and take them as his starting point, but this is consistent for Farrer believes that anytime knowledge of God occurs revelation will be present (as will human reason as well).[106] It is odd at first sight that Barbour would demand some basis for starting with revelation considering his own broader conception of rationality and his awareness of the contextual nature of knowledge, but it is not so surprising when one factors in his faulty description of Christian theology. I think Barbour does not treat theology as "faith seeking understanding" in part because in many ways, despite his broader understanding of scientific rationality, he still wishes to let science dictate the terms of rationality to religion.

Third, Barbour is wrong in thinking that Farrer wants to isolate imagination from other human faculties as the tool which God uses. Farrer held that human beings possessed a "luminous apex of consciousness" which is self-knowledge and includes conscious intelligence informed and supported by the senses and the imagination and the ability to make choices.[107] Farrer's treatment does not isolate one faculty, but involves all our cognitive abilities which are capable of being "supernaturalized" or enhanced by God.

And fourth, Barbour errs in thinking Farrer removes images from the human experience in which they occur. In fact, Farrer carefully traces the development of the dominant New Testament images and shows how much of their meaning is derived from their part in the earlier history of Israel, and he also discusses the development of these images apart from Israel in the mythology and art of more "primitive" or "polytheistic" cultures and the relationship of images to the writing of poetry.[108] Farrer sees divine activity at work in many places in human history which serve as preparation for understanding the great images when they impress themselves on the human mind.

Farrer's approach is not susceptible to Barbour's criticisms, and, while I personally find Farrer's treatment of revelation very convincing, the main value of Farrer's work for this discussion is how it is helpful in pointing out some deficiencies in Barbour's approach. The answers to Barbour's objections show that it is possible to not accept an "either-or" between "God-given" and "interpretation" and to recognize that there can be more "givenness" in revelation. Thus, Barbour's treatment of theology is not particularly helpful, and a position like Farrer's (and others who begin with "faith seeking understanding") which starts with the prior initiative of God to the believer rather than the more general category of "religious experience" offers a more fruitful starting point for Christian theology.[109]

Metaphysics

Barbour's understanding of metaphysics presents two important difficulties which undermine the usefulness of his approach to integrating science and theology: (1) weaknesses in Barbour's general understanding of metaphysics, and (2) weaknesses with Barbour 's specific choice of process metaphysics.

Barbour defines metaphysics as "the search for a set of general categories in terms of which diverse types of experience can be interpreted. An inclusive conceptual scheme is sought that can represent the fundamental characteristics of all events."[110] This understanding of metaphysics is consistent throughout his work and is taken from Alfred North Whitehead[111] and creates numerous difficulties for Barbour's position.

First, Barbour assumes a definition of metaphysics derived from process thought which provides him with a means to critique other attempts at relating theology and science which do not rely on the process understanding, but he does not offer convincing reasons for adopting his understanding of metaphysics. It is highly questionable to equate integration with process categories and then describe non-process thinkers as failing to achieve a satisfactory integration because they construe the integration of theology and science in other ways.[112] Perhaps this would be acceptable if it were obvious that the process understanding of metaphysics were correct, but this is far from the case. As pointed out in Chapter 2, process thought enjoys support from a small number of theologians and has little acceptance among current philosophers.[113] In fact, in a recent survey of the current scene in philosophy which includes a voluminous bibliography and a discussion of the rebirth of metaphysical debates, there is not a single mention of the process perspective, thus illustrating the lack of interest in process thought in discussing metaphysical problems in contemporary philosophy.[114] Now while this inattention may not quite be fair to process thought, it at the least shows that a process conception of metaphysics cannot simply be assumed as an adequate definition but must provide some justification of its use as the correct understanding of the nature of metaphysics. The need for defending the choice of a process conception of metaphysics is even more pressing if one considers the remarks of Nicholas Rescher, a leading contemporary philosopher very sympathetic to process thought who thinks it deserves more attention but concludes

> ... the process approach has many assets. But it has significant liabilities as well. It is not unfair to the historical situation to say that process philosophy remains no more than a glint in the mind's eye of various philosophers. A full-fledged development of the process doctrine does not yet exist as an accomplished fact, its development to the point where it can be compared with other major philosophical projects like materialism or absolute idealism still remains.[115]

Second, and even more importantly, Barbour's definition of metaphysics falls prey to the criticisms of conceiving metaphysics as a "comprehensive scheme," "overall framework of reality" or "system" given in Chapter 2: (1) greater generality is not a universal characteristic of metaphysics, (2) metaphysical hypotheses need not form a tightly knit system but can be independent of one another, (3) theological and scientific statements have a relative independence from metaphysical questions, (4) the vast majority of philosophers do not construe metaphysics in this way, and (5) philosophers of science understand the problem of metaphysics to be the question of realism versus anti-realism, not general categories or system-building. Barbour does not address important problems for his conception of metaphysics such as these or argue for the justification of process thought; rather, he endorses the process perspective of metaphysics from the very beginning of his discussion because: (1) he understands process thought to be formulated under the influence of scientific and religious thought, (2) he sees it as consistent with recent themes in science and (3) he finds it to offer distinctive insights to theology.[116] Barbour does not so much argue for or defend his choice of process thought or the need for general categories for all of reality as much as he points out weaknesses in other positions and then describes or suggests how he thinks process philosophy is at least as good as or better than other positions.[117] Perhaps this is not so surprising, for Whitehead, the source of Barbour's treatment of metaphysics, defined the discipline as a "description," the elucidation of which's accuracy was foreign to the description.[118] As John Passmore remarks, Whitehead does not argue, in any ordinary sense of the word, but uses a philosophical method Passmore disrespectfully describes as the "I'm telling you method,"[119] and, while I would not refer to Barbour or Whitehead in this disrespectful manner, I do think Barbour needs to justify his choice of his conception of metaphysics in light of the above mentioned criticisms. I conclude that Barbour's general treatment of metaphysics does not make its case, but his particular metaphysical choice of process philosophy still needs to be explored to examine the adequacy of the description he gives of process thought as consistent with scientific themes and offering distinctive insights to religion.

The description advanced by process thought, Whitehead claimed, has the elucidation of its accuracy as foreign to its description. Barbour suggests process theology can be justified as a reformulation of classical theology by four criteria which he developed for the assessment of scientific theories and religious beliefs within paradigm communities in Chapters 2 and 3 of *Religion in an Age of Science*.[120] The first criterion is agreement with data, and process theology should have a better fit with the findings of contemporary science and of religious experience (including the Bible) than traditional Christian theology in order to justify reformulation. The second criterion is coherence, which is understood by Barbour to require consistency with the central core of the Christian tradition, internal consistency, and the integration of all dimensions of life into a set of basic categories. The third criterion is scope, which seeks comprehensiveness in offering a coherent account of diverse types of experience in articulating an inclusive world-view. The fourth criterion is fertility, which means that a school of thought should stimulate creative theological reflection, extend into new domains and disciplines, encourage ethical action, and nourish religious experience and personal transformation. And, though I have been critical of various aspects of Barbour's thought, I think these informal criteria (and others) derived from the emerging consensus in the contemporary philosophy of science can be helpful in suggesting ways in which to assess world-views.[121] Because of this, I will use these four criteria to evaluate Barbour's choice of process metaphysics in general and then turn to the application of his method of integration to specific issues in science and religion.

Before applying the four criteria to Barbour's approach, it would be helpful to give a brief summary of what how Barbour understands the essential features of process philosophy and theology and what he sees as the attractive features of this thought.

Barbour commends process thought because he finds it congenial to science and to offer distinctive contributions to theology. Process thought, according to Barbour, is congenial to science for its emphasis on a number of key features. First, process theology emphasizes the primacy of time. Process thought starts with becoming rather than being. Second, process thought emphasizes the interconnection of events. The world is a network of interactions and all events are interdependent. Third, process thought sees reality as an organic process. The world is not a machine but a highly integrated and dynamic pattern of interdependent events. Fourth, process thought holds the self-creation of every entity. Each event is an entity in its own right and responds to other events as a center of spontaneity and self-creation. Reality consists of an interacting network of individual moments of experience, and these interacting moments are "actual entities" or "actual occasions." Each new entity comes about under the guidance of its "subjective aim," or creative freedom with its own unique perspective on the universe, and the prototype of this process is a moment of human experience. God is the ground of novelty and order for the world.

In addition, there are diverse levels of experience among the world's entities. Subjective experience occurs in progressively more attenuated forms from persons to animals to lower organisms to cells to atoms, but stones, plants, or other aggregates are excluded. Since mind and consciousness are only found at higher levels, Barbour prefers the term "panexperientialism" to "panpsychism," and he endorses viewing lower-level entities as "rudimentary forms of experience" even though this runs against the assumptions of many scientists. Barbour further departs from

Whitehead's philosophy, for he does criticize Whitehead's treatment of human experience as excessively episodic, and he questions his treatment of inanimate reality as perhaps not treating the radical diversity of levels of activity and the emergence of genuine novelty adequately. Despite these objections, however, Barbour does not see any direct inconsistency between process thought and contemporary science, and he holds that process thought is very congenial with evolutionary biology and systems theory and can make a significant contribution to environmental ethics.[122]

Process theology contributes the following insights endorsed by Barbour. First, God is seen as the ground of order and novelty. Second, God is influenced by the events in the world, and God's power is limited as the world is said to be "in God" (panentheism) for God includes the world but is more than the world as opposed to identified with the world (pantheism) or separate from the world (theism).[123] God's activity is to be understood as persuasion or the evocation of response, not coercion, and God is seen to be one factor among many in a moment of experience. Barbour finds the biblical idea of the Spirit to mark the closest parallel to the process understanding of God's activity in the world and in Christ, and he insists process thought offers the best solution to the problem of evil for God is intrinsically limited in power and shares in human suffering.[124] Furthermore, God should be modeled as a creative participant who is leader of a cosmic community or a wise teacher who desires students choose for themselves and act harmoniously.[125]

This description of the integration of theology and science is impressive, but a number of significant problems undermine Barbour's position. There are serious difficulties for process thought in each of the four evaluative criteria of agreement with data, coherence, scope, and fertility.

First, the claim that process philosophy offers the best fit to contemporary science is highly suspect. Though Whitehead did develop his metaphysics after Einstein formulated his theories, Whitehead rejected Einstein's theory of relativity for many years and proposed an alternative theory (which was never taken up by physicists) and never accepted Einstein's interpretation of relativity.[126] Whitehead rejected Einstein's denial of universal simultaneity, and, as F. S. C. Northop has shown, Whitehead's refusal to accept Einstein's position undermines Whitehead's entire system and epistemology for it depends upon simultaneous immediate individual awareness as such, insists on a uniform spread to space, rejects a crucial role for special facts such as the speed of light, and proposes a noncontingent uniformity in spatial relations which is less open to experimental applications, all of which were rejected by Einstein.[127]

Northrop further adds that Whitehead's description of knowledge as a "relationship of subjectivity" ends in solipsism, for it fails to respect the differentiation between our individual impressions of an event and our designation of that event by public definition or scientific theory and leaves us with no public knowledge at all.[128] Barbour is correct to claim that both modern science and process thought stress the relationality of knowledge, but the relationship described by process thought is very different from the relationship of modern science and bears only a superficial resemblance to it.[129] In fairness to Barbour it must be noted that he does not adopt Whitehead's work uncritically, and he does suggest the Whiteheadian system could be modified without endangering its coherence,[130] but he does not address important issues such as the ones mentioned above, and therefore Barbour's case does not appear to me to be strong enough to justify the claim that Whitehead's work fits better with contemporary science.

Second, process thought is not as congenial to scientific thought as Barbour proposes because process thought actually views science as inadequate in its explanations. Process thought postulates such factors as "subjective aim" in entities which science does not entertain (for they are unnecessary) in its explanations of material processes, and though process thought would not defend a "God of the Gaps," it comes, despite Barbour's denials, dangerously close to postulating gaps in scientific explanations which need to be filled by process metaphysics. As Ernan McMullin points out, process thought requires that scientific explanations fail to adequately describe reality for its persuasiveness, and it revives "physico-theology," which has at best a dubious historical track record, to explain material processes, and this ought to make anyone wary of accepting such a proposal.[131] Coherence with science and agreement with data is indeed a problem for process thought.

Third, process thought has not shown itself to be fertile for scientific progress. Barbour, like Kuhn, Lakatos, Laudan, and others in the contemporary philosophy of science, holds that metaphysical beliefs are important and influence conceptual frameworks like paradigms, research programmes, and research traditions. The history of science is replete with examples of how certain metaphysical beliefs aided, and in some cases hindered, scientific progress, and even mistaken metaphysical conceptions have led to scientific progress.[132] Process thought, however, has not contributed to any advancements in the natural sciences, which is surprising for a conceptual scheme which is claimed to be the most congenial to modern science. If one of the marks of a good metaphysical system is fertility, process thought has failed to measure up to this criterion.

And fourth, process thought does get good marks for scope, for it does attempt to develop general categories for all of reality, but even this comes at a price, for it introduces a level of generality even further abstracted from particulars than physics and therefore is actually less helpful in describing particularities than science since it offers little that is helpful in interpreting historical events.[133] Abstractions can clarify, but they can also confuse, especially if the model is so general that it is incompetent to detect the particulars of significance. This excessive generality will continue to be a problem for Barbour's integration of science and theology as a discussion of the application of his method will show.

The Integration of Science and Religion: Application

This section will critique Barbour's application of his method to specific problems where science is relevant to theology. Barbour opens his treatment of the metaphysical implications of quantum theory and relativity with some wise observations on how certain interpretations of modern science go too far. He exposes the errors in those who claim that time is illusory, that reality is mental, that relativity supports relativism, that reductionistic approaches best describe reality, that free will should be equated with the categories of physics, and that Eastern mysticism offers the best fit with current science.[134] Barbour is less successful, however, when he applies the content of specific scientific theories to theology and synthesizes the two disciplines with process thought. Included in this discussion will be Barbour's treatment of creation, evolution and human nature, and God and nature.

Astronomy and Creation

In his discussion of astronomy and creation, Barbour argues the anthropic principle does not produce a conclusive argument for God's existence,[135] the Big Bang theory should not be equated with the Christian doctrine of creation,[136] and the contingency of the world raises questions which science cannot itself answer.[137] It is his discussion of *creatio ex nihilo*, however, which departs most from traditional Christian theism. Barbour does not believe *ex nihilo* to be a biblical idea, and he rejects the treatment of *ex nihilo* as a temporal beginning.[138] Barbour prefers to speak of a *creatio continua*, or God's continued creating through natural processes, though he does want to preserve what he thinks is the theological message of *ex nihilo*, which he sees as locating human life in a cosmic order and articulating a sense of wonder at, gratitude to, and dependence on God. He also notes the historical importance of *creatio ex nihilo*, for it was used to refute the Gnostic claim that matter is evil and not the work of God and to reject pantheism by asserting the world is not divine or part of God but distinct from God.[139] Despite the value of *ex nihilo*, however, Barbour thinks the doctrine of creation needs to be reformulated to the process conception which emphasizes the immanence and participation of God in the world and the world's participation in God, and he holds that the religious idea of creation starts with gratitude for life as a gift.[140]

The question that arises here is whether or not process theology offers a better alternative to the traditional doctrine of creation or is more fruitful in its theological insights, or, as David Burrell has put it, How effective is process thought in illuminating the tradition?[141] Burrell argues that concept of *creatio ex nihilo* actually anchors the conception of life as a gift even more solidly than the process view, and he cites a number of works and Jewish-Christian dialogues to illustrate this point.[142] Furthermore, God's graciousness is even more profound in the traditional view, for God does not create out of need or lack but because of a free act of love. The traditional doctrine of creation affirms the continuing nature of creation with God as the source of all that exists, and it has the added plus of stressing the ontological uniqueness of God. Process thought, with its panentheistic conception of God, blurs the distinction between God and the world and marks a rejection of one of the most basic features of the Christian idea of God.[143] In addition, Ted Peters, in addressing Barbour's treatment of creation, argues that Barbour would be more consistent to defend an absolute beginning rather than just continuing creation.[144] For these reasons, Barbour's treatment of creation, while commendable in many respects, does not meet the criteria of fertility or coherence by which he evaluates doctrinal reformulation.

Evolution and Human Nature

Evolution

In discussing evolution and human nature, Barbour endorses the modern evolutionary synthesis while at the same time acknowledging the issues which remain unresolved. Barbour also rejects methodological, epistemological, and ontological reductionism, and defends a hierarchy of ever increasing complexity and inclusive wholes with complex interactions taking place at all levels.[145] Chance does not pose a threat to theology, and Barbour carefully explains why chance and law should be seen as complementary, not conflicting.[146] Evolution and creation should not be in conflict with one another, and Barbour recommends a systematic synthesis of the two by process metaphysics.

Process thought, with its emphasis on change and development, would seem to be ideal for relating evolution and theology; however, this is not the case. First, as Holmes Rolston has pointed out, process thought is too general to interpret the incredibly complex course of evolutionary passage and the particulars involved in the development from nature to culture.[147] Second, and more importantly, Barbour's "panexperientialism" does not seem to be in agreement with the data in its description of the world. Barbour holds that unified entities at all levels should be considered "*experiencing subjects*, with at least rudimentary sentience, memory, and purposiveness,"[148] and reality consists of "an interacting network of moments of individual *moments of experience*."[149] A stone, however, has no "unified activity beyond the physical cohesion of its parts."[150] But then what of the claim that reality consists of interacting moments of experience? Holmes Rolston illustrates the difficulties with this claim with an illustration of an astronaut landing on the moon and finding nothing remotely resembling an "experiencing subject." It is only on Earth (as far as we know) that reality is organized enough to rise to the level of interacting moments of experience, and elemental subjective aim appears to absent from the greatest part of reality. Furthermore, plants and wholes such as species understood as historical lines and ecosystems have no subjective experience (rudimentary sentience, memory, and purposiveness) either.[151] As Rolston asks, "Where is the promised agreement with data, scope, coherence, and fertility, if the scheme that interprets the general characteristics of reality cannot include stones, plants, species, and ecosystems?"[152] And third, Barbour's understanding of emergence and incrementalism is faulty. "There are no sharp lines between an amoeba and a human being.... The universe is continuous, insists Barbour."[153] The problem with this claim is that sharp lines do indeed exist. Examples include: (1) the skin of an organism though it be part of an ecosystem and semipermeable, (2) one gets a whole proton or none at all, and (3) a woman is pregnant or not.[154] Gould and others who stress "punctuations" in evolutionary history see rather sharp changes of state taking place not just incrementalization in slow emergence. In addition,

Barbour's need for coherence in his metaphysics leads to the postulation of "subjective aim" all the way down to atoms and undermines the acceptance of radical new emergents such as consciousness, and Barbour concedes the use of human experience as the model for all other experience is "somewhat strained."[155] As the writers of Genesis knew, the world stuff is created by God and creative, but it is not subjective or enchanted. Thus, Barbour's process thought fails to offer the best interpretative scheme for evolution and to fit the biblical picture of the nature of the created order.

Human nature

In his discussion of human nature, Barbour rejects materialism and dualism, and defends human beings as (1) creatures, but unique among creatures, (2) individuals, but in community, (3) in God's image, but fallen, and (4) unitary persons, not a body-soul dualism.[156] He also discusses the role of Christ in his treatment of human nature, and he offers some observations on the human future.[157] He develops these biblical conceptions by the use of process categories, but this development once again undermines his attempt at a coherent integration which agrees with the data of scripture and religious experience. I will illustrate this with Barbour's treatment of sin and Christology.

Barbour rightly rejects treating Adam and Eve as historical figures and interprets them instead as representatives of humanity to be taken seriously, not literally. The Fall is "Everyman's journey from innocence to responsibility and sin," and sin, in all its forms, is a violation of relatedness.[158] But there are clear difficulties for understanding sin and a Fall within process thought. For example, since panentheism blurs the distinction between God and the world, God's activity (though limited) is identified with the evolutionary process in process thought, and this ascribes the world as it is to God (even though it is on its way to improvement)[159] and overlooks the fact that the biblical picture of God portrays God as morally and redemptively opposed to some of the process and acting to overcome it in ways that go beyond a mere "lure" to goodness. Furthermore, without a Fall which changes the nature of the relationship between God and the world, it is difficult to speak of God in the creative process without morally implicating God in the creation's turmoil or injustice or reducing God to a unifying symbol for the process. The idea of the Fall fits better with a God who transcends, not envelops, the world, and Barbour, if he wishes to retain the idea of a Fall, needs to either develop the concept further or find some way to deal with the difficulties posed to theology by adopting process thought.

Christology is also in need of reformulation in Barbour's thought. Barbour rejects the classical understanding of Christ as drawing too sharp a line between Christ and other humans, and he prefers to think of the difference between Christ as others as one of degree.[160] He defends an evolutionary Christology which views Christ as the continuation of what had been occurring previously and as a new stage in evolution and God's activity. The human side of Christ means he was perfectly obedient to God; the divine side means God was acting in and through Christ. Barbour, following Lampe, prefers to speak of Christ as one whom God acted through decisively, not the eternal son of God. But here one is left the question of reconciling Barbour's view with the totality of the biblical witness to Christ and to the Christian tradition and religious experience. Scripture portrays Christ as the eternal Son or Word of God who enjoys a unique ontological relationship with the Father, not just one in whom God decisively acted or inspired by the Spirit.[161] Barbour's position in effect rejects the decisions of Nicaea and Chalcedon which treat the Son as "of one substance with the Father" and "complete in Godhead and complete in manhood, two natures without division, confusion or separation, in one person," and therefore radically departs from the Christian tradition and ignores the important soteriological issues which led to these formulations and the acknowledged inadequacy by the church fathers of human conceptuality to explain the mysteries of the divine nature.[162] In addition, more traditional conceptions of the trinity and Christology are producing fruitful work, and therefore it is far from exhausted in theological fertility.[163] Adopting Barbour's approach to Christology would mark a real loss of the insights of the traditional understanding, and his position does not offer sufficient gains to pay this price.

God and Nature

Barbour critiques the way God is understood to relate to the world in a number of perspectives, and his criticisms of Bultmann, Wiles, Gordon Kaufman, Sallie McFague, and Grace Jantzen are particularly good.[164] Unfortunately, his own position, process theism, does not fit well with the four criteria he has developed for critiquing doctrinal reformulations, and since I have discussed a number of problems with his position in the preceding sections, I will not repeat them here. However, I will mention three other areas of concern I have with Barbour's position.

First, the idea of God as a leader of the cosmic community who is like a wise teacher hardly fits with the biblical description of God or the experience biblical characters have in the presence of Yahweh. The God of the Bible is one whose holiness produces not merely feelings of awe and dread but brings about repentance on the part of the human being who encounters God.[165] Barbour's God is rather tame compared to Yahweh, and much is lost in taking sin seriously without the Biblical model of a God who can shake us to the very core of our being with our recognition of the seriousness of our moral responsibility and accountability.

Second, Barbour's contention that God's power is persuasive, not coercive, is suspect. If coercion is understood as the complete divestment of the power of self-determination, I agree, but I think it is a mistake to deny coercive power to God if coercion is understood as the ability to unilaterally restrict the ability of others to act in accordance with their desires. Human beings exercise this type of coercion all the time, sometimes for evil (such as Hitler imprisoning Jews) and sometimes for good (such as preventing a small child from playing in a dangerous street). Coercive power is sometimes required to bring about a good end, and there does not seem to be any intrinsic reason why persuasion is morally superior to coercion. In fact, one could use persuasion to bring about evil results (such as convincing someone to try narcotics). God, as portrayed in the Bible, clearly at times uses coercive power and Christ does as well.[166] Furthermore, it seems some coercive power on the part of God is required in order to finally overcome evil. Barbour and other process theists may give up any hope of an absolute victory over evil and the triumph of justice, but this again is one of the dominant themes of the Bible and the Christian tradition. A more fruitful theological formulation should attempt to find ways to communicate this message to the modern world rather than abandoning one of the most important of human hopes.[167]

And third, the kenotic model of God's voluntary self-limitation as a way of describing the relationship between God and the world offers a more promising model than process theism, for it is able to overcome some of the weaknesses in the traditional model while at the same time maintaining more continuity with it and the primary/secondary cause model than process thought. The idea that God's omnipotence includes the ability to limit God's power is highly compatible with the understanding of God that has prevailed in Christian tradition, and it fits better with the picture of the graciousness of God discussed above, for God freely chooses to limit

God's self out of love to allow the creation to be; God is not forced to create out of necessity or any limits intrinsic to God's being. Barbour has no criticisms of this position except to say it is does not develop its insights into a coherent metaphysical system, and he even believes this position will become more like process thought over time.[168] I think Barbour is mistaken in this, for there really is no compelling reason at this time to move toward the conception of metaphysics Barbour supports.

Conclusion

Barbour's integration of theology and science has many valuable insights into the relationship of theology and science, but it is ultimately unsatisfactory due to its lack of ability to meet Barbour's own criteria of agreement with data, fertility, scope, and coherence. Many of the difficulties in Barbour's thought come from his treatment of science and religion as paradigms and from his method of integration which relies on fitting science and religion into a comprehensive scheme by use of process metaphysics. Despite the critical remarks made about some elements of Barbour's approach, I think it important to close by noting that Barbour's contribution is one of the important and positive to be made to the discussion of religion and science. His status as the *doyen* of contemporary writers on science and religion is richly deserved both for the quality of his work and the graciousness of his person. A different approach to theology and science is offered by Thomas Torrance, and it is to his work we now turn.

Notes

1. Ian Barbour, *Issues in Science and Religion* (Englewood Cliffs N.J., 1966). Hereafter abbreviated as *ISR*.
2. Ian Barbour, *Myths, Models, and Paradigms: A Comparative Study in Science and Religion* (New York: Harper & Row, 1974). Hereafter abbreviated as *MMP*.
3. Holmes Rolston III, "Religion in an Age of Science; Metaphysics in an Era of History," *Zygon*, 27 (March 1992), pp. 65-87. The quote is from page 65.
4. For a discussion of Barbour's somewhat confusing use of the terms "religion" and "theology," see footnote 12.
5. *ISR*, pp. 131-134, 269-270.
6. *ISR*, p. 264.
7. *MMP*, p. 170.
8. *MMP*, p. 170.
9. Ian Barbour, *Religion in an Age of Science: The Gifford Lectures, 1989-1991*, Vol. I (San Francisco: Harper & Row, 1990).

10.Barbour's earliest discussion of the ways religion and science can be related can be found in his first book *Christianity and the Scientist* (New York: Association Press, 1960), pp. 86-88. Barbour adapts H. Richard Niebuhr's types from *Christ and Culture* (New York: Harper & Row, 1951) into the following strategies for relating religion and science: "Religion against Science" (the Amish and similar groups), "Religion under Science" (religious liberalism), "Religion above Science" (Roman Catholicism), "Religion separate from Science" (Luther and Barth), and "Religion transforming Science" (Calvin and Wesley). Barbour chooses the fifth option for his own approach, and he views the relationship between religion and science as an open and dynamic interaction in which the values of the Christian tradition reorient the purposes science should serve. It should be pointed out that what Barbour means by "science" in this specific context is technology, and he does not appear to use this Niebuhrian typology except when referring to science in this limited sense.

11.See Ian Barbour, *Religion in an Age of Science* (New York: Harper & Row, 1990), pp. 3-30 and hereafter abbreviated as *RAS*; "Ways of Relating Science and Theology," in *Physics, Philosophy, and Theology: A Common Quest for Understanding*, ed. Robert John Russell, William R. Stoeger, S.J., and George V. Coyne, S.J. (The Vatican: Vatican Observatory, and Notre Dame: University of Notre Dame Press, 1988), pp. 21-48; and "Consultation Summation," in *The Church and Contemporary Cosmology*, ed. James B. Miller and Kenneth E. McCall (Pittsburgh: Carnegie Mellon University Press, 1990), pp. 297-312. It should be noted at this point that I am stating Barbour's views in order to clarify his position, and I am not endorsing all of his models of the ways science might be related to religion or his treatment of many of the thinkers discussed in this section. In fact, there are a number of difficulties with his approach. First, many of the particular authors discussed do not really fit very neatly into his categories (Thomas Torrance, Wolfhart Pannenberg, Langdon Gilkey, and Ernan McMullin, to name a few). And second, the use of Barbour's models tend to caricature some of the thinkers discussed. For example, the defenders of creation science would no doubt argue that they hold to an Integration position which incorporates science and theology into a comprehensive world-view, for they view themselves as being in conflict with a false scientific theory (evolution) not with true science. Barbour concedes that his categories are best viewed as a broad sketch of alternatives and that particular thinkers may not fit them (*RAS*, p. 3), and it appears the real value of his classifications lies in how they help one understand Barbour's own views, not the views of others.

12.*RAS*, p. 3. It is Barbour's use of these terms which clears up his somewhat confusing use of the broader term "religion" (which designates a "way of life" as opposed to just a set of beliefs, see p. xiii) instead of "theology," for it is the theologian, who draws upon philosophy in his or her critical reflection on the beliefs and traditions of the religious community (which include formative scriptures, communal rituals, individual experiences, and ethical norms), who actually has the task of relating religion to science. Barbour also has stated in response to a criticism by Nancey Murphy that he prefers to use the term "religion" as opposed to "theology" in order to not exclude Buddhist and nontheistic traditions. See Ian Barbour, "Response to Nancey Murphy," *Zygon*, 31, no. 1 (March 1996), pp. 52-54.

13.Barbour makes two changes in his treatment of the possible positions one may take in describing the relation between religion and science. In the two earlier essays found in *Physics, Philosophy, and Theology* and in *The Church and Contemporary Cosmology*, Barbour lists only two variants – doctrinal reformulation and systematic synthesis – for the Integration model. Though he does mention natural theology, he does not treat it as a third variant of the Integration position until *Religion in an Age of Science*. In addition, he renames the doctrinal reformulation variant of the earlier essays "theology of nature." Since *Religion in an Age of Science* contains Barbour's most recent statement of his position, it will form the basis of the following discussion rather than the earlier works. See *Physics, Philosophy and Theology*, pp. 40-45; *The Church and Contemporary Cosmology*, pp. 306-308; and *Religion in an Age of Science*, pp. 23-30.

14.*RAS*, p. 4.

15.*RAS*, pp. 4-10. Barbour's insight is correct, and he does point out the philosophical errors in both positions; however, he should have developed another important facet of the problem with the Conflict position – both variants are bad theology as well. For a number of discussions of the theological issues involved, see Roland Frye, ed., *Is God a Creationist?: The Religious Case Against Creation-Science* (New York: Charles Scribner's Sons, 1983), and Ernan McMullin, ed. *Evolution and Creation* (Notre Dame, Indiana: University of Notre Dame Press, 1985). A discussion of how atheistic scientists make theological claims by overstepping their boundaries can be found in Diogenes Allen, *Christian Belief in a Post-Modern World* (Louisville: Westminster/John Knox Press, 1989), pp. 35-84.

16.*RAS*, p. 10.

17.*RAS*, pp. 11-12.

18.*RAS*, pp. 12-13.

19.*RAS*, pp. 13-15.

20.*RAS*, pp. 15-16.

21.*RAS*, p. 16.

22.*RAS*, pp. 17-20. Examples of theologians exploring these issues include Thomas Torrance, Wolfhart Pannenberg, Ernan McMullin, Karl Rahner, and David Tracy.

23.*RAS*, pp. 20-22. Michael Polanyi and John Polkinghorne are listed as examples of this approach.

24.*RAS*, p. 20.

25.*RAS*, p. 23. Barbour actually numbers three objections in the text, but his numbers 1 and 2 can be condensed as variations of what I have numbered as 1.

26.*RAS*, p. 23.

27.Barbour discusses John Leslie and Hugh Montefiore as examples of this position. See *RAS*, pp. 25-26.

28.See Barbour's essay in *The Church and Contemporary Cosmology*, p. 306.

29.*RAS*, p. 26.

30.*RAS*, p. 26. Examples of this position include Arthur Peacocke and Teilhard de Chardin, see p. 27.

31.*RAS*, p. 28.

32.*RAS*, p. 28. Examples of this view include Alfred North Whitehead, Charles Hartshorne, and John Cobb.

33.*RAS*, p. 30.

34.*RAS*, pp. 31-32. Barbour changes his terminology in relation to models from his earlier work. In *Myths, Models, and Paradigms*, Barbour refers to the models which generate theories as "theoretical models" rather than "conceptual models" (see pages 30-31). Barbour gives no reason for the change so it is unclear whether it represents a genuine modification of his position or is simply a synonymous use. The only ascertainable difference I can find in the two uses is that he states models refer to "mechanisms and processes" in *MMP* and his earlier work *Issues in Science and Religion* (pp. 158-159) and to "postulated entities" in *RAS*, but on page 41 of *RAS* he uses the terms synonymously. Treating "entities" and "mechanisms and processes" as synonymous is consistent with a process metaphysics, but there are a number of theologians and philosophers who would question this identification. Barbour's apparent equation of the two will require a defense, and thus his more highly developed use of process philosophy and theology in *RAS* becomes integral to his discussion of science and religion in a way not found in his earlier works.

35.*RAS*, pp. 32-33.

36.*RAS*, pp. 33-36.

37.*RAS*, pp. 36-38.

38.Barbour used to refer to the central narratives of a religious tradition by the term "myth" (see *MMP*), but since many people think of "myth" as meaning "untrue," he now uses the term "story" because it does not imply any judgment about the narrative's historical validity (*RAS*, p. 39).

39.*RAS*, pp. 39-41.

40.*RAS*, p. 41. See also *MMP*, pp. 30-34.

41.*RAS*, pp. 410-41; *MMP*, pp. 30-34.

42.*RAS*, p. 43; *MMP*, pp. 35-42.

43.Barbour explains how religious models interpret experience in *MMP*, pp. 51-53.

44.*RAS*, pp. 45-47.

45.*RAS*, pp. 47-51. Barbour also introduces some important limitations on the use of complementary models in religion. See also *MMP*, pp. 71-78.

46.*RAS*, p. 51.

47.*RAS*, pp. 51-54.

48.*RAS*, pp. 54-55. Barbour lists these criteria in his discussion of religious pluralism on pages 88-92 of *RAS*.

49.*RAS*, pp. 57-58.

50.*RAS*, pp. 58-65.

51.*RAS*, p.65.
52.*RAS*, 66-67.
53.*RAS*, pp. 67-68.
54.*RAS*, pp. 68-69.
55.*RAS*, pp. 69-70.
56.*RAS*, pp. 70-71.
57.*RAS*, pp. 71-73.
58.*RAS*, p. 73.
59.*RAS*, pp. 73-81.
60.*RAS*, pp. 83-84.
61.*RAS*, pp. 84-87.
62.*RAS*, pp. 90-91.
63.*RAS*, pp. 89-90.
64.*RAS*, p.88.
65.*RAS*, p. 89.
66.*RAS*, p. 89.
67.*RAS*, p.89.
68.*RAS*, pp. 90-91.
69.*RAS*, p. 57.
70.*RAS*, pp. 57, 59-60, 90-92; *MMP*, chapters 7-8. Barbour treats whole religious traditions as paradigms more explicitly in *MMP* than in *RAS*, in which he tends to speak of a community containing paradigms; however, the use of paradigm for a larger community is implied.
71.*RAS*, pp. 60-62.
72.Barbour takes a school of thought to constitute a research program, but Nancey Murphy's conception is much narrower, for she treats as research programs one theory of the atonement or the attempt to authenticate religious experience. See Nancey Murphy, *Theology in the Age of Scientific Reasoning* (Ithaca: Cornell University Press, 1990); "Revisionist Philosophy of Science and Theological Method" (Paper delivered at the Pacific Coast Theological Society, Spring 1983); "Acceptability Criteria for Work in Theology and Science," *Zygon* 22 (1987), pp. 279-297. Murphy rejects Barbour's broadening of research program to a school of thought for she holds: (1) religious thought is made up of large-scale and fine-scale structures, and (2) the concept of paradigm too broad to be applied fruitfully to theology, see "Ian Barbour on Religion and the Methods of Science: An Assessment," *Zygon*, 31 (1996), pp. 11-19.
73.*RAS*, p. 62.
74.Murphy thinks this problem arises from Barbour's focus on "religion" rather then "theology," but I think this is mistaken, for Barbour has adequately explained his preference for the term religion and he has made it clear what he considers to be the role of the theologian (see note 12 above). The actual reason for Barbour's difficulty will be discussed in my treatment of the disanalogy between "paradigm" in science and religion.
75.Gary Gutting, *Religious Beliefs and Religious Skepticism* (Notre Dame, Ind.: University of Notre Dame Press, 1982), p. 124.

76.Ibid., pp. 124-125.

77.As do W. H. Newton-Smith, Ernan McMullin, and Michael Banner, and many others.

78.William Rottschaefer, "Religious Cognition as Interpreted Experience: An Examination of Ian Barbour's Comparison of the Epistemic Structures of Science and Religion," *Zygon* 20 (1985), pp. 265-282.

79.An example listed by Rottschaefer is the seismologist whose equipment keeps showing major activity for hours on end and therefore calls other scientists to discover what their seismographs are doing.

80.There is a distinction between an experiential and a postulated analogy. In an experiential analogy, one has experienced both terms of the comparison, as for example, when Muhammad Ali says of his opponent, "He's a marshmallow." In a postulated analogy, one has not experienced the object itself, as for example, the wave-particle model of the atom, in which one has experienced only the perceptual materials from which the analogy is drawn and not the atom itself. If religious models are experiential, they leave open the possibility of direct cognition; if they are postulated, they leave open inferential cognition.

81.Ludwig Wittgenstein, *Philosophical Investigations*, trans. G.E.M. Anscombe, 2nd ed. (Oxford: Basil Blackwell, 1968), pt. 2, p. 194. Barbour uses the Basil Blackwell edition of 1953, p. 194e. The drawing can be seen as a duck or a rabbit depending upon how one takes it.

82.*MMP*, pp. 51-53.

83.Garrett Green, *Imagining God: Theology and the Religious Imagination* (New York: Harper & Row, 1989), p. 71.

84.N. R. Hanson, *Patterns of Discovery: An Inquiry into the Conceptual Foundations of Science* (Cambridge: Cambridge University Press, 1958), pp. 9-10, cited in *Imagining God*, p. 71.

85.Green holds that what does happen is an act of "paradigmatic imagination," or, in this specific case, perceptual as opposed to interpretive imagination, which is the ability to see one thing as another and also to understand properly the relationship between wholes and parts. See *Imagining God*, pp. 73-74, 49-54.

86.Green, *Imagining God*, pp. 72-73.

87.Unless, of course, someone wished to argue our multiple perceptions of the world exist because the objects of perception in the world or our minds are *intended* to lend themselves to accepting a number of perceptions.

88.*RAS*, p. 3.

89.*MMP*, p. 176. Philip Clayton endorses Barbour's view in a qualified way and adds: "Certainly Barbour cannot be faulted for inadequate regard for the practicing community and its practices." *Explanation from Physics to Theology* (New Haven: Yale University Press, 1989), p. 165 and continued on 166; however, it is precisely this fault which I find in Barbour.

90.Translations of Anselm's works are numerous, but I am relying on the edition by edited by S. N. Deane, *St. Anselm: Basic Writings* (LaSalle, Ill.: Open Court, 1962). Anselm enjoys long-standing support among Roman Catholic, Eastern Orthodox, and liberal and conservative Protestant Christians. By appealing to

Anselm's theology, I am not necessarily endorsing all of his views; my intent is show how Barbour's description of theology is inadequate to encompass how theology is understood by the majority of Christians. Examples of Anselm's influence are many but a few representative contemporary approaches illustrate it well: Thomas V. Morris, *Our Idea of God* (Downers Grove, Illinois: Inter-Varsity Press, 1991); Robert Sokolowski, *The God of Faith and Reason* (Notre Dame, Indiana: University of Notre Dame Press, 1982), Chapter 1; and Daniel L. Migliore, *Faith Seeking Understanding* (Grand Rapids: Eerdmans, 1991). The importance of Anselm for Barth's theology is well known.

91.Important treatments which describe theologians as responding to the prior initiative of God and defend the intellectual adequacy of this starting point include William C. Placher, *Unapologetic Theology* (Louisville: Westminster: John Knox Press, 1989) and Ronald Thiemann, *Revelation and Theology: The Gospel as Narrated Promise* (Notre Dame, Ind.: University of Notre Dame Press, 1985).

92.For example, in the "billiard-ball model" of a gas both the gas molecules and the billiard-balls have mass and velocity though they may differ in many other aspects.

93.*ISR*, pp. 208-211 in addition to the treatments of religious experience in *RAS* and *MMP* discussed above.

94.*MMP*, p. 18.

95.*MMP*, p. 18.

96.Austin Farrer, *The Glass of Vision* (London: Dacre Press, 1948), p. 36-37.

97.Ibid., p. 42.

98.Ibid., p. 57.

99.Farrer develops and supplements his treatment of divine and human interaction even more completely in *Faith and Speculation* (London: A. & C. Black, 1967), especially Chapter VI. In this volume, Farrer develops his concept of the "paradox of double agency" in which the divine and human are both active but the causal joint between the two cannot be specified.

100.*Glass of Vision*, pp. 43-44.

101.Ibid., pp. 57-61.

102.Basil Mitchell, *How to Play Theological Ping-Pong: And Other Essays on Faith and Reason* (Grand Rapids: Eerdmans, 1990).

103.See Farrer's discussion of "involuntary thinking," *Glass of Vision*, pp. 87-90.

104.Ibid., pp. 110-112. Farrer uses the content of rational theology and the conception of God as a supreme being as his canon; in addition, the greater images help to criticize the lesser.

105.*Glass of Vision*, p. 33.

106.Ibid., pp. 1-3. Farrer develops the need to start with faith even more explicitly in *Faith and Speculation*.

107.*Glass of Vision*, pp. 22-23.

108.Ibid., pp. 43-43, 96-112, 113-131.

109.One objection which can be raised against the "faith seeking understanding" position would be to claim that starting from faith means one is automatically methodologically compromised. Wentzel van Huyssteen effectively answers this charge in *Theology and the Justification of Faith* (Grand Rapids: Eerdmans, 1989) and describes how theologians can be aware of their commitments and avoid methodological compromise and fideism.

110.*RAS*, p. 28.

111.See *MMP*, 140-142, 165-170 and *ISR*, p. 262, in which he explicitly makes reference to Whitehead's *Process and Reality*.

112.Barbour does propose a "natural theology" approach to integration which could be seen as independent of process thought, but he rejects natural theology as of little use for the religious community. The two preferred options, "theology of nature" and "systematic synthesis" exclusively discusses process thinkers and thought.

113.See pages 59-60.

114.John Passmore, *Recent Philosophers* (La Salle, Illinois: Open Court, 1985).

115.Nicholas Rescher, "Process Philosophy," in *A Companion to Metaphysics*, eds. Jaegwon Kim and Ernest Sosa (Oxford: Blackwell Publishers, 1995), pp. 418-19.

116.*RAS*, pp. 28, 221-242.

117.*RAS*, p. 230 provides a good example: "There are, to be sure, dangers in the anthropomorphic extension of human qualities to the nonhuman sphere, but there are also dangers in 'mechanomorphic' attempts to explain everything with the concepts of physics and chemistry. On balance, then, process philosophy seems to be a promising attempt to provide a coherent system of concepts for interpreting a wide variety of phenomena in the world." See also page 270 where process thought is endorsed because it has "fewer weaknesses" than the other models discussed.

118.Alfred North Whitehead, *Religion in the Making* (New York: Macmillan, 1926), especially Chapter 3, pp. 88-89.

119.John Passmore, *A Hundred Years of Philosophy* (Middlesex, England: Penguin, 1968), p. 340.

120.pp. 265-267.

121.I am not proposing an exhaustive list, but I would include in addition to Barbour's criteria at least such criterion as economy, or not wantonly multiplying entities and explanations. See John Polkinghorne, *One World: The Interaction of Science and Theology* (Princeton: Princeton University Press, 1986), p. 36, quoting J. R. Carnes, *Axiomatics and Dogmatics* (Christian Journals, 1982), Chapter V.

122.*RAS*, pp. 221-230.

123.*RAS*, pp. 230-232.

124.*RAS*, pp. 232-242.

125.*RAS*, p. 260.

126.A good discussion of this point can be found in Harold Nebelsick, *Theology and Science in Mutual Modification* (New York: Oxford University Press, 1981), pp. 54-62.

127.F. S. C. Northop, "Whitehead's Philosophy of Science," in *The Philosophy of Alfred North Whitehead*, ed. Paul A. Schlipp (Evanston, Ill.: Northwestern University Press, 1941), pp. 190f., 199ff. Barbour is aware that there is no universal simultaneity (*RAS*, pp. 108-110) but he does not discuss the difficulties this poses for the process view.

128.Northrop, pp. 168, 204f.

129.In addition, John Polkinghorne points out how the "event" concept of process thought is really at odds with quantum physics, see *Science and Creation* (Boston: Shambhala, 1988), pp. 73-74.

130.*RAS*, pp. 224-27 has an example.

131.Ernan McMullin, "Natural Science and Belief in a Creator: Historical Notes," in *Physics, Philosophy, and Theology: A Common Quest for Understanding*, eds. Robert John Russell, William Stoeger, and George V. Coyne (Notre Dame, Ind.: University of Notre Dame Press, 1988), pp. 72-73.

132.The works listed by Kuhn, Lakatos, and Laudan cited in Chapter 1 contain numerous examples, as does Stanley Jaki, *The Road of Science and the Ways to God* (Chicago: University of Chicago Press, 1978). See also Michael Polanyi, *Personal Knowledge* (Chicago: University of Chicago Press, 1962), especially pages 6-9 for a description of Platonic influence on Kepler's discoveries and how even mistaken metaphysical assumptions can contribute to scientific progress.

133.Holmes Rolston III, "Religion in an Age of Science; Metaphysics in an Era of History, " pp. 71-75.

134.*RAS*, pp. 95-124.

135.*RAS*, pp.135-138.

136.*RAS*, pp. 125-129.

137.*RAS*, pp. 141-144.

138.*RAS*, pp. 129-135, 144-146.

139.*RAS*, p. 131.

140.*RAS*, p. 133.

141.David Burrell, "Does Process Theology Rest on a Mistake,?" *Theological Studies*, 43 (March 1982), pp. 125-135.

142.Ibid., pp. 130-132.

143.A full discussion of the distinction between God and the world and its theological importance can be found in Robert Sokolowski, *The God of Faith and Reason* (Notre Dame, Ind.: University of Notre Dame Press, 1982). Sokolowski's work shows there is still plenty of creative insight to be gained from the traditional doctrine of creation.

144.Ted Peters, "Cosmos as Creation," in *Cosmos and Creation: Theology and Science in Consonance*, ed. Ted Peters (Nashville: Abingdon, 1989), pp. 45-113. He treats Barbour's position on pages 78-85. See also Robert John Russell, "Religion and the Theories of Science: A Response to Barbour," *Zygon* 31 (1996), pp. 29-41, especially pages 35-37 for similar criticisms.

145.*RAS*, pp. 154-172.

146.Ibid., pp. 172-176. Barbour's approach to law and chance is much more fruitful for theology than fundamentalist approaches which see indeterminacy as a threat to Christianity. An attempt to calm fundamentalist fears about the "new physics" can be found by Allen Emerson, "A Disorienting View of God's Creation," *Christianity Today*, (February 1, 1985), pp. 19-24, and "A Conversation with Carl Henry about the New Physics," p. 26.
147.Rolston III, "Religion in an Age of Science; Metaphysics in an Era of History," pp. 71-75.
148.*RAS*, p. 172.
149.Ibid., p. 223.
150.Ibid., p. 224.
151.Rolston III, "Religion," pp. 76-81.
152.Ibid., p. 80.
153.*RAS*, p. 226.
154.Rolston III, "Religion" p. 81. Rolston includes other examples as well.
155.*RAS*, p. 227.
156.*RAS*, pp. 204-209.
157.Ibid., pp. 209-217.
158.Ibid., p. 206.
159.That evolution means progress or improvement is itself a highly problematic notion.
160.*RAS*, pp. 209-214.
161.John 1 is one biblical example of this point.
162.A good discussion of these developments can be found in Bernhard Lohse, *A Short History of Christian Doctrine*, rev. American ed. (Philadelphia: Fortress Press, 1985).
163.See Thomas V. Morris, *The Logic of God Incarnate* (Ithaca: Cornell University Press, 1986) and the essays collected in *Trinity, Incarnation, and Atonement*, ed. Ronald J. Feenstra and Cornelius Plantinga, Jr. (Notre Dame, Ind.: University of Notre Dame Press, 1989) as two good examples of this point.
164.*RAS*, pp. 259.
165.See Michael Foster, *Mystery and Philosophy* (London: SCM Press, 1957) for a good discussion of this point.
166.The Old Testament includes many examples of God acting in ways against Israel's desires from the wanderings in the wilderness to the Babylonian captivity, and Jesus did not rid the temple of the money-changers by logical argument.
167.I recognize that God's ability to use coercive power re-opens the problem of the relationship of God and evil, and I do not pretend at this point to have an answer to all theodicy issues nor have I developed a way to communicate God's absolute victory over evil in modern categories.
168.*RAS*, pp. 251-254, 268.

Chapter 4

Theological Science and an Ordered Reality

Introduction

Thomas F. Torrance is truly one of the pioneering figures in the exploration of the relationship between theology and natural science, and his influence can be seen on a number of writers who acknowledge his contributions.[1] Unlike Barbour, however, whose work is relatively uncontroversial to interpret and generates mostly praise when reviewed at all, Torrance's writings have produced a wide variety of interpretations and reactions, from unadulterated praise[2] to a number of criticisms, some of which are contradictory, that view his work as of little value for it "is foundationalist,"[3] "too intellectualist in his view of faith,"[4] "fideist,"[5] "wreaks havoc on the scientific method,"[6] "embodies an utterly frustrating level of confusion, mistake, and superficiality,"[7] and "creates a word jungle which deters criticism of his thought."[8]

While I agree Torrance's style can be very repetitive and his vocabulary obscure (especially when he is shifting across different languages and employs terminology specific to the work of Barth and Polanyi without explaining the term's special use in these thinkers), I find Torrance's work to represent one of the most admirable efforts to integrate theology and science written to date and to be more fruitful for theological reflection than Barbour's. In addition, many of the criticisms of Torrance's approach by current thinkers are mistaken, and therefore the significant contributions which Torrance's work could make to the current theology and science dialogue are overlooked while less helpful approaches command more attention.

This chapter will make a case for Torrance's continuing value for theology by: (1) carefully explicating both Torrance's method for integrating theology and natural science and his application of his method to specific issues in relating theology and science in order to clear up some of the problems of interpretation his work poses, and (2) critiquing Torrance's method of integration by the criteria developed in Chapters Two and Three to reveal its continuing value as well as some unresolved problems which it leaves for theology. This may appear to be a daunting task, for the volume of Torrance's work is considerable, but this problem is resolvable since Torrance picks up many of the same themes from book to book and his position has remained consistent with only a few minor adjustments throughout his career.[9] Furthermore, the essentials of his treatment of method are concentrated in a single text, *Theological Science*,[10] which will be used extensively and supplemented with his other works when necessary to clarify some of the more obscure parts of his exposition. The application of his method to specific issues in theology and science will be illustrated by Torrance's treatment of contingency which comes primarily from his book *Divine and Contingent Order*[11] and his discussion of the incarnation and resurrection in *Space, Time, and Incarnation*[12] and *Space, Time, and Resurrection*.[13] These works will be supplemented by other texts when needed as well.

Theological Science: Method

In the Preface to *Theological Science*, Torrance presents some of the essential features of his thought which will be developed at greater length. First, scientific theology or a philosophy of theology is needed because our relations with God are problematic.[14] The problem is with us and not God, for we distort and obstruct the knowledge God would give us by getting ourselves between God and ourselves, but God continues to present God's self to us and attempts to heal our distortions with God's revelation. Theological science steps in to help us refer our thoughts beyond ourselves to God.[15] Second, reality is rational and capable of being apprehended by human beings otherwise we could not understand it. Third, scientific knowledge is relational, for we penetrate into the rationality of that we investigate and the realities we investigate also challenge the questions and presuppositions we bring to them.[16] Fourth, theology and science share the same basic problem:

how to refer our thoughts and statements genuinely beyond ourselves, how to reach knowledge of reality in which we do not intrude ourselves distortingly into the picture, and yet how to retain the full and integral place of the human subject within it all.[17]

Torrance's intention in *Theological Science* is: (1) to clarify how to solve theology's basic problem and refer human theological activity back upon God, its direct and proper object, and (2) to reintroduce objectivity and rationality back into the positive and constructive task of theology.[18]

The Knowledge of God

In his discussion of how one knows God, Torrance begins with some introductory observations on the question of the knowledge of God and then treats the actuality, objectivity, and possibility of the knowledge of God.

Knowledge is Concrete

The first point Torrance makes about knowledge is that questions about the possibility of knowledge cannot be raised in the abstract but only in the concrete act of knowing. The sciences do not start with philosophical or epistemological questions; rather, each science presupposes the reality and accessibility of the object it investigates and the possibility of knowing the object further and leaves the question of its justification to be answered by its own inner content and rationality. Theology as a science should operate in the same way, and faith is the way that one opens one's self to knowing God, who communicates God's self to us in Jesus Christ.[19] One cannot begin with the abstract question, "How can God be known?", for, since the nature of what is known and the nature of the knower determine how something can be known, the question of how God can be known must be determined completely by the way in which God is actually known.[20] One does not begin with questions of epistemology, for one must proceed with an open epistemology which can be clarified and modified as one continues to get deeper insights into the reality one investigates. Theological activity must not be abstracted from its material content, and the material content of theology can clarify our understanding of theology's methodology.[21]

Rationality, Knowledge, and Conceptuality

Torrance also makes three preliminary observations on the knowledge of God. First, knowledge of God is a rational event. Reason is defined as "the capacity to behave in terms of the nature of the object, that is to say, to behave objectively."[22] God is the subject who confronts us with full objectivity, and it is when our own objectivity meets the objectivity of another subject that we have our most rational experience.[23] Second, knowledge of God is knowledge in the proper sense of the term. Torrance uses the term "knowledge" formally in the same way it is used for every branch of knowledge or *scientia*, but he is careful to point out that knowledge is not materially the same, for each science has its own particular reality which it investigates.[24] Knowledge is once again emphasized as a relation to an object, and we must be careful to distinguish what we know from our knowing of it. All true knowledge involves an attachment, or submitting of ourselves to an object, and a detachment, in which we distinguish the object from our awareness of it. And third, knowledge of God is conceptual in its acts of cognition and its acts of expression.[25] A "concept" is that which enables us to lay hold of, to seize, to take in, or to comprehend, and there are two kinds of concepts: (1) closed, and (2) open. Closed concepts can be reduced to clipped propositional ideas, but open concepts are used for reality that cannot be exhausted by our knowledge of it. Open concepts are limited in their ability to capture reality, but they do yield knowledge. Concepts are open toward the reality to which they refer and operate on the boundary between the known and the new, and theological concepts are open toward God.[26] Torrance also insists on the auditory, rather than visual, nature of concepts, and he holds visual "images" or pictures are not the best ways to communicate the reality of God.[27]

The Actuality, Objectivity, and Possibility of the Knowledge of God

Torrance then turns to a discussion of the actuality, objectivity, and possibility of the knowledge of God. Each of these three points are fundamental to Torrance's approach and require careful scrutiny.

The actuality of the knowledge of God involves two key points: (1) theological knowledge comes from what is *given*, that is, it comes from what is beyond it and does not depend on our discovering it; and (2) the given fact of the knowledge of God is not a mute fact.[28] The reality of God is always given to us within our complex of experiences, but we should not confuse the givenness of God revelation with either our subjective states or complex of experiences, for it cannot be reduced to our experiences of feelings, concepts, or even words, for it is *through* these experiences that we perceive genuine objective reality. Faith is not the subject-matter of theology – God , who is not mute, and in whom we have faith is. Faith is a condition of rationality and can be described as the orientation of reason toward God's revelation. God communicates God's self to us, giving God's self to us as Word and in Word. Just as the scientist recognizes that he or she must let nature speak for itself and criticize and guide our formulations and apprehensions, the theologian must listen for the Logos that he or she encounters. There is a difference of degree between science and theology at this point, for theology is more like listening than any other knowledge in that the theologian must learn how to distinguish *the given in its own self-interpretation* from the interpretative processes in which we engage in receiving and understanding it. Without a real Word from God, our theological formulations are merely reflections of our own complex of experiences, genuine theology must be grounded in the divine reality.

The objectivity of the knowledge of God involves six main factors, and Torrance points out that objectivity does not mean detachment or indifference toward the object, for one must engage the object in order to truly know it. Objectivity cannot be abstracted from the subject-object relationship, and both sides of the relationship need to be explored. Torrance first considers the relationship from the side of the object, which in the case of theology is also a subject, namely, God.[29] First, the object has absolute primacy for it is the Lord God's self. The object takes us under its command and directs our relation to a degree not found in any other field of knowledge.[30] Second, the object is given to us in a unique sense of given. God is known within a subject-object relationship like all other objects, but there is a crucial difference for God's nature is given in "grace." Human beings do not find God by their own efforts, and God is not susceptible to coercion through empirical methods of observation like natural objects. The kind of inquiry directed to God must realize that God is a subject, and the appropriate means of questioning is more akin to prayer than to coercive examination.[31] Third, God is a person, and when God becomes an object of our thought God remains a subject. Theological knowing is dialogical, that is, it is an answer to an object who converses and communicates with the subject investigating it by acts of revelation and reconciliation.[32] Fourth, the object of theological knowledge is a speaking subject who addresses human beings personally as the Word of

God. A distinction must be made between the Word and the words used to communicate to us, and all concepts used of God must remain open for the divine reality transcends all our speech.[33] Fifth, the object of theological knowledge is the living, loving, God in action toward us, and knowing God will be an act which is spontaneous, free, and active in a way analogous in nature to the freedom and motion in God's self-giving.[34] And sixth, the object of theological knowledge is engaged in the purposive action of fulfilling God's creative and redeeming purposes. God cannot be known except within God's purposes or in accordance with them, and the objectivity of theological knowledge is soteriological in nature, which means we cannot truly know God without being reconciled and renewed in Jesus Christ. It is through Christological criticism of all of our knowledge of God that human beings can distinguish (as far as possible) between genuine and false objectivity.[35]

The question of the possibility of the knowledge of God is not meaningful apart from the actual knowledge of God, but it must be asked in order for a full understanding of the objectivity of the knowledge of God to be gained. If someone does not acknowledge the actuality of the knowledge of God, all one can do is bear witness to the actual knowledge of God and explicate and elucidate the possibility arising out of its actuality, for one cannot demonstrate the possibility of the knowledge of God apart from its actuality, nor should one expect to, for it is unscientific to proceed in this way. However, there is a legitimate question to asked about the possibility of the knowledge of God, for one can ask how God gives God's self to be known and how human beings receive what is given.

The answer is to be found in Christ, since Christ is God as God objectified God's self for us, it is through Christ we will have genuine knowledge of God, and there is a negative and positive aspect to our knowledge of God. Negatively, the two basic errors of Christology must be avoided: (1) Docetic Christology, which takes a general idea of God and attempts to deduce Christ from it, and (2) Ebionite christology, which wants to start with the manhood of Christ and take the way of induction to rise to God. Positively, one should begin with God as God has actually met us in Jesus Christ as God and man.[36] Our realization of our knowledge of God in Jesus Christ has three moments. First, God condescended to reveal God's self to human beings in Jesus Christ within our limited existence and contingencies, and the possibility of our knowing God is grounded ultimately in God crossing the boundary between God and humanity and objectifying God's self for us. God establishes the possibility of human beings knowing God by entering into the subject-object relationship and converting or reversing our relation of knowing by assuming our subjectivity and making it free, spontaneous, and responsible to God.[37] Second, in Jesus Christ God has come to reconcile humanity to God's self, and the Incarnation reveals both our hostility to God and our need to have our estranged and alienated humanity adapted to the Word and truth of God in Jesus Christ. Humanity needs to be reconciled to God and lifted up to know God above and beyond our natural powers.[38] And third, in Jesus Christ God provides humankind with the ability to receive adequately the truth. It is through the gift and power of the Holy Spirit that human beings are able to share in the knowledge of God, and the Holy Spirit is absolutely epistemologically relevant for knowledge of God in Christ to occur. Furthermore, human knowledge of God is always penultimate, not ultimate, for we are unable to make the knowing of God fully comprehensible as a human action. God always transcends our knowledge of God, and an account of the knowledge of God must never reduce God's holiness, transcendence, or majesty.[39]

The Interaction of Theology and Scientific Development

In this chapter,[40] Torrance addresses important points relevant to his understanding of the interaction of theology and science in connection with his discussion of how the Reformation idea of God helped the development of modern science, and, while his historical reconstruction of the development of science can be challenged,[41] the points made by Torrance about the interaction of science and theology are not really dependent on the correctness of his historical analysis. Leading themes discussed by Torrance in this section include: (1) why theology is interested in science, (2) the subject-object knowledge relationship in Reformed theology and modern science, and (3) natural theology.

Theology's Interest in Science

Torrance holds that theology has two primary reasons for being interested in science. First, theology as a scientific activity demands objectivity and therefore it is inherently interested in the development of adequate tools and methods in the service of knowledge.[42] And second, theological knowledge is concerned with God as the Creator of the world and with God's relation to the world of creaturely realities.[43] Natural science deals with the contingencies of created reality and gives information about some aspects of creaturely being, and Christian theology nurtures scientific activity by its faith in the reliability of God the Creator and in the ultimate intelligibility of the creation.

The Subject-Object Relationship in Knowledge

Reformed theology was particularly helpful in giving rise to modern science, especially by freeing the ideas of God and the world from Aristotelian presuppositions, by stressing that nature and grace are related by the biblical conception of the covenant, and by emphasizing the objectivity of the Word of God as opposed to tradition.[44] Of even more importance is the way Reformed theology develops the place of the human subject in knowledge by the doctrines of accommodation and election. Torrance insists that all talk about knowledge of God must acknowledge that it is human beings who seek to know God, and an anthropomorphic element remains present in all talk of God. Following Calvin, Torrance holds that God reveals God's self to human beings in such a way that human beings do not need to stretch themselves beyond their humanity to know God. The doctrine of "accommodation" teaches that God condescends to our ignorance and adapts God's self to our knowing, and the doctrine of "election" teaches that God acts upon human beings and thus rejects human projections onto to the divine. These two doctrines bring out the two sides (subject-object) of the knowing relationship, and, though all our theological statements contain an element of impropriety, they are not false.[45]

Modern science also relies on the idea of the subject-object knowing relationship, and it has produced a critical reassessment of the place of subjectivity in knowledge and of our attitude toward nature. Modern thought recognizes the presence of subjectivity in all knowledge, and it also sees the need for a controlled and self-critical subjectivity which conforms to the object, thus producing a double critique of subjectivity and objectivity.[46] Modern theology, according to Torrance, needs to apply the subject-object relationship to theological reflection to acknowledge that God acts upon human beings in such a way as to posit and fulfill their subjectivity without allowing it to impose itself upon God. In the interplay between the human subject and the divine object, the human subject must respond in obedience to an act of God's grace, and this response requires self-criticism and repentance. Due to human limitations and the greatness of God, it is very difficult to express the relation between the divine object and our statements about it, but Torrance will attempt to resolve this in his discussion of the nature of theological statements.[47]

Natural Theology

It is within the context of the new attitude toward nature that Torrance expresses his view of natural theology. Once again he emphasizes the contingency of nature, and he argues that the investigation of nature as nature reveals the limits of nature.[48] Natural science and scientific theology call natural theology into question, and natural theology is to be either relativized or excluded by "pure" theology, but Torrance is not completely negative about natural theology. Natural theology does have a positive role for it can help to remove the grounds of rational doubt, but its role is clearly limited cannot give us the knowledge of God available in scientific theology. Torrance does not deny a form of a natural knowledge of God, for the reality of God presses upon human beings everywhere in nature, and all people have a sense of the presence of God unless they actively suppress it. However, once again, this natural knowledge cannot reach the living God.[49] Despite his relatively negative assessment of natural theology, Torrance does believe natural theology has a place within revealed theology, and that it can be developed as a compliant conceptual instrument which theology uses to express knowledge of God in an acceptable way.[50] Torrance is clear in his rejection of an independent natural theology which serves as the foundation for revealed theology, but a *Christian* natural theology can be of limited fruitfulness in exploring the areas of overlap between natural science and theological science.[51]

The Nature of Scientific Activity

Torrance's discussion of the nature of scientific activity treats three issues: (1) the distinction between general and special science, (2) the relationship between theology and general scientific method, and (3) the scientific requirements of theology.

General and Special Science

Torrance agrees with Barbour and other contemporary philosophers of science that there are actual scientific methods and no one scientific method, but he does think that there is a scientific way of acting to be found in all sciences. He agrees with the teaching of Aristotle[52] in distinguishing between a general and a special science. There is a unity and plurality to science. The unity is derived from the one world of nature which lies behind and requires a corresponding unity for human knowledge of it. The plurality derives from the different things within the world which require different sciences, each with its own distinctiveness and characteristics of method, to study them.[53] The different particular sciences each have fundamental principles in common which constitute a *formal* scientific procedure, but each particular science will differ due to their *material* scientific procedures which are determined by the nature of the object investigated.[54]

Theology and General Scientific Method

Scientific method in theology is marked by a number of basic features. First, theology must have a sheer respect for objectivity by proper devotion to its object. Second, theology must be rigorous, disciplined, methodical, and organized knowledge. Third, theology must exhibit the trait of simplicity; that is, it must use a minimum of primary concepts and relations to find the elemental form or basic order of thought in relation to reality.[55] Fourth, theology must use the proper form of inquiry. This involves five main considerations: (1) questions must be modest, intentional, and appropriate – directed toward the object and not ourselves, asked in order to follow up or pursue them to their end, and fit the object under examination; (2) questions should always reflect backwards on ourselves and challenge us to recognize our limitations in knowing the object; (3) questions must be ruthless or unrelenting in the sense that they demand a willingness to repent on our part or make any change necessary to know the object; (4) questions are not the same as doubt, for Descartes' certainty based on self-certainty is the very reverse of scientific procedure since it is an exercise in self-absorption; and (5) questions must be asked within the context of the questioner realizing he or she is already questioned by the object.[56] And fifth, questions must recognize the problematic and interrogative forms of thinking; that is, our questions must be ordered in such a way as to enable us to know the object genuinely as a whole. Theology should not be dialectical or primarily concerned with working out a system or addressing problems; theology should be dialogical or see itself as communion with the living God who operates with the logic of grace. Problematic thinking is concerned with clarifying what one already knows, and interrogative thinking is open to exploring new knowledge and cannot say exactly how it has come to the truth. Interrogative inquiry is present in both theology and science, and when the truth is encountered as the new in natural science it is called discovery and in theology as revelation.[57]

The Scientific Requirements of Theology

Theology requires five elements in order to be scientific. First, theology requires an epistemological inversion, by which Torrance means a transformation in the subject-object relationship in which the one seeking to know is ultimately known by the object who enables the seeker to be lifted out of his or her incapac ity to know in order to know the object[58]. Second, theology requires respect for the personal nature of its object, Jesus Christ, who is both person and word. This creates three requirements for theology, since it must be derived from the Word, must not step outside of a dialogical relationship, and must have a personal medium or community of persons in which to be continued and maintained. This community is the church.[59] Third, theology requires a recognition of primary objectivity, in which God is recognized as the Lord, and secondary objectivity, in which God gives God's self to human beings in human form within our space and time. This double objectivity makes theology unique from other forms of knowledge, and it requires theology to devote itself to the specific nature of God's revelation in Christ as opposed to some general understanding of creaturely objectivity.[60] Fourth, theology requires the acknowledgment of the centrality of Jesus Christ in the knowledge of God, for Christ is the norm and criterion of theological knowing, and theological knowledge should exhibit the modes and internal structural coherence that is to be found in the nature of Christ. Mystery is a part of our understanding of Christ, and theology must reflect this and reject attempts to reduce knowledge of God to merely a logical system of ideas.[61] And fifth, theology requires that the demonstration of its truth be a demonstration in accord with the nature of its object, that is, by the Spirit, and, though this knowledge is open to all, only those who actually attempt to know God in the way God is known will understand the demonstration of God's reality.[62]

The Nature of Truth

Torrance's discussion of the nature of truth treats two major points: (1) the truth of God, and (2) the truthfulness of theological statements, which includes a treatment of existence and coherence statements and the nature and justification of theological statements.

The Truth of God

Torrance is convinced that truth must not be reduced merely to ideas or statements, and it is important for theology to recognize that truth comes in the form of personal being, namely in Jesus Christ. Jesus Christ serves as the source and norm of all true statements about God, and this truth cannot be demonstrated, for one only comes to grasp the truth by allowing the truth to come before one in His being and authority. The nature of the truth of God poses three problems for theologians: (1) theology seeks to know the ultimate Truth, (2) human statements of the Truth are not ultimate and final but point to the ultimate Truth, and (3) how is the gap between human statements and the Truth to which they refer to be bridged? Torrance insists the answer to these problems cannot be found in abstraction and one must look to how God has actually bridged the gap in Jesus Christ.[63]

God has revealed God's self to human beings in Jesus Christ, who is the Truth, the Way, and the Life. Christ as truth involves four basic claims. First, in Christ, word and person are united so that person and message are one, and truth is therefore both personal and propositional; that is, the truth communicates and interprets itself and is known through personal relation, and in its personal and propositional nature is dialogical. Second, the truth of God in Jesus Christ is bi-polar or both divine and human, for knowledge of *God* is given to us in *man*, and therefore truth is sacramental or communicated in the form of mystery. This means that our knowledge contains far more than we can ever adequately articulate or conceptualize, and genuine theology will arise out of contact with the reality of God in God's revelation. Third, there is a two-fold movement in the truth of God, for the eternal becomes temporal without ceasing to be eternal and the temporal is brought into inseparable union with the eternal without ceasing to be temporal. Logic, or abstracted thinking separate from the subject, is not enough to move from the unknown to the known, for real knowledge requires an act of will involving the whole subject and takes place as a decision in history, such as Kierkegaard's "leap" and Einstein's "imagination" which are not irrational acts but obedient reactions to the nature of truth in time. And fourth, Truth is related to the Way and the Life. God in God's grace comes to us in Jesus Christ and makes the way possible for us to know God, and God also enables us to live in such a way that we share in God's living truth. Jesus Christ thus serves as the matter and form of the truth of God which means: (1) theological truth has its basis in the kerygmatic and didactic material of the New Testament scriptures through which Christ is mediated to us, and (2) genuine theological statements will take their form from the life of Jesus as a humble inquiry which glorifies the Father.[64]

The Truthfulness of Theological Statements

The discussion of the truthfulness of theological statements takes place within the context of a treatment of existence-statements and coherence-statements and moves to the nature and justification of theological statements. Before turning to these issues, however, Torrance first gives a definition of the terms he will employ. "Statement" is used in a general sense to refer to a positive or declarative communication and includes what is stated, the stating of it, and is always the act of a subject. A "judgement" refers to what takes place within the mind in response to another statement. A "proposition" refers to a communication from one subject to another about something, and the decisions for or against a proposition's acceptance are made in dependence with other minds. In other words, some object is presented by one person to another in order to get a judgment or decision in agreement with that of the proposer. Knowing takes place within the structure of a community in which mutual questioning, criticism, and communication provide the necessary condition for verification and progress in knowledge. Theology, like other sciences, also takes place in community, and propositions claiming to arise out of a real dialogue with God are presented to others within the community for scrutiny.[65]

After defining his terms, Torrance refashions David Hume's distinction between statements as "matters of fact" and "relations of ideas" into existence-statements and coherence-statements. Existence-statements always point beyond themselves to the object intended.[66] Coherence-statements refer primarily to other statements and seek to establish orderly patterns among abstract ideas. Evidence for the two statements is different, for coherence-statements are susceptible to demonstrative arguments or proofs, but existence-statements are not; one can only try to convince others to see or hear the reality referred to as one sees it. Others must be brought to share our *intuition*, or the apprehension of reality in its objectivity and unity as a whole, of the object given.[67] Furthermore, there is no sharp dichotomy between existence-statements and coherence-statements:

> coherence-statements are properly made, as it were, at right-angles to existence-statements for that angular relation is the hinge of their meaning.

If they are entirely detached as pure abstractions,self-sufficient and self-contained, and do not even have a general ontological reference, they lose real meaning. Existence-statements, on the other hand, are shot through and through with conceptual interpretation, so that unless they yield coherence-statements they are incapable of significance.[68]

Torrance further adds that the relation between existence-statements and coherence-statements is not theoretical but practical, for they overlap in function and reference, though the truth reference of existence-statements is primarily to existents and the truth reference of coherence-statements is primarily to other statements. No existence-statements are made apart from other statements within a pattern of meaning, and the pattern must be grounded on existence-statements. Existence-statements and coherence-statements are mutually dependent, but existence-statements are basic and primary for coherence-statements are ectypal not archetypal.[69]

Specifically theological statements can also be divided into existence-statements and coherence-statements where they are called kerygmatic and didactic statements. Kerygmatic statements and didactic statements are more closely interwoven than regular existence-statements and coherence-statements, for they derive their meaning from Jesus Christ. Kerygmatic statements have their reference beyond themselves to God through Christ, and didactic statements have their interior reference as a coherent whole in him. Theological statements also differ from other statements to the extent that they collide with our natural forms of knowing and thinking, for theology, due to its object, demands an even greater stretch of our language than that found in other disciplines. Theological statements are true in that they have a real term of reference beyond themselves to which they point, and their truth will derive from their being "hearing-statements" in response to God's Word and analogically from God's Truth.[70]

Theological statements are not true in themselves but only in reference to what is beyond them. This poses three problems: (1) how can these statements truthfully refer to what is utterly transcendent of them?, (2) how can theological statements relate their language to the external facts?, and (3) how can theological statements have an objective standard to measure them if they are analogical? Torrance grants these are difficult problems for theology, for he admits that in themselves theological statements have no real truth and in themselves "...we cannot say just how they relate to the reality which they indicate...;"[71] however, this is not ultimately disastrous for theology, for natural science has the same problem in justifying its existence-statements relation to their referents. Inability to give a "theoretical bridge" of how human beings can refer to reality need not produce skepticism in either discipline, for bare thought does not adequately grasp reality, and, rightly taken, the proper response is what "Einstein called 'awe' before a mystery which we shall never understand."[72] Theology, like science, must start with how objects actually come to be known, and for theology this means it must start with how God is actually known in Jesus Christ. Furthermore, the nature of theological statements requires that they should cohere with other areas of truthfulness in human knowing such as historical facticity, logical consistency, ethical validity, and others.[73]

Theological statements are formally and materially related to the truth. Formally considered, theological statements are true in so far as they are faithful responses to the witness of the Holy Scriptures as they are heard in the historical life of the church. The church is the community where the Word of God in scripture is proclaimed, but the truth is found there because it is the place where God has chosen to reveal God's self in Jesus Christ, and the church must point beyond itself to the reality of God in its midst. Materially considered, theological statements are true if their content comes from God's grace. God may reject human statements and human beings must cast themselves upon God asking for God's criticism and correction, and truth can only be verified by the one who is Truth[74]. Truth for theological statements requires "justification by Grace and demonstration of the Spirit, that is, verification and action by the Truth Himself."[75] Justification by grace through faith in Christ is not just about our life and action; it includes epistemology as well. Torrance concedes that the need for justification in epistemology may be charged with irrationalism by some, but it is really the opposite and the height of rationality, for this is precisely what is required for knowledge of God to be possible. God is to be sought where God can be found, in Jesus Christ and the witness to him in the scriptures in the midst of the church. Furthermore, justification requires a commitment to truth in action, for the theoretical and the practical cannot be separated from one another.[76] Commitment in action by itself cannot be used as a pragmatic test for truth, for it is only by God's grace that our action can encounter the real which yields truth.[77]

Problems of Logic

In discussing the logic of theological statements, Torrance first treats the logic of God followed by a discussion of the logic of man which includes the logic of existence-statements, the logic of coherence-statements, and logical formalization in theological thinking. The specific mode of rational activity by human beings seeking to know God is faith, and theology cannot step outside of faith in its effort to truly understand God. Theology has two problems: (1) ontologic, or relating speech to being which is true of every science, and (2) theologic, or relating statements to God which is its own particular difficultly.[78] It is to how theology can overcome these problems that Torrance turns.

The Logic of God

Jesus Christ, as the Logos, is the logic of God incarnate and provides the nomothetic structure of human understanding of the logic of God. First, the logic of God is the logic of grace, for God comes to human beings to enable them to know God. Second, the logic of God is an interior logic based on the union of God and man in Jesus Christ, for it is this union that makes possible knowledge of God. Third, the logic of God is the logic of love, for Christ, the One Person who unites the divine nature and the human nature, is the One Word of God who communicates knowledge of God to human beings in an inter-personal relation which involves love. And fourth, the logic of God is a four-dimensional logic, by which Torrance means a logic of verbs, for one is related to the truth of God in time and in action, and knowing the truth is a dynamic relationship which involves movement in time and constant decisive action within a community.[79] Knowledge of God requires an act of obedience or decision, in contrast to knowing timeless and necessary truths such as 2 x 2 = 4, and decision is the only way theology can discern the truth. However, the fact that decision is the way to discern truth does not mean that the act of faith makes real the truth of the Gospel, for acts of faith are rooted in God's election, or prevenient movement of love, and it is only through grace that theological statements may be true of God.[80] Grace has an unconditional priority in theological knowledge, but it remains grace; that is, it does not override the human, for God speaks to human beings in human thought-forms, and so human knowledge must be respected within theology and the logic of man is important as well.[81]

Human Logic[82]

To understand human logic, or our activity in formulating an understanding of the divine Logos, one must consider the diverse types of order that reasoning takes, which involves a discussion of the logic of existence-statements, the logic of coherence-statements, and logical formalization in theological thinking.

Existence-statements are not isolated but come in clusters or groups which unfold from interrogative operations and develop through analogical operations. Existence-statements follow a logic of question and answer and take as their most basic form "What have we here?" The object under investigation often forces us to ask new questions and break out of old modes of thinking, and a heuristic induction or discovery is necessary to know the object. No fixed logical rules can be made for scientific discovery, nor is the evidence immediately evident to us, for discovery involves a heuristic act which leaps across the logical gap between our questioning and the object itself. Theological statements also refer to an object which cannot be exhausted by human knowing, and the logic of their reference must correspond to God's self-communication or revelation. In addition, since our knowledge cannot exhaust the object, existence-statements must be tested against reality and developed in their correspondence with each other through analogical relations if they are to be confirmed. Existence-statements taken together and developed analogically should produce a conceptual pattern of epistemological harmony through which the objective pattern in reality discloses itself. These conceptual patterns are paradeigmatic in character, which means they provide us with means of grasping objects in our apprehension yet they never exhaust the realities and always fall short of them. The necessity of analogical reasoning in knowing involves four features: (1) the patterns must remain "open" to new disclosures; (2) the patterns are not replicas of objective structures nor are they merely imposed upon these structures, for they are perspicuous forms through which we discern, however scantily, the inherent rationality and order of the real world; (3) the patterns are tested by various criteria to confirm their acceptance, such as the applicability of a model to the real world (as confirmed by empirical test), the relevance of an analogue to enable us to grasp an object under investigation, or the fertility of a theory in illuminating problems and opening up new facts; and (4) the patterns will overlap with coherence-statements and therefore the distinction between existence-statements and coherence-statements can never be drawn very sharply, though the general patterns of existence-statements are built up through analogical reasoning and the general patterns of coherence-statements are built up through deductive reasoning. Theological statements also require analogical reasoning and paradeigmatic help in order to yield knowledge, and

Torrance offers the Chalcedonian definition of the two natures of Christ as "without confusion or division" as an example of a helpful theological analogue.[83]

Coherence-statements deal with formal logic which is not an active process of inquiry, for formal logic investigates the rules of valid implications between propositions. A proper logic of coherence-statements will recognize the following points. First, there are differences between numerical and verbal relations and they must not be reduced one to another. Second, logical systems must have real applicability to the physical world and not simply impose an artificial formal structure on the world. Third, logic must have both a certain detachment from ontological reference in specific sciences in order to deductively evaluate propositions and a certain attachment to existence in the sense that logical systems are incomplete[84] which makes complete logicalization of a special science impossible and requires reference to the object under consideration. And fourth, there are three different logical levels which must be respected: (1) the level of fundamental knowledge of things in accordance with what they are, (2) the level where we test and formalize this knowledge mathematically into a coherent system, and (3) the level at which we interpret the formulations of the system and determine its mode of connection and consistency. Theological science uses three levels as well: (1) the knowledge obtained through the rational assent of faith, (2) the orderly and systematic account of this knowledge in dogmatics, and (3) the philosophy of theology or its meta-science including its logic and epistemology. In addition, four final observations need to be made about the three logical levels of a special science. First, the levels needed in a special science will depend on the nature of the subject-matter. Second, the levels are hierarchical, and they extend upwards and reach downwards to help clarify the lower levels. Third, logical formalization takes place only after an analogue or model has first been developed through analogical reasoning. And fourth, there are different types of order comprising different types of concepts which must not be overlooked in their correlation.[85]

Torrance concludes his discussion of logic with a treatment of logical formalization in theological thinking. The strict demands of secular formal logic are not applicable to theology, but theology does rely on a principle which is as or even more reliable than formal logic – the faithfulness of God. The faithfulness of God controls theological reflection, and even philosophical difficulties such as the problem of evil must be interpreted *a posteriori*, or in light of the knowledge of God which human beings possess. Logical thinking contributes to theological thinking, for it can help to prune theological statements and arguments which do not conform to an integrated pattern of the whole. A rigorous formulation of theological language can also play a positive role, for it can help to reshape the language used in grasping the object by sharpening and clarifying it. Logic and metaphysics should not dictate the terms of theological discussion; however, for theology should be understood as primary over these disciplines due to the fact that theology, as a valid science, has its own inner logic which demands faithfulness to its subject-matter, and the applicability of theological statements will involve an actual conformity to the object under investigation. Formal logic is limited, for it can never exhaust or completely describe reality, but theology is in a superior position to other sciences in that knowledge of God, though limited, is helped by the fact that God has bridged the gap between our statements about the object under consideration through the Incarnation. The Incarnation must serve as the norm for the theological thinker, and he or she should not be unduly concerned if the secular thinker disagrees or questions this approach, for genuine theological thinking demands this as its rational standard.[86]

Theological Science among the Special Sciences

Theology is a special science devoted to a unique object, but it is a human quest for truth which takes place within the environment of other special sciences and within the bounds of human learning and reasoning. Theology cannot justify itself on the grounds of the other special sciences, but it must be open to all truth and to self-criticism in light of new learning and reasonable argumentation and continue to test its claims severely if it is to be true knowledge of God. God is the source of all being and the ground of all truth, and because of this theology must be concerned with a level of wholeness and unity not to be found in other special sciences. Due to the Christian doctrine of creation which respects the created order, each of the natural special sciences functions as an independent branch of the knowledge of contingent realities, and these sciences are not qualified to speak outside of their proper object of study; however, theology should be in genuine dialogue with the natural sciences, for an indirect comparison with the natural sciences can help to purify theology of ideology by refocusing it on its proper object and enable it to communicate its rationality to others. In order to accomplish these goals, a careful examination must be given of the similarities and differences between theology and other sciences, the relevance of historical science to theology, and the nature of theology as a dogmatic science.[87]

Similarities between Theology and other Sciences

First, like the natural sciences, theology is a human activity, which presupposes its object exists, is capable of rational investigation, and uses models through which to know the object, and, even though theology investigates a self-communicating object, it remains a human form of inquiry which can only grasp what is communicated through orderly constructions of human forming, and thus all dogmas must be relativized in light of the object we seek to know through them. These dogmas never exhaust the object, but they are not merely symbolic with no basis in reality. Second, there is an active and passive element in theology and the natural sciences, for one forms models to attempt to grasp the object but at the same time must be open to allowing reality to revise or criticize the model, and in theology openness to the object is even greater than in natural science. Third, neither theological science nor the special sciences operates with a preconceived metaphysics. Both the special sciences and theology do unavoidably contain metaphysical ideas, but openness to the reality under investigation constantly questions these ideas and often requires their reformulation into a proper ontology. Fourth, both theology and the natural sciences must recognize they come upon limits beyond which they cannot investigate. And fifth, both theology and the special sciences have a problem in relating scientific language to ordinary language. Many of the concepts used in physics are hard to describe in any common sense way, and theology must also make use of language that fits poorly with the language of our ordinary experience. The Holy Spirit does help with statements about God in a way without counterpart in the other special sciences, but Torrance insists that the Holy Spirit does not take human beings out of the subject-object relation, and thus theological concepts must interact with ordinary language or human beings could say nothing of God. There is no one-to-one correlation of scientific (either special or theological) language to ordinary language at every point, but correlation can be had at some particular points which are of crucial importance; for example, theology can never dispense with its historical roots in the historical Jesus and must be willing to engage in rigorous historical-critical investigation.[88]

Differences between Theology and the Special Sciences

The fundamental difference between theology and all other sciences is that theology's object of study is God and not creaturely realities, and this gives rise to basic differences in both the objectivity and subjectivity of theology in comparison to other sciences. In regard to objectivity, theology differs from the other sciences in that: (1) theology, since it comes up against ultimate reality and therefore has a final term of reference which natural science does not, is the most profoundly objective and the most profoundly relative of sciences, and it is both the most certain but also the most humble of the sciences; (2) theology involves a two-fold objectivity which natural science does not, for theology must deal with God, the ultimate reality of objectivity, and the clothing of that reality within the contingent structures of the world; (3) theology deals with an object that gives itself freely (by grace) and is not subject to human control; and (4) theology has the particular or unique take precedence over the general, whereas in natural science the general takes precedence over the unique. In regard to subjectivity, theology differs from the natural sciences in that: (1) theology, unlike natural science, demands reciprocity from the theologian; that is, theology requires an epistemological inversion in which the object always remains a subject who challenges and retains primacy over the investigating subject, and (2) theology, unlike natural science, has an irreducible element of anthropomorphism, for the object under investigation appears to us as human in the Incarnation, and the humanity of Jesus Christ challenges and heals our defective humanity.[89]

The Relevance of Historical Science

After contrasting theological science with the sciences dealing with impersonal objects, Torrance then turns to a science which deals with personal objects, namely, history. Torrance acknowledges that it is difficult to establish the nature of a "historical fact," and he is especially careful not to reduce history to nature or to allow the dualistic difficulties of idealistic conceptions of history and materialistic views of science to undermine a true understanding of the nature of history. Collingwood and Dilthey fall prey to these mistakes, and the *Historie-Geschichte* disjunction proposed by Hermann, Troeltsch, and Bultmann is flawed by a similar mistake.[90]

The historian, like the scientist, must move beyond description and narration to explanation in his or her reconstruction of the past, but in doing so he or she must be careful not to impose modern standards of credibility and significance upon the data. The historian needs to recognize that what

> is required in historical explanation is a penetration into the movement or happening in a series of events in such a way we lay bare the inner logic of the interaction between mind and nature that runs throughout them and then in the light of it gain for ourselves such a grasp of those events in their intelligible patterns that they become, as it were, dramatized before us. Considerable use of art and dramatic imagination, of empathy and intuition, will undoubtedly be necessary but all in order to provide us with an adequate lens, as it were, through which our understanding can break through the original happenings themselves. In undertaking this we have to be aware of the changes in modes of thought and behaviour that have come over the human race, and therefore have to be constantly on guard against any selection and organization of the facts governed only by what modern people think, feel, and accept in case we work up those facts wrongly into a coherent whole by interpolating into them alien thoughts and intentions. Rather must we develop modes of interrogation that subject the source-material to such critical examination that they are made to interpret themselves through their own latent hermeneutic.[91]

Torrance also argues there is a different kind of rationality inherent in historical events than found in natural events. Natural events are amenable to mathematical representation or the rationality of number; historical events need to be understood in terms of intentionality or purpose or the rationality of word or logos.[92]

Returning to the question of Jesus Christ, we must treat this historical event like any other, but we must learn quickly that the Son of God becoming man is a unique historical event and therefore ask questions in two opposite directions at the same time, in accord with both the nature and acts of God and the nature and acts of human beings. But at his point, one may raise the questions: (1) how are we to determine which events are decisive in interpreting the divine intentionality, (2) what prompts us to ask questions in two directions, and (3) what is meant by source materials that interpret themselves? Torrance's answer to these questions is an act of discernment beyond common historical observation that is true to the nature of the event under consideration, that is, faith. Faith is adapted to the object considered, which is not the mere act of God or historical event as such but the word-act of God in which God encounters people in every age. Word and act are inseparable in the historical event of Jesus Christ, and the hermenuetic to be followed is intrinsic to the work of the incarnate

Son. Inquiry into the person of Jesus Christ must be theological-historico, for in Christ we are confronted with a "*complex fact that includes its own interpretation as part of its facticity.*"[93] Torrance's notion of complexity is related to his treatment of logical levels which are actually related but theoretically distinct. Godel's Theorem shows that logical systems cannot be both consistent and complete and must remain open upwards for their explanations. Applied to language, this means existence-statements and coherence-statements can be related without paradox or contradiction if we view them on different levels; applied to historical events, this means faith must also operate on different levels in investigating Christ as we examine: (1) the biblical texts, (2) the witness of the text beyond itself to the reality to which it points, and (3) the ground level where we meet God God's self in the person of Jesus Christ. The historical events in the Gospels must be interpreted on all three levels, and thus we cannot allow other presuppositions foreign to the reality of actual contact with God to determine the meaning of the text, and therefore the resurrection of Christ must be seen as an actual historical event and eschatological and teleological elements will inevitably be part of the Christian approach to history.[94]

Theology as a dogmatic science

Torrance closes his treatment of theological science with a repetition of earlier themes advanced and he adds the importance of the church for theology. Theology is to be done in community, not in isolation, and theology is a dogmatic science. To explain this, Torrance distinguishes between *dogma*, which is the ultimate ground and creative source of the existence of the church in the communication of God's own being, and *dogmas*, which are the church's historical inquiries and formulations of the datum of divine revelation. Dogmatics is the science of dogma, not dogmas, and is open to reconstructions of the past dogmas of the church which may rest on limited range and need to be re-worked in light of the advance of knowledge.[95] One of the areas of new knowledge which needs to be taken into account is the advances in the natural sciences, and it is to Torrance's integration of scientific knowledge into theological thinking we now turn.

Theological Science: Application

A cursory reading of Torrance may give one the impression that he is not interested in integrating theology and science into a coherent world-view, for he is constantly emphasizing the differences between theology and natural science and the unique nature of theology as a science. However, this is only part of the story, for Torrance does have some very specific reasons as to why he thinks the integration of theology and science is necessary. This section will explore Torrance's reasons for integration by paying close attention to his treatment of specific issues in the relationship between science and religion.

Reality as an Integrated Whole

Torrance sees reality as an integrated whole, and theology and natural science fit into this integrated whole in the following ways: (1) theology and science have a shared intelligibility; (2) the universe itself is a multileveled and an integrated whole reflecting divine and contingent order; and (3) reality is relational, which is exhibited in both theology and science.

Shared Intelligibility

Torrance rejects the adversarial understanding of the relationship between theology and science as examples of both bad science and bad theology, and he argues that science and theology should be viewed as allies rather than foes. Theology and science each have their own subject-matter and do not contribute to the material content of one another, but they do interpenetrate one another in significant ways.[96] First, both disciplines are an integration of theory and praxis where integration means a unifying or creating of a whole where none was recognized before. This organization is a spontaneous integration of coherences actually embedded in nature, and it is grasped through informal or non-analytical acts of knowledge. Second, both disciplines are creative sciences. Theory or doctrine comes about as a result of reflecting upon experience in the light of one's basic intellectual convictions and intuitions concerning reality. Both the theologian and scientist make a leap of imaginative insight to postulate a new theoretical structure, and the new theory must be tested by having propositions deduced from it tested empirically. The method of both is cyclical, for it originates and terminates in experience, and, upon successful testing, different observers are able to acquire a common or shared understanding of the theory or doctrine in question. From this common understanding a consensus is built. Third, Torrance holds that theology motivates and provides wholeness and meaning to natural science; natural science can sharpen and clarify theological reflection. Honest and open dialogue between scientists and theologians can be very fruitful, for they have a shared intelligibility based on the divine order revealed in God's redemptive interaction with human beings in history and the contingent order revealed through human exploration of the physical universe. This shared intelligibility can be seen in that old dualisms have broken down, one of which is the old claim that theology answers why-questions and science answers how-questions. Torrance insists both types of questions occur in each discipline, and the questions can be transformed when they are linked together and seen as part of a larger unitary intelligibility.

Universe as Multi-leveled Whole: Divine and Contingent Order

As is clear by now, Torrance is convinced we advance in knowledge as our thoughts grasp the structures of reality for it is presumed "that a correlation is possible between our human conceiving and the inner structure of reality itself, and we carry out all our operations in that belief,"[97] for, as Torrance quotes and endorses Polanyi, there is a real "correspondence between the structure of comprehension and the structure of the comprehensive entity which is its object."[98] Furthermore, there is a hierarchical and multileveled character to the universe and to the nature of knowledge.[99] These levels are: (1) the primary or the level of scientific activity, (2) the secondary or meta-theoretical level in which we reflect on our investigations, and (3) the tertiary or meta-meta-theoretical level in which we subject our reflections to an ultimate logical economy or simplicity. Thus, there is a stratified structure to the levels of inquiry,[100] and Polanyi's principle of marginal control (that each level of inquiry is coordinated to the one above, by reference to which it becomes comprehensible and meaningful) applies in the stratified structure of knowledge. Torrance modifies Polanyi's principle to include theology as the highest level, and he describes it as the principle of coherent integration from above.[101] This refutes any form of reductionism in science, and shows why theology can give meaning and purpose to science since there is

an ontological stratification in the universe comprising a sequence of rising levels, each higher one controlling the boundaries of the one below it and embodying thereby the joint meaning of the particulars on the lower level.[102]

The stratification of knowledge and being culminates in divine order, which is the basis of the contingent order studied by natural science. Both science and theology have a stake in and reveal the contingent nature of the universe, and in his work *Divine and Continent Order* Torrance gives a sustained development of this point.

Contingent events are not necessary but ones which "happen to be like that," and "did not have to be like that, for they might have been very different."[103] Contingence is grounded in God's creative activity and is a fundamental feature of the world as described by science, and means

> that as created out of nothing the universe has no self-subsistence and no ultimate stability of its own, but that it is nevertheless endowed with an authentic reality and integrity of its own which must be respected.[104]

In addition, contingent order means that the universe is not "self-sufficient or self-explaining but is given a rationality and reliability in its orderliness which depend on and reflect God's own external rationality and reliability."[105] This can be seen in that space and time are not infinite but belong to the created order of things, and that at its boundaries science raises questions with religious import which it cannot itself answer. If one presses back to the earliest history of the universe, for example, astronomy forces one to ask why those particular initial conditions were present, and at this point science finds an order which is both rational and contingent which it cannot itself explain. This combination of intelligibility and contingency prompts the search for new and unexpected forms of rational order, and Torrance argues that the theologian can best make sense of the rational contingent order since he or she sees it as grounded in the rationality of God. Furthermore, theology can actually be of aid to natural science, for there has been a tendency in the history of science to attempt to deny contingency, and theology offers solid reasons for resisting these efforts to impose an artificial necessity on the world. Theology also provides a reason why natural science's presuppositions of the intelligibility and order of the universe are valid, and it may suggest fruitful analogies for scientific reflection.[106] In addition, natural science as a free and creative inquiry can also aid theology, for it may help theology to purge itself of doctrines expressed in outdated scientific concepts,[107] and it may also suggest fruitful analogies for theology's use.[108] This productive dialogue is possible for theology and natural science because reality is a multileveled and integrated whole, and the analogical fruitfulness that exists between the two disciplines is possible because reality is inherently relational.

The Relational Nature of Reality

The relational nature of reality is expressed in two ways: (1) a relational, rather than a receptacle, view of space-time, and (2) the importance of field theories in modern physics.

Relativity theory understands the space-time continuum to be relational in nature in contrast to the old receptacle view of space. In the receptacle model, space and time are conceived as a huge container which holds all the objects that exist and events that occur. In the relational model envisioned by Einstein and Torrance, space is not empty but filled with matter and energy with time as an inalienable ingredient in the relations between particles and the events affecting their configurations. Space and time are not containers but relations intrinsic to the ongoing process of the universe.[109] The contingent order is relational, and so is the divine order, for the Godhead is a unitary, triune, community of divine love.[110] In addition, the Incarnation of Jesus Christ is more comprehensible by using a relational, rather than a receptacle, understanding of the space-time continuum, for the old dualisms which have plagued theology and science are overcome with this new model.[111]

Field theories also demonstrate the relational character of reality. An emphasis on fields, or relations between bodies, is an important part of Torrance's approach, and he derives much of his treatment of fields from Polanyi,[112] Maxwell, and Einstein, whose theory of general relativity is a field theory.

Torrance understands field theory to be at the heart of modern science. According to Torrance, modern science rejects the dualism of previous scientific eras and understands nature in terms of "continuous invisible fields in a multi-leveled universe."[113] Furthermore, Torrance holds that field theories are needed in all sciences, not just physics. Biology, for example, needs to give up its tendency to apply mechanistic explanations to living systems and investigate "the field set up by living force."[114] Biology needs organic thinking in which structures are set up which do not abrogate the laws of nature expressed by physics and chemistry but are coordinated with them at their boundary conditions which the laws of physics leave underdetermined. Torrance calls for a "biologic" that grasps the dynamic laws of living organisms, and he follows Polanyi in arguing that the DNA molecule transcends explication merely in terms of physics and chemistry.[115] Theology also needs to adopt the idea of a field, and it needs an appropriate "theologic," and it is Torrance's hope that when modern biology achieves its break-through to a field theory that it will supply historical and theological science with more apt analogues than those now available in physics.[116]

For Torrance, theology is concerned with the "the theological field of connections in and through Jesus Christ," or the field of God's interaction with humanity and the world through Jesus Christ.[117] Different field-languages should not be confused, however, for those that are designed to explain the non-observable (theology) are very different that those which arise out of observation (gravitational). Proper understanding of God's interaction with the world must be determined by the force or energy which constitutes it, the Holy Spirit of God. In this way one can discern the operational principles of the theological field.[118] Furthermore, theology does not learn from the material content of any particular field theory, but it learns "from the way the in which the approach is made to the question of connection."[119]

Different field-languages must be hierarchically coordinated.[120] One cannot apply the methods of verification in one field to another quite different one. Torrance approves of Polanyi's claim that it is illogical to attempt the proof of the supernatural by natural tests.[121] Experimental investigation is scientifically inappropriate to God, and for an example Torrance discusses the virgin birth of Christ. Torrance argues that biological questions will yield biological, not theological, answers and biological answers cannot be set against theological answers, for they must be coordinated, not confounded.[122] "Constitutive axioms" or the ultimates of Christian theology such as the Incarnation and Resurrection cannot be verified or validated on any other grounds than those they themselves provide.[123] These all-embracing miracles upon which the Christian gospel rests cannot be substantiated in terms of the evidences and arguments which obtain within the natural sciences but are only finally explicable from grounds in God, although they participate in the natural order of things. These events are not infringements of the laws of nature but are ordering events within the natural order restoring and creating order where it is damaged or lacking. They may be explained as "the *giving of order*."[124] Theological formulations cannot be without their empirical correlates, but they are inexplicable in terms of the operational principles in the natural sciences.[125]

Consequently the theological field requires its own distinctive language and methods and is not subject to control by other field-languages, for theology and natural science represent incommensurable frameworks. Polanyi provides Torrance with a helpful description of incommensurable frameworks:

Formal operations relying on *one* framework of interpretation cannot demonstrate a proposition to persons who rely on *another* framework. Its advocates may not even succeed in getting a hearing from these, since they must first teach them a new language, and no one can learn a new language unless he first trusts that it means something.[126]

Polanyi adds that if anyone is persuaded by the advocates of a novel and strange doctrine such an acceptance may be legitimately described as a conversion. Polanyi is talking about a conversion to a new scientific paradigm, but Torrance applies it to theological conversion as well.

Each field must set out its own principles of verification. One cannot investigate the truth or falsity of a claim from an outside perspective.[127] Investigations take place within our fiduciary frameworks, and disagreements between these frameworks are not trivial because frameworks are "indwelt" since "we are accustomed to live in our frames of reference; we and they belong together."[128] Christian fundamentals such as the resurrection of Christ are disclosed only by indwelling in the circle of knowing which establishes them. Only the believer is able to weigh the evidence properly.[129]

The field concept is used by Torrance in an analogical sense. Torrance prefers to speak of analogies in a disclosure, rather than a pictorial manner. Theological analogies are God-created correspondences existing between two knowledge structures representing distinct objects or relationships of reality. Analogy is a similarity within dissimilarity or a commonality arising from certain aspects of the entities being compared and represents a partial likeness or reflection which is true but not exhaustive. As W. Jim Neidhardt's excellent summary of Torrance's understanding of analogy puts it:

Torrance's analogies are always *across* logical levels of reality; they are *heuristic* (exploratory, discovery- oriented, stimulating further investigation) in character. Each of them establishes a *disclosure* relationship between entities at different logical reality levels. This contrasts with the kind of analogy that establishes a purely *formal* correspondence between entities at the same logical reality level. In Torrance's work, an analogy, with its capacity for *disclosure*, represents a heuristic *pointing from one level to another* occurring *between* similar aspects of two objects or relationships that either represent or constitute elements of different reality levels. Finally, it is necessary to recognize the distinctive character of dissimilarity within similarity in an analogy of relatedness between physics and theology. Torrance always emphasizes that theological concepts concerning relatedness have a life-transforming and life-directing quality of much deeper personal dimensionality than the analogous concepts associated with physical relatedness. Thus when *disclosure analogies* are used both the similarities and the differences are heuristically instructive; as does Torrance, I believe it cannot be emphasized enough that all truly creative thinking has an analogical component.[130]

Torrance draws upon the work of James Clerk Maxwell to create an analogy from field theory. Drawing upon the work of Farraday, who envisioned charged particles or magnets as interrelated to one another by invisible lines of force-fields which fill all space, Clerk Maxwell developed a mathematical theory that consistently represented the two fields of electricity and magnetism, and he was able to unite electricity, magnetism, and optics together in a theoretical framework through four equations. Clerk Maxwell showed that changing magnetic fields generate electric fields and vice-versa, and a disturbance in one field affects the other in such a way that a self-perpetuating cycle of electric and magnetic fields is created, and this disturbance does not need help from the matter that created it to keep going. Clerk Maxwell called this unified dynamic disturbance the electromagnetic field, and it showed that particles should be described in a relational way as inseparable from their interactions. As Torrance puts it,

> ...the relations he (Clerk Maxwell) referred to were not just imaginary or putative but real relations, relations that belong to reality as much as things (particles) do, for the interrelations of things, are, in part at least, constitutive of what they are. Being-constituting relations of this kind we may well speak of as "onto-relations."[131]

Torrance sees this field concept as heuristically analogous to the biblical concept of person as developed by the early Church Fathers to formulate the doctrine of the trinity. Central to this theological understanding of person is the reality of human relationships as an integral part of what persons really are. Human beings are not cut-off or isolated individuals like Newtonian particles; rather, persons are interrelated with other persons and these interrelationships constitute the very stuff of personal being. For Torrance, the natural order is not divine, but perceived through the eyes and ears of faith, one can see traces of the divine nature imprinted in the creation, and discovering the analogies that exist helps to show the unitary nature of reality and provide mutually enriching dialogue between theology and natural science.

The Necessity of Theology's Interaction with Science

Torrance believes that theology must interact with natural science, and it is to theology's advantage (and natural science's) to do so. Though Torrance remains insistent that no other discipline should set theology's rationality standard for it and he claims to make no apologies for divine revelation,[132] Torrance does not want a "great gulf fixed" between theology and natural science. The interaction of theology and natural science can be very fruitful for both disciplines for a number of reasons. First, Torrance insists that theology cannot be sealed off from natural science and must consider the relevant problems and questions posed by the other sciences in clarifying knowledge of its own subject-matter. Second, as noted above, theology may make legitimate use of analogies taken from other sciences where similar problems arise in order to help it penetrate into its own inner intelligibility.[133] Third, the two great ultimates of Christian faith, the Incarnation and the Resurrection, are events which occurred within the space-time continuum, and therefore the nature of space and time is relevant, indeed inescapable, as part of these great events.[134] That is why Torrance insists theology must have "empirical correlates."[135] Fourth, a careful study of natural science will reveal that many of the problems which worried theologians in previous generations were pseudo-problems which were tied to a mechanistic conception of the universe which is now discredited by science.[136] Those who are familiar with modern science are in a position to be more open to the objectivities present in reality, for they are used to dealing with an open universe, an open relationship between theoretical and empirical concepts, and open structures of thought, and the theologian can point out the consistency of the Christian doctrines of creation and incarnation with other thought in order to bear witness to the intelligibility of the Christian faith.[137] And fifth, theology honors scientific efforts to understand the contingent order as part of man's religious duty, for the quest for truth is part of the faithful human response to the Creator.[138] Torrance constantly insists on the need for a theology of nature, and he refers to human beings as the "Priests of Creation,"[139] whose job it is to act redemptively and mediate order. Human beings are in a unique position for good within the created order, for they can mediate divine order to the contingent order, but they also can be a source of evil, for they struggle with the fact that they live on the boundaries of divine and contingent order.

The Transformation of Culture

Torrance, the son of Christian missionaries,[140] can be rightly described as a missionary himself to the world of science. Torrance sees a real need to integrate theology and natural science for he understands it to be part of the Christian mission. Torrance sees his theological task as following the example of the early church which set out not just to communicate the gospel to the Graeco-Roman world but to transform the prevailing frame of thought and culture so the gospel could take deep root and develop within it. Torrance's describes his work as rising out of a sustained engagement with the tension between Christian theology and the general frame of thought that has dominated European culture for several hundred years, and the dominant force in modern culture has been the rise of natural science.[141] The Christian faith must be brought to bear transformingly upon the whole frame of human culture, science, and philosophy in every age in order to fulfill its mission to people, and the church must be involved in the struggle for the mind of contemporary society. Torrance's careful attention to specific developments in natural science are an important part of his attempt to bring theology to bear transformingly on the modern world, and, as has been mentioned above, he finds the history of science to show the important contributions Christianity has made to the development of modern science and its harmony with the truth found about the contingent order. Torrance is hopeful that all knowledge will eventually be seen within a unified whole.

Theological Science: Critique

This section will examine the relevance of Torrance's work for current discussions of the relationship between theology and natural science. It will first discuss various criticisms made of Torrance's work by a number of reviewers. Most of these criticisms will be shown to be misplaced and not posing any substantive challenge to Torrance's position at all. More serious charges against the relevance of Torrance's work will then be examined, for, if Ronald Thiemann and other writers in the theology and science area are correct, Torrance's theology is hopelessly outdated and irrelevant to the contemporary scene (except perhaps as a way not to do theology). I think Thiemann and others are mistaken in this, and I will show why Torrance is not guilty of the charges the more serious critics make against him and discuss why he remains relevant for current thought. I will close with some an assessment of Torrance's thought and discuss aspects of his work that still leave unresolved problems and will suggest some ways of at least partially resolving these problems by drawing on other work in the contemporary philosophy of science.

Insubstantial Criticisms of Torrance's Position

The criticisms of Torrance's work to be treated here are *insubstantial,* by which is meant they either represent a clear misunderstanding of Torrance's position or can be dismissed rather easily and as such pose no real threat to the relevance of Torrance's work for ongoing treatments of the integration of theology and natural science. They are worthy of attention, however, for Torrance has been entirely too neglected a figure in current treatments of the relationship between theology and science,[142] and these criticisms may have contributed to easy dismissals of Torrance's thought which do not really engage his work. These easy dismissals will be shown to be faulty.

John Hick, one of the most influential philosophers of religion, questioned one of the basic features of Torrance's thought – the definition of science as thought which is determined by the nature of its object of investigation. Hick sees Torrance's treatment of science as too all-embracing and writes that "there is a danger of proving too much by this procedure. Would not fairy-lore, for example, qualify as a science under Torrance's definition?"[143] Hick's example is ambiguous and easily answered. First, since Torrance's definition is solidly grounded in realism, it would not allow for fairy-lore to be a science in a primary sense unless fairies are taken to actually exist, but the study of fairy tales could be undertaken scientifically. To put it another way, on the one hand, *fairy-lore* would not be a science for fairies are fictional creatures; however, on the other hand, fairy-*lore* could be a science, for one could actually study the way fairy tales have emerged and been transmitted throughout various cultures.[144] Hick's rather ambiguous example either fails to understand Torrance's position or else offers a weak argument and is therefore an inadequate criticism of it.

A second criticism of Torrance is the charge that he has "too intellectualist a view of faith."[145] This criticism seems strange, for Torrance constantly emphasizes against positivism and idealism that knowing is an *act* which involves the whole person and fiduciary frameworks are *indwelt* and influence people in tacit, as well as intellectual, ways. Torrance does emphasize the cognitive aspects of faith, but this aspect is rooted in a broader understanding which includes action and a fiduciary framework, as Torrance's exposition of Polanyi's understanding of faith, which Torrance endorses, illustrates:

> we must recognize belief or intuitive apprehension once more as the source of knowledge from which our *acts* of discovery take their rise, for it is in belief that we are in direct touch with reality, in belief that our minds are open to the invisible realm of intelligibility independent of ourselves, and through belief that we entrust our mind to the orderly and reliable nature of the universe.
>
> Behind and permeating all our scientific activity, reaching from end to end of our analyses and investigations, there is an elemental, unshakeable faith in the rational nature of things, but faith is also in the possibility of grasping the real world with our concepts, and faith in the truth over which we have no control but in service of which our human rationality stands or falls. Faith and rationality are intrinsically locked with one another. No human intelligence, Polanyi claimed, however critical or original, can operate outside such a context of faith, for it is within that context that there arises within us, under compulsion from the reality of the world we experience, an *operative set of convictions or a framework of beliefs* which prompts and guides our inquiries and controls our interpretation of data.[146]

Faith, for Polanyi and Torrance, is an *interaction* between human beings and a reality independent of human beings which in the case of theology involves the whole person and God and is not excessively intellectual. While Torrance does treat in great detail the cognitive or intellectual aspects of faith, this should not be seen as a negative but a positive feature of his theology, for it is not hard to agree with John Barton's description of the current climate in theology:

> irrationalism rather than rationalism now seems (to me at least) to be the enemy of true religion. The religious world today is full of credulity
> and a seeking after six impossible things to believe before breakfast. For me the problem is not how to defend the supernatural character of the faith I profess, but how to connect it with knowledge in other fields, both scientific and humanistic. For that task an approach which fences off scriptural revelation from the rest of knowledge has its dangers.[147]

I do not know if Barton has directly commented on Torrance's work, but Torrance should be counted as one who seeks to champion the integrity of both faith and reason in theology.

Another charge labeled against Torrance's work is that it is simply a "sophisticated Barthian fideism."[148] This is unfair for two reasons. First, Torrance is not simply a Barthian, for, even though he was highly influenced by Barth, Tórrance is critical of Barth on a number of points, including a lack of attention to the doctrine of the Holy Spirit and a lack of positive interaction with modern science,[149] and Torrance develops the relationship between theology and science and a theology of nature far beyond anything to be found in Barth[150]. And second, Torrance is not properly classified as a fideist. Though Klinefelter does not define what he means by "fideist," it is clear Torrance is not a fideist in the traditional sense. As one can see from the exposition of Torrance's thought given above, Torrance does not see a clash between faith and reason with faith being tipped the upper hand; rather, he sees faith and reason working together in harmony in the knowing act. Torrance, like Polanyi, is really arguing for a broader conception of rationality which transcends the either/or conception of faith and reason found in much modern epistemology, for believing and reasoning are both indispensable parts of all knowledge. Torrance's work has more in common with postmodern approaches to epistemology than with the old dualistic conceptions of faith and reason.

Frederick W. Norris raises the possibility that Torrance is inconsistent, for Torrance claims the relationship of geometry to physics can instruct the theologian on how to relate natural and revealed theology, and this, Norris claims, compromises Torrance's insistence on the priority of theology and theology's need to operate within its own boundaries.[151] A proper understanding of Torrance's use of analogy, however, shows there is no inconsistency. As mentioned earlier, for Torrance analogies are *God-created correspondences* across different knowledge structures which are heuristic in character. Torrance's use of geometry is an example of his use of the heuristic relevance of science for theology and as such the analogy is illustrative, exploratory, discovery-oriented and suggestive of further research; it does not dictate nor is it determinative of the methods of theology. Torrance's treatment of analogy allows for heuristic aid to be helpful across disciplines without compromising the integrity of each discipline since, as noted earlier, these analogies help in the process of knowing and do not contribute material content across disciplines. Torrance is also usually very careful in spelling out the dissimilarities in his analogies; indeed, he even insists that significant analogies will often have more elements of dissimilarity than of similarity.[152] Thus, Torrance is able to avoid inappropriate transferences across disciplines, and he is not inconsistent for he does not compromise the priority of theology.

Frank Schubert has raised two objections against Torrance's position that a revealed God is the only proper subject matter for theology: (1) in the scientific sphere, science remains unaccommodating towards "once and for all" happenings, and (2) in the religious sphere, problems emerge for any fundamental exclusivity of revelation.[153] Schubert argues that the scientist must be completely open to the possibility of any number of sources of data whereas Torrance restricts his data to one possibility.[154] Schubert's criticism has little force, however, for two reasons. First, science does take seriously "once and for all happenings;" for, to use one example, while many aspects of the Big Bang may be controversial, no scientist would suggest it not be taken seriously. Second, Schubert fails to take into account Torrance's distinction between general science and special sciences. A science is determined by its object. A particular science need not be completely open to all possibilities; in fact, it must not be and must ignore some, for there is much data that is simply not relevant to a particular science though it may be totally appropriate for another one. Christian theology, as a special science, has its own appropriate object to investigate, and as a special science with its own methods and object is entitled to a corresponding selectivity in its data as is other sciences. Torrance's claims here are consistent with his understanding of a science, and for Schubert's case to be successful he will need to do more than object to the exclusivity of revelation and develop an argument which shows Torrance's understanding of science is faulty. Schubert's second claim is that the Einsteinian conception of relatedness refers to a relational nature to the entire universe and not to a specific relatedness in space and time such as the Incarnation.[155] Once again, Schubert's point has little force, for he fails to realize that the relational nature of the universe is an example of contingent order which can serve as a useful analogy for the divine order. Because of the uniqueness of God, Torrance would never claim that the relatedness of the Incarnate Word is exactly like the relatedness found in the natural order; indeed, he freely grants, as noted above, that dissimilarities are often more prevalent and instructive than similarities. Thus, Schubert's objections are easily answered by looking at Torrance's thought in more detail.

Donald Klinefelter and Andrew Louth have argued that Torrance's attempt at a theological science is faulty for the analogies he postulates between science and theology are strained to the breaking point. Klinefelter argues that Torrance constantly draws analogies between scientific and theological methodologies only to stress the uniqueness of theology compared to natural science in each case.[156] Klinefelter makes the same mistakes as Schubert – he fails to recognize the distinction between a general and a special science and Torrance's use of analogy.

Based on Torrance's analysis of theology and its object, one should not expect a discipline with an absolutely unique object to fit exactly with the methods employed in the natural sciences (indeed, each special science, natural or otherwise, will have its own methods), but theology does fit the criteria demanded of science in general, and Torrance does lay out a method for theology as a special science. To expect theology (or literary criticism, for that matter) to fit exactly with the methods of the natural sciences would be an unreasonable expectation. Louth also bases his argument that Torrance is mistaken in the fundamental thrust of his enterprise on a disanalogy between theology and science as well.[157] As Louth puts it, the "procedures of theology *are* the procedures of the humanities, not those of the sciences ('libraries, not laboratories')."[158] Louth focuses his criticism on the experimental method, which is so important in science and inappropriate in theology. Louth's criticism, however, misses the point. Torrance grants theology is bound to the nature of the object and as such operates from a source in God's grace, not experimental control, and he concedes theology has a number of disanalogies with science, but he would insist theology has a number of serious disanalogies with the humanities as well. Theology seeks to know God, and theological knowledge will be different in material content and method from studies in the humanities as well. Torrance would no doubt be supportive of exploring rationality parallels and dissimilarities between theology and the humanities for their analogical value and, as mentioned earlier, he does examine history in this way. But to know God is not exactly the same as knowing a character in the *Divine Comedy's* reference to a historical figure. The disanalogies between theology and natural science really do not jeopardize Torrance's position.

And finally, Willem Drees has dismissed Torrance's approach to the integration of theology and science as follows:

> A major problem for arguments based upon parallels or overlap between two enterprises is that partial analogies need not be significant. The apparent overlap between astronomy and astrology does not imply that they both make credible claims about reality.[159]

Drees's objection here is too easy a dismissal of a much more sophisticated position and betrays a certain carelessness which can be answered in two parts. First, take his claim that "partial analogies need not be significant." One must immediately ask, "Aren't all analogies partial?" If they were total they would be identity-statements, not analogies, so his understanding of analogy is immediately suspect for use as an argument. It is true, however, that analogies may be bad arguments if there really is very little similarity between the terms of the analogy.[160] Torrance's definition of a general science is sufficient to include theology and natural science for that is where the parallels are, but he does not force a case for methodological parallels across disciplines in terms of the material content of the special sciences. Drees's argument may have more force (assuming his sloppy treatment of analogy were cleared up) if Torrance were guilty of this. And second, Dree's "astronomy vs. astrology" example is faulty in making his point. Drees states that the overlap between astronomy and astrology is "apparent," but is it? Astronomy studies the positions and motions of celestial bodies; astrology looks for the *influences* the positions and motions of celestial bodies have on human affairs and terrestrial events. The former is a science which acts according to the nature of its object, that is, studying the motion and position of the object; the latter does not act in accordance with the nature of the object but proposes a cause-and-effect relationship which must establish a linkage between two objects, the motions of celestial bodies and events taking place on the terrestrial plane. The so-called "apparent" overlap consists in that astrology must use astronomy in order to engage in its speculations; astronomy has no stake at all in the claims of astrology. To put it another way, there are no *methodological* parallels between the two; there is only the appropriation of astronomy by astrology for its purposes. Dree's example simply misses the point and has no force against the fruitfulness of Torrance's methodological parallels.

Crucial Criticisms of Torrance's Work

The criticisms of Torrance mentioned in the last subsection were fairly easily dealt with and as such posed no real challenge to the continuing relevance of Torrance's thought. The criticisms discussed in this subsection are designated as *crucial*, by which is meant these criticisms, if successful, would show Torrance's work is of little, if any, value for current discussions of the relationship between theology and science. I do not think these criticisms are successful as will be argued below.

The most significant criticism of Torrance written to date is found in Ronald Thiemann's *Revelation and Theology*.[161] Thiemann's criticisms of Torrance are threefold and all involve the claim that Torrance's work undermine the prevenience of God's grace. First, he accuses Torrance of inconsistency in his methodology. Second, Thiemann argues that Torrance's position is foundationalist. And third, he disagrees with

Torrance's use of "intuition" and "existence-statements" and "coherence-statements" in his theological epistemology. Each of these criticisms will be examined in detail.

Thiemann argues that Torrance's thought is inconsistent for Torrance claims that theology exemplifies the formal characteristics of a rational discipline but Torrance contradicts himself when he argues that human subjectivity plays an essential but nonconstitutive role in the revelatory relationship. Thiemann thinks Torrance's methodology is faulty for it involves the following inconsistent triad:

1. Theology is a rational discipline exemplifying the characteristics of a true science.
2. The reciprocal relation between the investigating subject and the object of inquiry is a general
characteristic of rational scientific activity.
3. Theology's unique object is the truth which imposes itself on the subject independent of the subject's reciprocal influence.[162]

If this were an accurate portrayal of Torrance's views one would have to admit that Torrance is inconsistent, but there are two answers to Thiemann's objection. First, it is true that Torrance wants to protect God's revelation from being altered by the subject receiving it, for the human knower is

not just a logical or an epistemological subject but a living and active person in the most real sense, called into a *reciprocal* relation with God, but here too the activity of the human subject does not *affect or alter* the Object Himself although it is essential to his relation with the Object and his knowledge of the Object.[163]

The quote above may seem to lend force to Thiemann's argument, for human beings do not affect or alter God, but notice Torrance clearly labels the relationship as "reciprocal." The key question to ask is if "affecting or altering" is identical with reciprocity. Reciprocity involves mutual giving, and both God and human beings do give to one another in Torrance's thought. God's giving is primary and stems from God's grace, and human beings give of themselves in response to God's grace. As noted in the discussion of Torrance's methodology, God clearly gives to human beings in that God chooses to initiate contact with human beings, accommodates God's revelation to human limitations, becomes Incarnate to give the fullest possible revelation of God's self, and gives the Holy Spirit to enable human beings to come to know God. God does not need to alter God's revelation to us in the act of giving it, for God has already graciously taken the participation of the human knower into account before the revelation is given. Human beings give themselves to God, and their repentance, obedience, and devotion empowered by the Holy Spirit enables an "epistemological inversion" which allows us to grasp God's revelation. Thiemann may still object here that the reciprocity is far from equal and it is less than that found in other knowing relationships not involving God, but there is no requirement that reciprocity be equal in degree by both parties and some key differences are to be expected due to the uniqueness of God. Human beings do not affect or alter God's revelation (if they perceive it rightly), but giving does take place on both sides of the subject-object relation as God interacts with us and we participate in the knowing act.

Torrance's methodological parallels are not inconsistent for a second reason as well. Thiemann has misidentified what the proper formal characteristic between the sciences is. The formal characteristic of a general science is that one "behave in terms of the nature of the object," but *how* one is to behave toward an object varies from science to science and marks the differences of the special sciences. Personal participation takes place in, but is not exactly the same in, all disciplines. The appropriate behavior in theology is, as Torrance admits, more like listening than any other discipline, but that is not inconsistent with his treatment of a general science.

Thiemann's second criticism accuses Torrance of having a foundationalist epistemology. This is a very significant charge, for, as pointed out in Chapter Two, classical (sometimes called modern) foundationalism[164] has largely been discredited as an viable option for contemporary epistemology. If Torrance's thought is foundationalist in this sense, then his work is of little value for current discussions of the relationship between theology and science, but Torrance is not guilty of this as I will show.

Thiemann defines and describes foundationalism and Torrance's relation to it as follows:

> Foundationalism in epistemology is represented by philosophers as diverse as Plato, Descartes, and Locke, among many others, and is the most common model employed by theologians for formulating
> doctrines of revelation. However different their ideas may be in actual content of their theories of knowledge, foundationalists all agree that knowledge is grounded in a set of non-inferential, self-evident beliefs which, because their intelligibility is not constituted by a relationship with other

beliefs, can serve as the source of intelligibility for all beliefs in a conceptual framework. These noninferential beliefs function as the givens or foundations of a linguistic system because the mode of their justification is direct and immediate. The mental act by which means of which direct justification is bestowed is usually termed *intuition*. Through intuition the knower grasps with absolute certainty "clear and distinct ideas" (Descartes), "impressions" (Locke), or "sensations" (Russell). A necessary structural characteristic of foundationalism is that a relationship of representation or correspondence is established between the incorrigible belief and that to which it refers, whether ideas or sense impressions. Foundational propositions are true then by correspondence with (in the example of modern empiricism) states of affairs in the concept-independent world. All other propositions are true by virtue of their inferential relation to these foundational beliefs.[165]

The key aspects of a foundational epistemology are as follows: (1) a set of non-inferential, self-evident beliefs which serve as the foundation of all knowledge, (2) a distinction between foundational beliefs and other inferential propositions, (3) a claim that foundational beliefs are justified immediately by a form of direct experience, (4) an appeal to the mental act of intuition, and (5) an assertion of correspondence between the self-evident beliefs and the language independent world. Although these characteristics have been culled from various philosophical epistemologies, they could just as easily have been derived from Torrance's theological epistemology. His position corresponds completely to the structural characteristics sketched above.[166]

Thiemann's criticism can be answered in two ways: (1) his treatment of foundationalism as a discredited option in epistemology does not apply to all forms of foundationalism but only to classical or modern foundationalism,[167] and (2) Torrance is not a classical foundationalist.

First, Thiemann mistakenly treats all foundationalist epistemologies as if they were equal and had been overturned; however, a number of foundationalist epistemologies are alive and well in current epistemological debates. One of the reasons for this is that though classical foundationalism has been rejected, "minimal foundationalism,"[168] which comes in a variety of forms, has not been refuted.[169] William Alston distinguishes between "strong" or classical foundationalism and "minimal foundationalism" in the following way. In founationalism, the idea is that there is a foundation for knowledge which consists of beliefs that are justified but do not rely on any other beliefs. These basic or immediate and noninferential beliefs are then used to justify other nonbasic, mediate, and inferential beliefs. The epistemic status of these basic beliefs has been the subject of considerable debate with differing understandings of what qualifies a belief as being basic advanced: certainty, infallibility, indubitability, or incorrigibility. The idea is that beliefs with these sorts of qualities are self-justifying in the sense that their status (as certain, immediate, and so on) guarantees their justification independently of anything else and therefore are the answer to The Regress Problem that plagues epistemology.[170] Strong versions of foundationalism require that one be able to demonstrate or *show* that our beliefs are justified, and if one is going to do this without relying on other beliefs, these beliefs need to be self-justifying in the sense noted above. Minimal foundationalism retains the idea of a structure of beliefs, but it only requires that basic beliefs be justified, not that one be able to show or demonstrate that they are justified. Beliefs need not be certain, infallible, indubitable, or incorrigible. Minimal foundationalism holds that justification for a belief is to be distinguished from demonstration of a belief, for, as Alston puts it, one may be justified in believing one is depressed without being able to establish it.[171] What is important for minimal foundationalism is that what justifies basic beliefs not be other beliefs. It does not follow from this that nothing other than the basic belief can play a role in justifying a foundational belief. Experience, for example, may play an important role in justifying one's beliefs. Minimimalist versions of foundationalism have not been discredited and remain an important option in current epistemological debates.[172] Simply being a foundationalist is not enough to disqualify the relevance of one's thought; Torrance would have to be a classical foundationalist for the criticisms to apply.

Second, Torrance's epistemology is not that of a classical foundationalist so Thiemann's criticisms are mistaken. As noted above, Thiemann mistakenly treats all foundationalism as if it were one singular position which makes identical claims and is refuted, and this is clearly not the case. Having a structure to knowledge and an appeal to intuition are not sufficient to label one a classical foundationalist unless one uses these terms in as a classical foundationalist does, and Torrance does not. This becomes clear in Torrance's treatment of existence-statements, coherence-statements, and intuition, which are the subject of Thiemann's third criticism.

Thiemann builds his case for Torrance being a foundationalist on the basis that Torrance's work contains a division between existence-statements and coherence-statements and relies on intuition.[173] Thiemann notes that all foundationalists make a distinction between existence-statements and coherence-statements, and Torrance does use this distinction as well. Torrance is not guilty of being a classical foundationalist; however, for he does not treat this distinction the same way as classical foundationalists. Classical foundationalists like Descartes and Hume made a sharp distinction between the two kinds of statements (hence the division into rationalists and empiricists)[174] but Torrance does not do this, for, as noted above, he claims that there is no sharp dichotomy between the two kinds of statements for they are mutually dependent. The relationship between the two is not theoretical but practical since they overlap in function and reference.[175] Granted, Torrance sees existence-statements as primary, but this is not enough to classify him as a classical foundationalist, for he sees a much closer relationship between existence-statements and coherence-statements than do the classical foundationalists. To propose a distinction between the two kinds of statements is not enough to make one a classical foundationalist, for minimalist foundationalists also propose classifying beliefs according to various types, and this seems entirely appropriate, for there are differences in the kinds of beliefs human beings hold.[176] Torrance does not pose the sharp dichotomy of classical foundationalism, and his distance from classical foundationalism can be seen even further in his discussion of intuition.

Thiemann also rightly pinpoints intuition as one of the features of classical foundationalism, and he rightly understands Torrance's treatment of intuition as different than Scheliermacher's in that it denies the validity of precognitive experiences and holds that personal and propositional revelation go together, but Thiemann is on less firm ground when he calls intuition Torrance's term to "signify the indubitability and incorrigibility" of causally imposed knowledge.[177] In *Theological Science* Torrance states his definition of intuition as "our apprehension of a reality in objectivity and unity, as a whole."[178] This is good as far as it goes, but it is stated much too tersely and could leave one mistakenly identifying Torrance's use of intuition with classical foundationalist views such as Descartes's "clear and distinct ideas." Torrance's view of intuition is richer and more complex than that found in classical foundationalism, as will become clear from the discussion below.

To understand Torrance's use of intuition one must consider Polanyi's influence on Torrance and Torrance's fuller statements of what he means by the term. One of Torrance's more detailed treatments of intuition which distinguishes his use of the term from foundationalist views can be found in his exposition of important concepts found in the thought of Michael Polanyi:

> *intuition* - not the supreme immediate knowledge called 'intuition' by Leibniz or Spinoza or Husserl, but the inexplicable apprehension or insight into

hidden coherences or intelligible order, which is indispensable at all stages of establishing knowledge, in discovery and in verification. According to Polanyi, the structure of scientific intuition is the same as that of perception, for it involves the same spontaneous process of sensing and integrating clues in response to some aspect of reality seeking realisation in our minds. This intuition of the relation between observation and reality is a faculty that can range over all grades of sagacity, from the highest level in the inspired guesses of scientific genius down to the minimum required for ordinary perception.[179]

Four key features of Torrance's understanding of intuition emerge from his discussion of Polanyi and his expanded treatment of his own views. First, Torrance's view of intuition is closely tied to discovery, for a heuristic act involves a intuitive leap of "insight and imagination" which is *unaccountable and crosses a logical gap* between the mind and reality.[180] Second, knowledge arises compulsorily but not necessarily, that is, not automatically but only as reality impresses itself on us to the point that we feel we cannot rationally resist, and this knowledge occurs within the context of an assent or commitment to reality.[181] Third, Torrance understands intuition to be connected closely to faith. In some passages, intuition and faith are used synonymously,[182] and, when not used synonymously, intuitive grasp of reality is said to be grounded in an ultimate belief or trust in our ability to grasp reality, which is *indemonstrable*.[183] All knowing is made possible by faith and occurs in acts of faith and cannot be demonstrated (shown to be certain) to others. And fourth, Torrance understands intuition to be connected with the ability to relate parts and wholes and is similar to Iris Murdoch's claim that the "idea of a self-contained unity or limited whole is a fundamental instinctive concept. We see parts of things, we intuit whole things."[184] As one can see, Torrance's understanding of intuition is clearly not that of classical foundationalism. Perhaps one could argue Torrance's view qualifies as   minimal foundationalism, but   Torrance's work has similarities with some forms of contextualism as well; however, there is an interplay between reality and our beliefs in Torrance's thought which moves it beyond a mere contextual justification and closer to minimal foundationalism.[185] It is hard to classify Torrance in any strict way since contemporary epistemological debates are getting increasingly more subtle, but fortunately it is not the purpose of this discussion to settle these debates but to show that Torrance is not a classical foundationalist *contra* Thiemann, and the case has been made.

A second crucial criticism for Torrance's ongoing relevance is found in the work of Philip Clayton and Nancey Murphy.[186] Both of these writers disagree with Torrance's insistence on theology having its own unique methods and argue that theology should be subsumed under a general rationality model based, in differing degrees, on the work of Imre Lakatos.[187] Clayton's reasoning is two-fold: (1) theology cannot avoid an appeal to broader canons of rationality and Torrance (and Barth) do not ,[188] and (2) the object cannot determine the methodology for theology must be intersubjectively criticizable, by which is meant validity for all knowing subjects.[189] Murphy agrees that theology should not have its own peculiar form of rationality, for this leaves theology "unintelligible to those who operate with the standard epistemology."[190] According to both these writers, Torrance's work is ultimately unsuccessful in providing a useful way of describing the relation to theology and science. I will argue that Clayton's and Murphy's criticisms fail to make their case.

Let us first consider Clayton's claims that theology cannot avoid an appeal to broader claims of rationality and must be intersubjective. Torrance does not try to isolate theology from broader claims of rationality, for he sets theology clearly within a broader frame of rational discourse. Theology is a special science which fits within a broader rationality pattern common to general science, and as such theology does share formal features of rationality with other disciplines. All special sciences have distinctive features, but theology is not unique in that regard. In addition, all sciences can fruitfully interact with one another. Torrance's real concern is to make sure other sciences do not dictate theology's method to it, and he does not to seal off theology from critique or interaction with other disciplines.

It should also be noted that Torrance's theology does appeal to broader canons of rationality and allows for some intersubjective critique. As was pointed out in the section "The Necessity of Theology's Interaction with Science" given above, Torrance gives five reasons why theology must take the findings of other sciences into account. Theology is not completely sealed off, indeed, it cannot be, and there is an additional reason why theological beliefs cannot be isolated from other beliefs or critique within the broader rational community. Theological beliefs and scientific beliefs are both held with what Polanyi called "universal intent,"[191] which entails a commitment to stand under the judgment of the reality one seeks to discover. Though recognizing that personal factors remain in the scientist's judgment, the scientist acts under obligation to an external objective which means that the truth-claims discovered are not merely personal but are universally valid. If the claims truly bear the mark of reality, they should stand up to tests, and so they are put forth in the hope that others who share the same commitment to reality will recognize and accept these claims as well. Depending on the scope of the theory, it may reach across disciplines and be put to the test in a variety of contexts, and it should win allegiance among competent assessors. This use of universal intent is not the same as the Enlightenment's epistemological principle of universality; however, for the scientist cannot establish his or her claims to universal validity with certainty nor can he or she expect every examiner of the claim to share his or her beliefs. The scientist believes, though, that reality will ultimately judge the truth or falsity of his or her work and therefore states his or her claims for the assessment and acceptance of the relevant community or communities. Torrance applies Polanyi's concept of universal intent to theology as well as natural science, and the theologian confesses or declares his or her beliefs to the community and the world to put them to the test with the hope that all relevant assessors will see the claim as an accurate depiction of reality.[192] Confessionalism is not a retreat, but an advancing forth of one's beliefs for consideration by others. Anyone who follows theology's proper method as a special science should in principle be able to see the warrant of the truth-claims made, and be open to critical feedback from others. Of course, there may be those who resist or refuse to allow theology to use its proper method, but that is to be expected, for universal agreement is not guaranteed and dissent remains even within the scientific community.[193] What one must do is remain true to the reality one has discovered and continue to try to make the case as persuasively as possible, or, if after further consideration one comes to believe one was mistaken, then one should abandon the claim. It is, for Torrance, our faith in our contact with reality which will ultimately decide if we were correct or not.

    Clayton does not share Torrance's confidence in our contact with reality, and he holds that coherence, not correspondence, should be the mark of truth.[194] If coherence were sufficient to replace correspondence as a theory of truth, perhaps Clayton's subsumption of Torrance would be more plausible. The coherence theory, like the correspondence theory, is a long-standing conception of truth, and suffers from a number of difficulties which undermine its acceptance,[195] but this discussion will be limited to those that are relevant to the integration of theology and science. First, Clayton claims coherence is the "umbrella" criterion of theories of scientific explanation,[196] but this claim is mistaken. As pointed out in Chapter One, scientific explanations are much more complex than this, and any number of theories can be made to cohere with data and one another if the theorist is clever enough. Coherence is undoubtedly one of the criterion used to assess scientific explanations, but it is only one and its strength has been weighted differently both throughout science's history and across disciplines. Lakatos is no help here, for the hard core of a research programme can be salvaged and incorporate new data by a variety of auxiliary hypotheses and there is no clear way of marking when a programme is degenerative or not. And second, as Clayton admits, the coherence theory of truth does have a real problem dealing with the challenges of skepticism, though he does cite the work of Laurence Bonjour as making a real step in overcoming these problems.[197] Bonjour's work, though impressive and perhaps one of the most widely accepted current forms of a coherence theory, is still unable to establish sufficient justification for one's beliefs.[198] Consistency is not enough; the source of our beliefs continues to make a significant contribution to their warrant. Problems with the correspondence theory of truth remain, but the coherence theory of truth is far from establishing itself as a superior conception.

Murphy's criticism of Torrance fares no better than Clayton's. The criticism that Torrance's theology is somehow insulated or not open to public critique has been answered in response to the same charge from Clayton, but Murphy adds that a position like Torrance's leaves theology "unintelligible to those who operate with the standard epistemology." Granted, if Torrance's work were unintelligible to those who operate with the standard epistemology that might undermine his usefulness for current debates, but one must ask of Murphy "What is the *standard* epistemology?" As described in Chapter One, the philosophy of science is a discipline with many unresolved problems and very few points of consensus (and even the consensus has significant critics), and no one philosophy of science commands anywhere near the kind of allegiance to make it the standard epistemology.[199] Murphy endorses the methodology of Imre Lakatos as what should be the standard for theology and science, but, as shall be argued below, Lakatos's work should not be taken as the standard.

Lakatos's work should not be taken as the standard for a number of important reasons. First, Lakatos's position is by no means taken to be the standard in the current philosophy of science, and it is even less influential in broader epistemological debates. Second, four successful challenges to Lakatos's methodology have been described in Chapter One which explain why Lakatos's work is rightfully not taken to be a standard epistemology. Lakatos's work simply has too many difficulties to be taken as "the" philosophy of science. And third, Torrance's work, which draws on Polanyi, actually offers a better description of natural science than does Lakatos's. Lakatos's methodology can best be described as a *historical reconstruction* of science.[200] This makes it an "after the fact" treatment of scientific rationality. It tries to describe why certain research programmes succeeded, but it offers very little guidance as to how science should proceed or settle current problems.[201] Torrance's and Polanyi's work accurately report past scientific discoveries (such as Einstein's), but they add a description of the creative process involved in scientific thinking. By paying careful attention to the actual practice of scientists and giving a discussion of how creativity and imagination are involved in scientific discovery, Polanyi and Torrance are able to move beyond a mere reconstruction of past disputes and describe how progress in science will probably continue to be made. Granted, Polanyi's philosophy of science is not perfect and many of his claims can be and are challenged,[202] but Polanyi's work offers a much better fit with the emerging mainstream in the philosophy of science described in Chapter One than does Lakatos's. Since Torrance and Polanyi offer a more fruitful description of how science actually works than does Lakatos, it is a dubious move to impose Lakatos's methodology as the standard epistemology for science or theology.[203]

The third and final crucial criticism of Torrance objects to Torrance's realism. Daniel Hardy points out that Torrance's realism is one of the most highly developed forms to be found among any current thinker in either philosophy or theology,[204] and realism is a position much under attack in contemporary philosophy.[205] Realism as such is not a problem, for the vast majority of philosophers of science remain realists, but naive realism is. If Torrance were a naive realist, his work would be irrelevant to current discussions of the relationship between theology and science, and even though Torrance does share the realist conviction that it is ultimately reality which will settle the truth or falsity of a given theory, he is not a naive realist. For unlike the naive realist, Torrance does not hold that scientific theories are simply read off reality, for he understands the development of scientific theories to be much more complicated than that.[206] One believes that the universe exhibits order and discloses that order to human beings, but the belief that our minds can match up with the intelligibility of the natural order is not demonstrable and is grounded in faith. Our knowledge of reality is limited and does not exhaust reality, and it must be open and capable of revision as our understanding deepens.

Colin Weightman has raised an objection to Torrance's realism which challenges Torrance's appropriation of Einstein.[207] The nature of Einstein's realism is a subject of controversy in the current philosophy of science. Arthur Fine has argued Einstein advocates a "motivational," not "metaphysical," realist and this would undermine Torrance's own realism.[208] Gerhald Holton, on the other hand, has argued in favor of Einstein's realism.[209] My own reading of Einstein leads me to find support for both Fine's and Holton's interpretations, and I think it quite plausible that one can indeed find Einstein to be inconsistent and of two minds about the issue. Torrance's interpretation of Einstein is certainly credible, and even if Einstein did waffle at times one could argue the case that he should have followed the stronger realist approach. Even more importantly, it is the uncontroversial interpretation of Einstein's motivational realism that is actually more important for Torrance's epistemology than the metaphysical. To be sure, Torrance has both, and much of his case is tied to Einstein's relativity theories being correct, but he has an even stronger commitment to realism as what motivates theological and scientific pursuits and gives their claims validity than he does to any particular scientific theory or theological doctrine.[210] At any rate, Weightman's criticism is not enough to discount the continuing validity of Torrance's approach to integrating theology and science.

    I think Torrance's version of realism should be more widely considered, for it possibly could provide a fruitful way for the realist out of the impasse in the realist/anti-realist debates. Despite all the powerful objections to realism which have emerged in the philosophy of science, realism has remained the dominant position because most realist philosophers of science share Hilary Putnam's claim that "realism is the only philosophy which doesn't make the success of science a miracle."[211] In addition, Einstein made many well-known remarks about how the facts that science emerged at all, that physical reality can be depicted mathematically, and that the human mind matches up with nature are "mysterious" or "miraculous." Why does science work? The belief that we can and do encounter and know reality presses itself upon us with such force that it is hard for anyone (other than professional philosophers) to deny it. The leading philosophers of science tend to not put much credence in miracles, but they continue to hold a realist position despite the very effective criticisms of realism put forward by anti-realists and even though they recognize their allegiance to realism still leaves some problems which they cannot completely resolve.[212] To put it another way, most defenders of realism believe they *know* that this position is the most reasonable even if there is no decisive refutation of the anti-realist objections or complete account of why realism is correct.[213]

Torrance and Polanyi's philosophy of science give a solid justification for hanging on to critical realism even if it cannot be fully demonstrated as true, for all knowing as "personal knowledge"contains a fiduciary component which makes our knowledge indemonstrable but nonetheless reasonable – "we know more than we can say." Knowledge is warranted even if it is not "certain" in the way demanded by the Enlightenment or classical foundationalism, and since a fiduciary component is indispensable it permits us to construct a broader understanding of rationality and scientific progress. One does not even need to bring in theism at this point, but perhaps it is true that without faith science, like Christ, can do no miracle.[214]

Theism does enter in as a plausible way to answer Einstein's awe before the mysteries. Torrance argues that at its boundaries science raises religious questions which it cannot answer. Science shows us an order that is both rational and contingent, and the combination of intelligibility and contingency prompts us to ask for new forms of order. Pressing science to its limits raises legitimate questions which science does not appear able to answer. The boundary questions do not prove God's existence, but they do raise the possibility of God as the creative ground and reason for the contingent but rational unitary order of the universe. Once again, a fiduciary component is necessary for grasping the truth about reality, and it is, theology, which seeks to enter into a knowing relationship with the Object of divine order that can provide the answers to the boundary questions. It is there one learns that Judeo-Christian theology both can motivate and give meaning to natural science.[215]

Theological Science: Continuing Relevance and Unresolved Problems

Torrance's work stands up well to many of the criticisms that have been made of it; however, there are some problems related to the integration of theology and science which he does not resolve. In this section, Torrance's theology relevance for contemporary discussions of theology and science will be assessed in part by using the informal criteria derived from Barbour and according to the categories developed in Chapter Two.

First, Torrance's theology is very effective in its ability to handle the problems posed by direct and quasi-direct relevance. Torrance's careful distinctions between theology and science avoid instances of direct and quasi-direct relevance and eliminate the difficulties inherent in advocating these kinds of relevance. Quasi-direct relevance removes coherence from one's world-view, for it occurs when theology and science offer competing explanations of the same data. In Torrance's thought, the special sciences have their own objects of study and competing explanations of the same data by theology and science do not and can not occur. Direct relevance occurs when a theological statement is directly supported or contradicted by a scientific statement, and the danger of direct relevance is that theology will be tied too closely to science and its credibility with rise or fall with the rapidly changing developments in science. Direct relevance should not occur within Torrance's methodology, and thus theology will neither be contradicted by science nor tied to a theory that may turn out to be false. Torrance's theology earns high marks for coherence and scope in dealing with direct and quasi-direct relevance.

Second, Torrance's theology offers a very effective treatment of heuristic relevance, though at times his application of analogies needs more precise development. Torrance's conception of analogy is a solid contribution to theology which has the potential to be very fruitful for contemporary theological reflection. Torrance draws some very effective analogies from science for theology, and he also discusses ways theology has suggested fruitful analogies for natural science. He also pays particular attention in most cases to the heuristic importance of both the similarities and dissimilarities present in his analogies. There are times, however, in which Torrance pushes his analogies too far and emphasizes the similarities while paying insufficient attention to the dissimilarities. One particular instance of this is Torrance's treatment of "field theory."[216] Torrance's application of analogy does need more precision at times, but his understanding of analogy is sound and can be useful for creating new analogies for theology from the natural sciences. Torrance's theology's heuristic relevance earns high marks for fruitfulness.

Third, Torrance's understanding of metaphysics fits well with the position toward metaphysics presented in Chapter Two. It was argued that theology and natural science should not be subsumed under a metaphysical system due to: (1) the relative independence of metaphysical questions, (2) the current state of philosophy which tends to be skeptical of metaphysical systems and instead focuses on specific problems, and (3) the specific form the metaphysical question takes in the contemporary philosophy of science (should one be a realist or anti-realist about scientific theories?). Torrance is committed to critical realism, but he has an open and exploratory approach to metaphysical problems and questions, and he envisions the relationship between theology and science as an ongoing dialogue. A strong belief in realism, for Torrance, functions as the motivation for and goal of knowledge, and this allows his thought greater flexibility to deal with potential anomalies than that offered by a metaphysical system such as process philosophy. I do have a concern, however, about Torrance's attention to the question of whether to interpret a scientific theory or theological formulation as realist or instrumentalist, but I will treat this point in the discussion of Torrance's method. Torrance's treatment of metaphysics earns high marks for agreement with data, coherence, scope, and fertility.

And fourth, Torrance's treatment of methodological relevance has many strong features to commend it. Torrance's method preserves the integrity of both theology and natural science, spells out the similarities and differences between theology and science clearly, gives a good picture of how science is actually practiced, and does not allow science to dictate the standards of rationality to science. In fact, Torrance's insistence that theology should not allow its methods to be dictated to it by other sciences can be argued even more forcefully if supplemented by the current developments in philosophy mentioned in Chapters One and Two. Torrance's method also fits well with the requirement of consonance which has been argued so effectively by Ernan McMullin, for Torrance does see the interaction of theology and natural science to be a dialogue which is ongoing and not complete since both theology and science constantly gain new insights. Torrance's treatment of method deserves high marks on each of the four criteria we are using for assessment; however, there are some unresolved problems in his approach which should be addressed.

First, Torrance does not provide a practical way to adjudicate between differing theological positions. Torrance has an approach to truth which seems to indicate "either you get it or you don't." If this is the case, very few of us can hope to grasp reality, for we simply do not have the intellectual ability or the sufficient training to intuit the deep structures of reality. Granted a handful of true scientific and theological geniuses may grasp these deep structures, but how are the rest of us to know who among the competing voices is actually bearing witness to the truth? Torrance says the best one can do is state one's findings and hope others can share the truthful intuition, but the question still remains as to how can one help another get into the place where he or she can share the truthful insight.[217] It is here I think that contemporary work in the philosophy of science can supplement and enhance Torrance's position. Transformational events which produce new insight are always preceded by conflict and include an interlude for scanning, by which is meant a psychological process of searching out possible solutions, taking apart errors, keeping parts, and discarding others.[218] Informal criteria, such as those given by Barbour, and the insights from critical realists such as Gardner, Penrose, Hacking, and McMullin discussed in Chapter Two can provide very helpful ways of advancing the process of scanning and getting one into the place where one is open to deciding to support a realist interpretation of either a theory or an entity; and, while this is a helpful way of dealing with natural science, more work still needs to be done on this point in theology.

Second, Torrance's epistemology does need to give a more detailed explication of the human subject as the recipient of revelation. While Thiemann's criticism of Torrance that he had no participation by the human subject was too extreme, it is the case that Torrance's work seems to leave the recipient of revelation as entirely too passive. More needs to be said about how the human mind apprehends God than just to say it is an act of repentance and obedience enhanced by the Holy Spirit. A discussion of how or at least in what way the Holy Spirit elevates the human mind beyond its normal operations to grasp God's truth would be helpful, and would strengthen Torrance's work in the areas of theological method and epistemology. Garrett Green's *Imagining God* and Austin Farrer's *The Glass of Vision* make very convincing arguments that imagination is the place where the revelatory interaction between the divine image and the human imagination becomes effective or takes place in human lives, and I think Torrance's work could be supplemented by these works with great profit.[219] In addition, the discussion of naturalized epistemology in the first chapter pointed out that current epistemological debates have taken a "psychological turn" by which is meant that a growing number of philosophers argue that beliefs are justified insofar as they are produced by reliable belief-forming mechanisms. Torrance's work fits well with type of approach to epistemology, but he does not give a very thorough treatment of how psychological mechanisms come into play in the knowing act. Torrance's epistemology's value for and plausibility within current epistemological debates would be more apparent if it were supplemented by greater attention to the psychological mechanisms which so interest contemporary philosophers. An advance on Torrance's work in this regard has been attempted by James Loder and W. Jim Neidhardt, who treat psychological descriptions of human intelligence and knowing in some detail, and it is hoped that efforts like these will increase the recognition of the value of Torrance's work.[220]

Third, while Torrance's work is clearly a pioneering effort on the relationship between theology and science, it needs to move beyond Einstein and be supplemented and brought into dialogue with other developments in science and the philosophy of science. For example, Robert John Russell's work on contingency would be a fine supplement to Torrance's treatment of contingent order, for Russell develops an even more precise classification of contingency into global, nomological, and local contingency which also fits well with a variety of cosmological theories.[221] In addition, both Ian Barbour and John Polkinghorne have pointed out that Torrance needs to pay more attention to quantum theory,[222] and there have been many more exciting developments in science in recent years.

And four, Torrance does not give an extensive treatment of divine agency, or how God interacts with the world, which is one of the thorniest problems in the current dialogue between theology and science.[223] Torrance makes some provocative remarks about God's activity within the world and the need for theology to have "empirical correlates," and he is emphatic that God's action must be understood by looking at how God has in fact acted. Proper understanding of how God interacts with the world must be determined by the force or energy which constitutes it, the Holy Spirit.[224] Torrance does not provide a description of how the Holy Spirit interacts with the physical world, and perhaps this is one area where his understanding of heuristic relevance could be applied fruitfully.

Torrance's work, while it has some difficulties, still remains one of the most important treatments of the relationship between theology and science and has much of value to contribute to current discussions. Perhaps his greatest contribution is to show that orthodox Christianity continues to have a robust intellectual vitality even in an age if science, and I think his work provides an excellent place from which to start the ongoing dialogue between theology and science. If this chapter has sparked the reader's interest in exploring the potential heuristic value of Torrance's theology for contemporary discussions I think it will have made a worthwhile contribution to the dialogue between theology and science. I hope that Torrance's position will get the hearing it deserves, but there is much to indicate he will continue to be ignored by many exploring the integration of theology and science since he in so many ways seems to go against the tenor of the times. This is unfortunate, for, in a theological climate where the Princeton goal of piety and learning is all too often simply considered a quaint motto of times past, a theologian who understands his theological efforts in the following way should be taken seriously:

> If I may be allowed to speak personally for a moment, I find the presence and being of God bearing upon my experience and thought so powerfully that I cannot but be convinced of His sheer overwhelming reality and rationality. To doubt the existence of God would be an act of sheer irrationality, for it would mean that my reason had become unhinged its bond with real being. Yet in knowing God I am deeply aware that my relation to Him has been damaged, that disorder has resulted in my mind, and that it is I who obstruct knowledge of God by getting in between Him and myself, as it were. But I am also aware that His presence presses unrelentingly upon me through the disorder of my mind, for He will not let Himself be thwarted by it, challenging and repairing it, and requiring of me on my part to yield my thoughts to His healing and controlling revelation.[225]

Conclusion

This book, unlike the dialogue between theology and natural science, is almost finished. In many ways it seems the conversation between theology and natural science has just begun, but much progress has been made. I offer this book as one attempt to help advance the dialogue, and I do think that the recommendations made here will be somewhat helpful for those seeking to relate science and theology. New problems and issues in the interaction between theology and science will continue to emerge, but I expect that theologians will remain capable of developing a coherent and consonant world-view as they pursue the conversation, for I am convinced one can have complete confidence in the intellectual integrity of the Christian faith.

Notes

1. A few examples of Torrance's influence can be found in John Polkinghorne, *Science and Creation* (Boston: Shambhala, 1988); Jurgen Moltmann, *God in Creation,* trans. Margaret Kohl (San Francisco: Harper & Row, 1985); James Loder and W. Jim Neidhart, *The Knight's Move: The Relational Logic of the Spirit in Theology and Science* (Colorado Springs: Helmers & Howard, 1992); Christopher Kaiser, *Creation and the History of Science* (Grand Rapids: Eerdmans, 1991); Ian Paul, *Knowledge of God: Calvin, Einstein, and Polanyi* (Edinburgh: Scottish Academic Press, 1987); and Harold Nebelsick, *Theology and Science in Mutual Modification* (New York: Oxford University Press, 1981).
2. See Douglas Trook, *The Unified Christocentric Field: Towards a Time-Eternity Relativity Model for Theological Hermeneutics in the Onto-Relational Theology* (Ph. D. Dissertation, Drew University, Ann Arbor: University Microfilms, 1987);

and Robert J. Palma, "Thomas F. Torrance's Reformed Theology," *Reformed Review*, vol. 38 (1984), pp. 2-46.
3.Ronald Thiemann, *Revelation and Theology* (Notre Dame, Ind.: University of Notre Dame Press, 1985, pp. 32-43.
4.Thomas Langford, "T. F. Torrance's *Theological Science:* A Reaction, *Scottish Journal of Theology*, vol. 25 (1972), pp. 155-170; and Dennis Samsom, "Scientific Theology: An Examination of the Methodology of Thomas Forsyth Torrance" (Ph. D. Dissertation, Southwestern Baptist Theological Seminary, 1981); both make this claim.
5.Donald S. Klinefelter, "God and Rationality: A Critique of the Theology of Thomas F. Torrance," *Journal of Religion*, vol. 53 (1973), pp. 117-134.
6.Frank D. Schubert, "Thomas F. Torrance: The Case for a Theological Science," *Encounter*, vol. 45 (1984), pp. 123-137.
7.Del Ratzsch, "Grappling with Googolplexes, Gluons, and God," *Books and Religion,* (Summer 1990), pp. 12 and 18.
8.Ray Anderson, review of *Space, Time, and Resurrection*, by T. F. Torrance, *Christianity Today*, vol. 22 (1977), p. 40, 42, 44-45.
9.The dissertation by Trook and Colin Weightman's *Theology in a Polanyian Universe: The Theology of Thomas Torrance* (New York: Peter Lang, 1994), pp. 131-136, document this point.
10.Thomas F. Torrance, *Theological Science* (New York: Oxford University Press, 1969, pp. vii-xviii. Hereafter cited as *TS.*
11.*Divine and Contingent Order* (Oxford: Oxford University Press, 1981). Hereafter abbreviated as *DCO.*
12.*Space, Time, and Incarnation* (London: Oxford University Press, 1969).
13.*Space, Time, and Resurrection* (Edinburgh: Handsel Press, 1976).
14.*TS*, p. ix.
15.*TS*, pp. ix-x.
16.*TS*, pp. x-xii.
17.*TS*, p. xvii.
18.*TS*, pp. xvii-xviii.
19.*TS*, pp. 1-6.
20.*TS*, p. 9.
21.*TS*, pp. 10-11.
22.*TS*, pp. 11-12. Torrance takes this definition from J. MacMurray's *Reason and Emotion*, p. 19.
23.*TS*, pp.12. Torrance specifies what he means by subjectivity and objectivity – subject refers to the knowing agent; object is what is known or external to the knower.
24.*TS*, pp. 12-13.
25.*TS*, pp. 13-14.
26.*TS*, pp. 14-16.
27.*TS*, pp. 19-25. Torrance criticizes Farrer's treatment of images on pages 19-20, but Torrance is mistaken, for Farrer did not insist in *The Glass of Vision* that the images are "pictures;" rather, Farrer understood "image" and "word" belong

together and serve an analogical, not just a mimetic, purpose.

28.*TS*, pp. 27-34.
29.*TS*, pp. 34-37.
30.*TS*, p. 37.
31.*TS*, pp. 37-38.
32.*TS*, pp. 38-39.
33.*TS*, pp. 39-40.
34.*TS*, p. 40.
35.*TS*, pp 41-43.
36.*TS*, pp. 43-46.
37.*TS*, pp. 46-48.
38.*TS*, pp.48-50.
39.*TS*, pp. 50-54.   See also *Theology in Reconstruction* (Grand Rapids: Eerdmans, 1965), pp. 192-258, especially 234-236. Hereafter abbreviated as *TR*.
40.See also *TR*, pp. 62-75 as well.
41.Stanley Jaki, for example, is highly critical of Ockham and more favorable to Roman Catholicism than is Torrance. See *The Road of Science and the Ways to God* (Chicago: University of Chicago Press, 1978).
42.*TS*, p. 55.
43.*TS*, p. 56-57.
44.*TS*, pp. 62-85.
45.*TS*, p. 85-86.
46.*TS*, pp. 92-95.
47.*TS*, pp. 96-98.
48.*TS*, p. 101.
49.*TS*, pp. 101-105.
50.*TS*, pp. 9-10, 104.   Torrance does not fully develop the value of natural theology in *TS*, but see his more complete treatments in *Reality and Scientific Theology* (Edinburgh: Scottish Academic Press, pp. 32-63 (Hereafter *RST*); *Transformation and Convergence in the Frame of Knowledge* (Grand Rapids: Eerdmans, 1984), pp. 285-301 (Hereafter *TCFK*); *The Ground and Grammar of Theology* (Charlottesville: University Press of Virginia, 1980), pp. 75-109 (Hereafter *GGT*).
51.*GGT*, pp. 90-108.
52.A rare instance for Torrance, to be sure.
53.*TS*, pp. 107-108.   Notice here Torrance's endorsement of what I referred to as the "unity of truth."
54.*TS*, pp. 111-116.
55.*TS*, pp. 116-119.
56.*TS*, pp. 119-126..
57.*TS*, pp. 126-131.
58.*TS*, 131-133.
59.*TS*, pp. 133-135.
60.*TS*, pp. 135-137.
61.*TS*, pp. 137-139.

62.*TS*, pp.139-140.
63.*TS*, pp.141-146.
64.*TS*, pp. 156-161.
65.*TS*, pp. 161-164.
66.Torrance does not restrict existence-statements to objects of sense experience.
67.*TS*, pp. 164-169.
68.*TS*, pp. 169-170.
69.*TS*, pp. 170-172.
70.*TS*, pp. 173-183.
71.*TS*, p. 184.
72.*TS*, p. 184.
73.*TS*, pp. 184-191.
74.*TS*, pp. 195-198.
75.*TS*, p. 198.
76.Torrance understands this linkage of theory and practice to occur in all sciences.
77.*TS*, pp. 199-202.
78.*TS*, pp. 203-205.
79.*TS*, pp. 206-211.
80.*TS*, pp. 214-216.
81.*TS*, pp. 216-222.
82.I have modified Torrance's language in this instance and some others in order to use more inclusive language.
83.*TS*, pp. 226-246.
84.By incomplete is meant containing propositions which cannot be demonstrated within the system.
85.*TS*, pp. 246-263.
86.*TS*, pp. 263-280.
87.*TS*, pp. 281-286.
88.*TS*, pp. 286-295.
89.*TS*, pp. 295-312.
90.*TS*, pp. 312-318; 328-330.
91.*TS*, pp. 319-320.
92.*TS*, pp. 321-322.
93.*TS*, p. 326. Emphasis Torrance's.
94.*TS*, pp. 334-337.
95.*TS*, pp. 337-346.
96.Thomas F. Torrance, *The Christian Frame of Mind: Reason, Order, and Openness in Theology and Natural Science* (Colorado Springs: Helmers & Howard, 1989), pp. 24-29. Hereafter abbreviated as *CFM*. This collection of essays contains an excellent introduction to some of the leading themes in Torrance's thought by W. Jim Neidhardt on pages xi-xliv.
97.Thomas Torrance, *RST*, p 27.
98.*TCFK*, p. 85, quoting Polanyi's *The Tacit Dimension* (New York: Doubleday, 1966), p. 30.

99.*STR*, pp. 188-192.

100.See also *RST*, pp. 131-159.

101.*Christian Theology and Scientific Culture* (New York: Oxford University Press, 1981), p. 37. Hereafter abbreviated as *CTSC*.

102.*DCO*, p. 20.

103.*DCO*, p. vii.

104.*DCO*, p. vii.

105.*DCO*, pp. vii-viii.

106.*TCFK*, pp. 215-242. Torrance uses James Clerk Maxwell as an example of how Christian presuppositions may have provided fruitful material for scientific reflection. Torrance also claims that the Christian idea of *perichoresis* or coinherence may be fruitful for the onto-relations of particles in quantum physics (see *GGT*, pp. 173-176) and that the theological concept *homoousion* can describe the intimate interrealtion of the theoretical and empirical in general relativity's integration of space-time and energy-mass (*GGT*, pp. 159-167).

107.These points are developed at sustained length with examples in *DCO*, pp. 26-84.

108.Two of Torrance's common analogies from the natural sciences include the explication of understanding God as "light" (*CFM*, pp. 147-155) and how the incorporation of geometry into physics in Einstein's thought provides a useful way of understanding how natural theology should be incorporated into positive theology (*GGT*, pp. 75-109; *STR*, pp. ix-xiii; *RST*, pp. 61-67, *TCFK*, pp. 285-301. For a criticism of Torrance's geometry analogy see Colin Weightman, *Theology in a Polanyian Universe*, pp. 164-166. Weightman attacks Torrance's historical treatment of the development of Euclidean geometry as a science independent of physics by claiming that Euclidean geometry rose out of contact with the everyday world and that higher geometries did not develop hand-in-hand with physical theories. One can plausibly question Torrance's treatment of the history of geometry, but Torrance's main point is sound – that with the work of Einstein geometry's relation to space came to be understood not as abstract and idealized structures inserted into a independent receptacle but instead as more dependent on the distribution in space of matter.

109.*DCO*, pp. 8, 12-13; *STI*, pp. 4-14, 22-25; *TCFK*, p. 270; *GGT*, pp. 22-26.

110.*GGT*, pp. 146-178; *RST*, pp. 160-206.

111.This is the theme of *STI*.

112.Polanyi includes in his conception of a field all the operations of the "tacit component." See *Personal Knowledge*, p. 398. The tacit dimension provides the unifying ground of all knowledge and is the informal, unaccountable, inarticulate, component which provides integration in perception and knowledge. As Polanyi put it, "we know more than we can tell." *The Tacit Dimension* (Garden City: Doubleday, 1966), p. 4. A good introduction to Polanyi's thought is Richard Gelwick, *The Way of Discovery: An Introduction to the Thought of Michael Polanyi* (New York: Oxford University Press, 1977).

113.*RST*, p. 80.

114.*STI*, p. 84, see also *DCO*, pp. 18-19 and *STI*, pp. 71-85.

115.*DCO*, p. 18.
116.*STI*, p. 85.
117.*STI*, pp. 71-72, 85.
118.*STI*, p. 85.
119.*God and Rationality* (London: Oxford University Press, 1971), p. 16. Hereafter abbreviated as *GR*.
120.*STR*, p. 60, *STI*, p. 85.
121.*STR*, p. 22, *GR*, p. 72, *TS*, p. 300.
122.*STR*, pp. 59-60.
123.*STR*, pp. 15, 22.
124.*STR*, p. 23. Emphasis Torrance's.
125.Ibid.
126.Michael Polanyi, *Personal Knowledge*, p. 151 quoted by Torrance in *GR*, pp. 203-204.
127.*TS*, pp. 197.
128.*TR*, p. 29.
129.*STR*, p. 57.
130.W. Jim Neidhardt, "Introduction" to *CFM*, pp. xi-xliv. The quote is from page xxvii. Emphasis Niedhardt's.
131.*TCFK*, p. 230.
132.In the Introduction to *Space, Time, and Resurrection*, he makes this claim a number of times to the point where one begins to think "he doth protest too much." See *STR*, pp. 1-26. Torrance's desire to integrate theology and natural science does seem to move "through and beyond" Barth's impressive but isolated theology. See *TCFK*, pp. vii-xiv. Despite Torrance's claim that Barth endorsed Torrance's position near the end of life, it is clear there is nothing like the dialogue with natural science envisioned by Torrance in Barth's work. How closely Torrance is faithful to Barth's theology or whether or not Barth really would have moved in the direction Torrance does is a question I will leave to specialists on Barth's thought.
133.*STI*, p. viii.
134.*STR*, pp. 20-24, 179-193; *STI*, pp. 52-90.
135.*STI*, pp. 89-90. He again uses his common example of how we can never dispense with the historical Jesus.
136.*STR*, p. 183.
137.*STR*, pp. 184-186.
138.*STR*, pp. 179-180.
139.*CFM*, pp. 59-63, *DCO*, pp. 128-142, *GGT*, pp. 1-14.
140.Some biographical elements about Torrance can be found in "A Pilgrimage in the School of Christ -- An Interview with T. F. Torrance," by I. John Hesselink, *Reformed Review*, vol. 38 (1984), pp. 49-64.
141.*TCFK*, pp. vii-xiv, *CTSC*, p. 14-15.
142.The lack of Torrance's impact is discussed in Daniel W. Hardy, "Thomas F. Torrance" in *The Modern Theologians: An Introduction to Christian Theology in the Twentieth Century*, Vol. I, David Ford, ed. (Oxford: Basil Blackwell, 1989),

pp. 71-91. Hardy understands Torrance's lack of influence to be tied up with his realism, which goes against many of the trends in the contemporary philosophy of science.

143.John Hick, review of *TS*, by Thomas F. Torrance, *Expository Times*, vol. 81 (November 1981), pp. 57-58.

144.An example of this type of fairy-lore can be found in the work of Dr. Leonard Roberts of Pikeville College, one of my early mentors, who was an internationally recognized authority on the "Jack Tales."

145.See footnote four for references.

146.Thomas F. Torrance, "The Framework of Belief," in *Belief in Science and in Christian Life: The Relevance of Michael Polanyi's Thought for Christian Faith and Life* (Edinburgh: Handsel Press, 1980, pp. 9-10, emphasis added. Torrance explicitly distinguishes between faith and logic and shows the need of response or act in knowing in this essay which runs from pages 1-27.

147.John Barton, *People of the Book? The Authority of the Bible in Christianity* (Louisville: Westminster/John Knox Press, 1988), p. 38. Barton is particularly critical of those who refuse to take the historical context of the biblical texts seriously and those he sees as fideists.

148.Klinefelter, "God and Rationality," p. 128.

149.*TCFK*, p. x.

150.A solid treatment of this point can be found in Chapter 12 of Colin Weightman, *Theology in a Polanyian Universe: The Theology of Torrance* (New York: Peter Lang, 1994), pp. 139-147.

151.Frederick W. Norris, "Mathematics, Physics, and Religion: A Need for Candor, and Rigor." *Scottish Journal of Theology*, vol. 37 (1984), pp. 457-470.

152.*STR*, p. 190.

153.Schubert, "Thomas F. Torrance," p. 125.

154.Ibid., p. 132.

155.Ibid., pp. 133-134.

156."God and Rationality," pp. 122-125, 127.

157.Andrew Louth, *Discerning the Mystery: An Essay on the Nature of Theology* (Oxford: Clarendon Press, 1983), pp. 48-57.

158.Ibid., p. 52.

159.*Beyond the Big Bang* (LaSalle: Open Court, 1990), pp. 168-169.

160.This is essentially Hume's point in rejecting the argument from design in his *Dialogues Concerning Natural Religion*, ed. Norman Kemp Smith (Indianapolis: Bobbs-Merrill, 1947).

161.Thiemann, *Revelation and Theology*, pp. 32-46.

162.Thiemann, p. 38.

163.*TS*, p. 308. Emphasis added.

164.Described as "narrow foundationalism" in Chapter Two.

165.Thiemann, *Revelation and Theology*, pp. 158-159.

166.Ibid., pp. 165-166.

167.Thiemann either is unaware of non-classical foundationalist treatments of epistemology or he mistakenly conflates all these approaches.

168."Mininimal foundationalism" is sometimes called by other names, such as "broad foundationalism," or "weak foundationalism."

169.See William Alston, "Has Foundationalism Been Refuted?" in *Contemporary Readings in Epistemology*, ed. Michael Goodman and Robert Snyder (Englewood Cliffs, N.J.: Prentice Hall, 1993), pp. 42-53.

170.The Regress Problem can be described as follows. If a belief is justified, there must be reasons why it is justified; otherwise, one has merely at best mere true belief, and this is not enough for justification. But one's reasons must also be justified if one wants to show the original belief is justified. And one's reasons for one's reasons must also be justified, *ad infinitum*. An infinite set of reasons is required to have even one justified belief. This problem is at least as old as Aristotle, and is mentioned by Sextus Empiricus in *Outlines of Pyrrhonism*, vol. 1, ch. 15. A modern discussion is presented at length in Laurence Bonjour's *The Structure of Empirical Knowledge* (Cambridge, Mass.: Harvard University Press, 1985), Chapter 2.

171.Alston, p. 45.

172.A number of current advocates of various versions of minimal foundationalism are mentioned by Alston; examples include Roderick Chisholm, *Theory of Knowledge*, 2nd ed.(Englewood Cliffs, N.J.: Prentice Hall, 1977); and Alvin Goldman, "What is Justified Belief?" *Justification and Knowledge*, ed. G.S. Pappas (Dordrecht: D. Reidel Publishing Company, 1979), pp. 1-23. Goldman's work incorporates many of the holistic elements of naturalized epistemology as does that of Alvin Plantinga, one of the leading critics of classical foundationalism, who has recently proposed a version he calls "Reidian foundationalism," which allows for many properly basic beliefs which classical foundationalism would not allow. Plantinga focuses on epistemic warrant; that is, what turns true belief into knowledge, and he argues that what is crucial to warrant is the proper functioning of one's cognitive faculties in the right kind of cognitive environment. See *Warrant: The Current Debate* (New York: Oxford University Press, 1993) and *Warrant and Proper Function* (New York: Oxford University Press, 1993). Plantinga's work represents one of the most significant contributions to current epistemological debates, and it is attracting major attention. Nancey Murphy criticizes Plantinga for retaining foundationalist vocabulary, argues no distinction can be drawn between basic and nonbasic beliefs, and advocates a holistic epistemology based on the work of Imre Lakatos. See *Theology in an Age of Scientific Reasoning* (Ithaca: Cornell University Press, 1990), especially pp. 192-195. Plantinga defends his approach and gives his reasons for accepting the distinction between basic and nonbasic beliefs in the works cited above. I agree with Alston that minimal versions of foundationalism have not been refuted, and I find Plantinga's arguments more persuasive than Murphy's, but many unsettled issues in epistemology remain. It is generally agreed by philosophers that classical foundationalism is no longer tenable, but we are far from a consensus as to what should take its place. I will return to this in my discussion of Clayton's and Murphy's treatment of Torrance and Torrance's realism.

173.*Revelation and Theology*, pp. 38-43.

174.Thiemann is to be commended for his discussion of the foundationalism of Descartes, Locke, and other modern epistemologists, see pages 9-31.

175.*TS*, pp. 169-172, 226-246, 246-263.

176.See Plantinga, *Warrant and Proper Function*, Chapters 4-9 for an even more detailed classification of types of beliefs than that offered by Torrance.

177.*Revelation and Theology*, p. 40.

178.*TS*, p. 165.

179.*Belief in Science and Christian Life*, p. 139. Torrance criticizes Descartes in *TS*, pp. 109-110, 120, 122-123, 184, and 306; *TCTK*, pp. 7-11.

180.*Belief in Science and the Christian Life*, p. 138, *GGT*, pp. 29-30, *CFM*, pp. 50-51, 71-75.

181.*Belief in Science and Christian Life*, p. 13.

182.*Belief in Science and the Christian Life*, pp. 9, *CTSC*, pp. 63-66, *CFM*, pp. 71-75.

183.*CFM*, pp. 73-75.

184.Iris Murdoch, *Metaphysics as a Guide to Morals* (New York: Allen Lane/Penguin Press, 1992), p. 1.

185.Contextualism is usually traced to the thought of Wittgenstein, who said belief systems should be imagined as a river flowing through a channel of bedrock. The bedrock is the context in which justification takes place and is composed of beliefs which are not questioned; the river represents beliefs which require justification. For Wittgenstein, for justification to take place some beliefs must remain unquestioned. Basic beliefs are not justified but are simply accepted. This may make the basic beliefs appear arbitrary, but Wittgenstein tries to mitigate this by arguing that justification is a practice which takes place in a social context. See Ludwig Wittgenstein, *On Certainty* (Oxford: Basil Blackwell, 1969), pp. 94-99, 204-205, 245-254. Contemporary contextualists also emphasize that when we try to justify a claim, we need to answer all relevant objections, but we do not need to justify all our beliefs. We are justified in holding a belief when we can defend it successfully against all relevant objections from the appropriate objector group. Relevant objections are those which are current and which present a real, as opposed to merely an academic, doubt. Community standards of justification will vary and the appropriate objector group will change depending on the context, but it must always have the quest for truth and the avoidance of error as its goal. When such an objector group does not require justification for a belief, it is because they feel the belief no longer requires defending, and all such beliefs are therefore contextually basic and justified. See David Annis, "A Contextualist Theory of Epistemic Justification," *Contemporary Readings in Epistemology*, pp. 105-113. It is interesting to note that some foundationalists are as flexible in allowing for basic beliefs as contextualists. For example, neither Torrance nor Plantinga would agree that all possible objections to a belief would need to be answered in order for one to properly hold that belief.

186.Philip Clayton, *Explanation from Physics to Theology: An Essay in the Rationality and Religion* (New Haven: Yale University Press, 1989) and Nancey Murphy, *Theology in the Age of Scientific Reasoning*.

187.See Clayton's comments in which he references Torrance on the "faith seeking understanding" model of doing theology (pp. 10-14) and his objection to the "object determining method" approach (p. 159). Murphy subordinates Torrance's work to Lakatosian methodology on page 195.

188.Clayton, *Explanation*, pp. 10-14.

189.Ibid., pp.158-167.

190.Murphy, *Theology*, p. 14.

191.*Personal Knowledge*, pp. 302f, 308f.

192.*Belief in Science and Christian Life*, pp. 16-17.

193.To think universal agreement can actually be obtained is a holdover from the discredited epistemologies of the Enlightenment, classical foundationalism, and positivism.

194.Clayton, *Explanation,* pp. 47-48, 109-112, 118-121, 156-158. Clayton does think that correspondence views of truth may be subsumed under a coherence theory, however (see p. 110). Clayton claims a coherence theory can do everything a correspondence theory can, but it cannot as will be argued below. In essence, the problem with the coherence theory can be distilled is coherence, in of itself, is simply not enough to warrant a belief, and as Barbour puts it, the "meaning of truth is correspondence with reality" (*RAS,* pp. 34-35). Coherence can function as one of the tests for truth but it alone is not enough.

195.See the article "Coherence Theory of Truth" by Alan White in *Encyclopedia of Philosophy*, vol. 1, pp. 130-133, for an overview of some of the traditional objections to the coherence theory. It should also be noted that there are a number of coherence theories of truth which differ in some details, but for ease of exposition I am classifying them all as the coherence theory.

196.Clayton, *Explantion*, pp. 47-48.

197.Clayton, p. 178. He cites Laurence Bonjour, *The Structure of Empirical Knowledge* (Cambridge, Mass.: Harvard University Press, 1985). See also "The Coherence Theory of Empirical Knowledge," *Philosophical Studies*, vol. 30 (1976), pp. 281-312. It is significant to note that Bonjour stresses that a coherent theory of beliefs will lead to a *correspondence* between one's beliefs and the world given enough time.

198.Alvin Plantinga, *Warrant: The Current Debate*, Chapter 5. Two of Plantinga's key criticisms include that Bonjour's work does not adequately deal with *degrees* of justified beliefs and that coherence alone is not sufficient for warrant.

199.The problem is further complicated if one looks at the diversity of opinion in the epistemological debates not limited to the philosophy of science. Unfortunately, if one attends the American Academy of Religion, one gets the impression that too many scholars operating in the fields of theology and religion have assumed that the thought of Rorty, Foucault, and Derrida represent the only real options in recent philosophy.

200.This description of Lakatos's work was pointed out to me by John Losee, Professor of Philosophy at Lafayette College. See his *Philosophy of Science and Historical Enquiry* (Oxford: Clarendon Press, 1987), pp. 90-103 and *A Historical Introduction to the Philosophy of Science* (Oxford: Oxford University Press,

1980), pp. 208-212.

201.This tendency in Lakatos shows up in Murphy's *Theology in the Age of Scientific Reasoning* as well. Murphy is most successful when doing historical reconstructions of how various theologians dealt with the particular problems facing them, but she offers little that would help settle current and future theological debates. A further difficulty for Lakatos's position is that his reconstruction of scientific history is not all that accurate (see Chapter 1).

202.See Richard Gelwick's *The Way of Discovery* for some criticisms of Polanyi's work.

203.It is not surprising that Polanyi's work is an accurate description of science for he was a distinguished chemist. Polanyi's description of science is highly attractive to those who have spent their time as working scientists such as W. Jim Neidhardt and John Polkinghorne (See Polkinghorne's *One World* (Princeton: Princeton University Press, 1986), p. 12, for an endorsement of Polanyi, and *Science and Creation* (Boston: Shambhala, 1989), Chapter 6 for a favorable treatment of Torrance. I have been helped to see that Polanyi's description of science is accurate by conversations with two practicing researchers: Dr. Scott Moor, Assistant Professor of Chemical Engineering, Lafayette College, and Dr. Hugh Gregg, Livermore Labs and NASA.

204."Thomas F. Torrance," p. 86.

205.A helpful discussion of the problems with realism that is not just limited to the philosophy of science can be found in John Passmore, *Recent Philosophers* (LaSalle: Open Court, 1985), Chapter 5.

206.A convincing and well-documented treatment of Torrance as a critical realist is argued in P. Mark Achtemeier, "The Truth of Tradition: Critical Realism in the Thought of Alasdair MacIntyre and T. F. Torrance," *Scottish Journal of Theology*, vol. 47 (1994), pp. 355-74. Achtemeier draws primarily on Torrance's *Reality and Scientific Theology*, which came after *Theological Science* to make his case. He does an excellent job of picking the relevant passages which clarify the nature of Torrance's realism and rightfully points out that even in this latter work Torrance is still sometimes guilty of a sloppy use of the word "fact."

207.Colin Weightman, *Theology in a Polanyian Universe*, Ch. 14. Though he is highly critical of Torrance, Weightman at least seems to think Torrance is consistent, for Weightman argues that Torrance has misunderstood and misappropriated practically every thinker he treats – Einstein, Barth, Polanyi, and the Church Fathers, and Weightman argues Torrance's work is unsuccessful as a result. Two points in reply should suffice. First, Weightman's own interpretations of these thinkers are very controversial and by no means certain, and there are many interpreters who would support Torrance's understanding of the thinkers he appropriates. I will discuss Einstein above; one other example is Richard Gelwick's *The Way of Discovery* which is in agreement with Torrance's reading of Polanyi. Second, Weightman evaluates Torrance's work as if it is supposed to be totally dependent on the thinkers who influenced him, but Torrance is critical of both Barth and Polanyi, and it is better to understand Torrance as appropriating and developing the ideas which he believes to be correct.

208.Arthur Fine, *The Shaky Game: Einstein, Realism, and the Quantum Theory* (Chicago: University of Chicago Press, 1986).

209.Gerhald Holton, *Thematic Origins of Scientific Thought* (Cambridge, Ma.: Harvard University Press, 1973).

210.See the article by Achtemeier for a discussion of this point. In addition, see *GGT*, pp. 102-103, for Torrance's suggestion that relativity, which in Torrance's mind will never be rejected, may not necessarily be the final word in science and may end up a limiting case which needs to be coordinated to a profounder or deeper level of physics.

211.This claim of Putnam's may be the most quoted remark by philosophers of science. One essay which states Putnam's position is found in *Scientific Realism*, Jarrett Leplin, ed. (Berkley: University of California Press, 1984), pp. 140-153.

212.See the volume edited by Leplin and the essays found in *Images of Science*, Paul Churchland and Clifford Hooker, eds. (Chicago: University of Chicago Press, 1985).

213.Polanyi's dictum that "we know more than we can say" is especially relevant to this point, and it is consistent with a common-sense perspective which remains important but is often denigrated in current epistemological debates. A couple of examples illustrate this point. First, as G. E. Moore pointed out, if I am looking at my hand and know I am looking at my hand, no amount of philosophical argument, no matter how sophisticated, really challenges that knowledge. A second, and more sophisticated example, deals with the nature of language. As Iris Murdoch shows, one of the significant differences between Wittgenstein and Derrida is that Wittgenstein took ordinary language for granted in that language could refer to the world; Derrida did not (see *Metaphysics as a Guide to Morals*, pp. 289-291). It seems clear that language does refer or we could not communicate, and we do communicate whether we can give a philosophically adequate description or not.

214.Matthew 13:58.

215.See especially *DCO and TCFM* for this point.

216.John Polkinghorne, *Reason and Reality* (Philadelphia: Trinity Press International, 1991), pp. 93-94.

217.This is a problem which has troubled me ever since my Junior M. Div. year and I heard Dr. James Loder lecture on the subject of whether or not Christianity could be taught.

218.James Loder, *The Transforming Moment: Understanding Convictional Experiences* (San Francisco: Harper & Row, 1981), pp. 29-44.

219.*Imagining God: Theology and the Religious Imagination* (San Francisco: Harper & Row, 1989), and Austin Farrer, *The Glass of Vision* (London: Dacre Press, 1948).

220.*The Knight's Move: The Relational Logic of the Spirit in Theology and Science* (Colorado Springs: Helmers & Howard, 1992). Torrance praises Loder and Neidhardt's efforts in the Forward to the book as "the most exciting and uplifting book of its kind that I have read in recent years" (p. xii).

221. Robert John Russell, "Cosmology, Creation, and Contingency" in *Cosmos as Creation*, ed. Ted Peters (Nashville: Abingdon Press, 1989), pp. 177-209. Russell's work is valuable for he makes the point that contingency will never be eliminated from cosmology, and he discusses the form contingency make take in a variety of cosmological theories noting that the understanding of contingency will vary according to the theory adopted as true. Willem Drees very effectively makes this same point in *Beyond the Big Bang*.

222. Ian Barbour, *Religion in an Age of Science*, pp. 13, 17-18, 141-142, 272n.27; and John Polkinghorne, *Reason and Reality*, pp. 93-94.

223. Some representative treatments of this issue can be found in Robert John Russell, Nancey Murphy, and Arthur R. Peacocke, eds., *Chaos and Complexity: Scientific Perspectives on Divine Action* (Vatican City: Vatican Observatory and Berkeley: Center for Theology and Natural Science, 1995).

224. *STI*, pp. 71-85.

225. *TS*, p. ix.

Bibliography

Abraham, William J. *An Introduction to the Philosophy of Religion.* Englewood Cliffs, N. J.: Prentice-Hall, 1985.

Achtemeier, P. Mark. "The Truth of Tradition: Critical Realism in the Thought of Alasdair MacIntyre and T. F. Torrance." *Scottish Journal of Theology*, vol. 47 (1994), pp. 355-374.

Alexander, Peter. "Complementary Descriptions." *Mind*, vol. LXV (1956), pp. 145-165.

Allen, Diogenes. *Christian Belief in a Postmodern World.* Louisville: Westminster/John Knox Press, 1989.

_____. *The Reasonableness of Faith.* Washington: Corpus Publications, 1968.

Anderson, Ray. Review of *Space, Time, and Incarnation* by T. F. Torrance. *Christianity Today*, vol. 22 (1977), pp. 40, 42, 44-45.

Alston, W. P. "Has Foundationalism Been Refuted?" *Contemporary Readings in Epistemology.* Eds. Michael Goodman and Robert Snyder. Englewood Cliffs: Prentice Hall, 1993, pp. 42-53.

_____. "Problems of the Philosophy of Religion." *Encyclopedia of Philosophy*, vol. 6. Reprinted ed. Ed. Paul Edwards. New York: Macmillan, 1972, pp. 285-289.

Annis, David. "A Contextualist Theory of Epistemic Justification." *Contemporary Readings in Epistemology*. Eds. Michael Goodman and Robert Snyder. Englewood Cliffs: Prentice Hall, 1993, pp. 105-113.

Anselm. *St. Anselm: Basic Writings*, ed. S. N. Deane. LaSalle, Ill.:Open Court, 1962.

Aquinas, Thomas. *The Trinity and the Unicity of the Intellect*. Trans. R. E. Brennan. London: Herder Book Co., 1946.

Augustine. *The Literal Meaning of Genesis*. 2 vols. Trans. J. H. Taylor. New York: Newman, 1982.

Austin, William H. *The Relevance of Natural Science to Theology*. London: Macmillan, 1976.

Ayer, A. J. *Language, Truth, and Logic*. New York: Dover, 1946.

Ayer, A. J., ed. *Logical Positivism*. New York: Free Press, 1959.

Banner, Michael. *The Justification of Science and the Rationality of Religious Beliefs*. Oxford: Clarendon Press, 1990.

Barbour, Ian. *Christianity and the Scientist*. New York: Association Press, 1960.

_____. "Consultation Summation." *The Church and Contemporary Cosmology*. Eds. James Miller and Kenneth McCall. Pittsburgh: Carnegie Mellon Press, 1990, pp. 297-312.

_____. Issues in Science and Religion. Englewood Cliffs, New Jersey: Prentice-Hall, 1966.

_____. *Myths, Models, and Paradigms: A Comparative Study in Science and Religion*. New York: Harper & Row, 1974.

_____. Religion in an Age of Science: The Gifford *Lectures, 1989-1991*, Volume I. San Francisco: Harper & Row, 1990.

_____. "Response to Nancey Murphy." *Zygon*, 31 (March 1996), pp. 52-54.

_____. "Ways of Relating Science and Theology." *Physics, Philosophy, and Theology: A Common Quest for Understanding*. Eds. Robert John Russell, William Stoeger, and George Coyne. Vatican City: Vatican Observatory and Notre Dame: University of Notre Dame Press, 1988, pp. 21-48.

Barbour, Ian, ed. *Science and Religion*. New York: Harper & Row, 1968.

Barton, John. *People of the Book? The Authority of the Bible in Christianity*. Louisville: Westminster/John Knox Press, 1988.

Barth, Karl. *Church Dogmatics*, vol. 1, part 1. Edinburgh: T. & T. Clark, 1975.

_____. "Philosophie und Theologie." *Philosophie und Christliche Existenz: Festschrift fur Heinrich Barth*. Ed. Gerhard Huber. Basel and Stuttgart: Verlag, Helbing, & Lichtenhahn, 1960, pp. 93-106.

Bartsch, H. W., ed. *Kerygma and Myth*. Trans. R. H. Fuller. London: Billing & Sons, 1964.

Bedau, Hugo. "Complementarity and the Relation Between Science and Religion." *Zygon*, vol. 9 (1974), pp. 202-224.

Bealer, George. "The Philosophical Limits of Scientific Essentialism." *Philosophical Perspectives, vol. 1: Metaphysics*, 1987. Ed. James Toberlin. Atascadero: Ca.: Ridgeview, 1987, pp. 289-365.

Bloor, David. *Knowledge and Social Imagery*. London: Routledge and Kegan Paul, 1976.

Bly, John. "Instrumentalism: A Third Option." *Journal of the American Scientific Affiliation*, vol. 37 (March 1985), pp. 11-18.

Bonjour, Laurence. *The Structure of Empirical Knowledge*. Cambridge, Mass.: Harvard University Press, 1985.

Boyd, Richard. "Confirmation, Semantics, and the Interpretation of Scientific Theories." *The Philosophy of Science*. Eds. R. Boyd, Philip Gasper, and J. D. Trout. Cambridge, Mass.: MIT Press, 1991, pp. 3-22.

Boyd, Richard, Philip Gasper, and J. D. Trout, Eds. *Philosophy of Science*. Cambridge, Mass.: MIT Press, 1991.

Braithwaite, R. B. "An Empiricist's View of the Nature of Religious Belief." *Classical and Contemporary Readings in the Philosophy of Religion*. Ed. John Hick. Englewood-Cliffs, N. J.: Prentice-Hall, 1970, pp. 394-405.

Bridgman, P. W. *The Logic of Modern Physics*. New York: Macmillan, 1927.

_____. *The Nature of Physical Theory*. Princeton: Princeton University Press, 1936.

Brody, Baruch, ed. *Readings in the Philosophy of Religion*. Englewood Cliffs, N.J.: Prentice-Hall, 1974.

Brown, Harold I. *Perception, Theory, and Commitment*. Chicago: University of Chicago Press, 1977.

Bube, Richard. *The Human Quest*. Waco: Word, 1971.

Burrell, David. "Does Process Theology Rest on a Mistake?" *Theological Studies*, vol. 43 (March 1982), pp. 125-135.

Butterfield, Herbert. *The Origins of Modern Science: 1300-1800.* New York: Macmillan, 1957.

Carnap, Rudolf. *Philosophical Foundations of Physics*. New York: Basic Books, 1966.

Chisholm, Roderick. *Theory of Knowledge*, 2nd ed. Englewood Cliffs: Prentice Hall, 1977.

Churchland, Paul M. and Hooker, Clifford A. *Images of Science: Essays on Realism and Empiricism, with a Reply from Bas C. van Frasssen.* Chicago: University of Chicago Press, 1985.

Clark, Gordon H. *The Philosophy of Science and Belief in God.* Nutley, N. J.: Craig, 1964.

Clayton, Philip. *Explanation from Physics to Theology.* New Haven: Yale University Press, 1989.

Clifford, W. K. "The Ethics of Belief." *Readings in the Philosophy of Religion.* Ed. Baruch Brody. Englewood Cliffs, N. J.: Prentice- Hall, 1974, pp. 241-247.

Coulson, C. A. *Science and Christian Belief.* Chapel Hill: University of North Carolina Press, 1955.

Cupitt, Don. *Only Human.* London: SCM Press, 1985.

_____. *Taking Leave of God.* London: SCM Press, 1980.

_____. *The World to Come.* London: SCM Press, 1982.

Davidson, Donald. *Inquiries into Truth and Interpretation.* Oxford: Clarendon Press, 1984.

Devitt, Michael. *Realism and Truth.* 2nd ed. Oxford: Blackwell, 1991.

Diamond, Malcom and Thomas Litzenburg, Jr., Eds. *The Logic of God: Theology and Verification.* Indianapolis: Bobbs-Merrill, 1975.

Drees, Willem. *Beyond the Big Bang: Quantum Cosmologies and God.* LaSalle, Ill.: Open Court, 1990.

Duhem, Pierre. *The Aim and Structure of Physical Theory.* Trans. Phillip P. Weiner. Princeton: Princeton University Press, 1982.

Emerson, Allen. "A Disorienting View of God's Creation." *Christianity Today*, Feb. 1 (1985), pp. 19-24.

Evans, Donald. "Differences between Scientific and Religious Assertions." *Science and Religion*. Ed. Ian Barbour. New York: Harper & Row, 1968, pp. 101-133.

Farrer, Austin. *Faith and Speculation*. London: A. & C. Black, 1967.

_____. *The Glass of Vision*. London: Dacre Press, 1948.

Feenstra, Ronald J. and Cornelius Plantinga, Jr., eds. *Trinity, Incarnation, and Atonement*. Notre Dame, Ind.: University of Notre Dame Press, 1989.

Feyerabend, Paul. *Against Method*. London: Verso, 1983.

_____. "Consolations for the Specialist." *Criticism and the Growth of Knowledge*. Eds. I Lakatos and A. Musgrave. Cambridge: Cambridge University Press, 1970, pp. 215-223.

_____. "Philosophy of Science: A Subject With a Great Past." *Historical and Philosophical Perspectives on Science*. Ed. R. Stuewer. Minneapolis: University of Minnesota Press, 1970, pp. 172-183.

Fine, Arthur. "And Not Anti-Realism Either." *Nous*, vol. 18 (1984), pp. 51-65.

_____. "The Natural Ontological Attitude." *Scientific Realism*. Ed. Jarrett Leplin. Berkeley and Los Angeles: University of California Press, 1984, pp. 83-107.

_____. *The Shaky Game: Einstein, Realism, and the Quantum Theory*. Chicago: University of Chicago Press, 1986.

Foster, Michael. *Mystery and Philosophy*. London: SCM Press, 1957.

Frye, Roland, ed. *Is God a Creationist?: The Case Against Creation Science*. New York: Charles Scribner's Sons, 1983.

Gardner, Michael. "Realism and Insrumenatalism in Pre-Newtonian Astronomy." *Minnesota Studies in the Philosophy of Science*, vol. X. Ed. John Earman. Minneapolis: University of Minnesota Press, 1983, pp. 201-265.

Gelwick, Richard. *The Way of Discovery: An Introduction to the Thought of Michael Polanyi*. New York: Oxford University Press, 1977.

Ghiselin, Brewster, ed. *The Creative Process*. (Berkeley: University of California Press, 1952.

Giere, Ronald. "The Epistemological Roots of Scientific Knowledge." *Minnesota Studies in the Philosophy of Science*, vol. VI. Eds. G. Maxwell and R. M. Anderson. Minneapolis: University of Minnesota Press, 1975, pp. 212-261.

_____. "Testing Theoretical Hypotheses." *Minnesota Studies in the Philosophy of Science*, vol. X. Ed. John Earman. Minneapolis: University of Minnesota Press, 1983, pp. 269-298.

Gillispie, C.C. *The Edge of Objectivity*. Princeton: Princeton University Press, 1960.

Gilson, Etienne. *Reason and Revelation in the Middle Ages*. New York: Charles Scribner's Sons, 1938.

Glymour, Clark. "Explanation and Realism." *Scientific Realism*. Ed. Jarrett Leplin. Berkeley: University of California Press, 1984, pp. 173-192.

_____. *Theory and Evidence*. Princeton: Princeton University Press, 1980.

Godfrey, Laurie, ed. *Scientists Confront Creationism*. New York: W. W. Norton, 1983.

Goldman, Alvin. "What is Justified Belief?" *Justification and Knowledge*. Ed. G. S. Pappas. Dordrecht: D. Reidel Publishing Company, 1979, pp. 1-23.

Goodman, Michael and Robert Snyder, Eds. *Contemporary Readings in Epistemology*. Englewood Cliffs, N. J.: Prentice-Hall, 1993.

Goodman, Nelson. *Fact, Fiction, and Forecast*. Cambridge: Harvard University Press, 1955.

Green, Garrett. *Imagining God: Theology and the Religious Imagination*. San Francisco: Harper & Row, 1989.

Gutting, Gary. *Religious Beliefs and Religious Skepticism*. Notre Dame, Ind.: University of Notre Dame Press, 1982.

Gutting, Gary, ed. *Paradigms and Revolutions*. Notre Dame, Ind.: University of Notre Dame Press, 1980.

Habgood, John S. "The Uneasy Truce Between Science and Theology." *Soundings*. Ed. A. R. Vidler. Cambridge: Cambridge University Press, 1962, pp. 21-41.

Hacking, Ian. "Experimentation and Scientific Realism." *Scientific Realism*. Ed. Jarrett Leplin. Berkeley and Los Angeles: University of California Press, 1984, pp. 154-172.

_____. *Representing and Intervening*. New York: Cambridge University Press, 1983.

Halverson, William H. *A Concise Introduction to Philosophy*. 3rd ed. New York: Random House, 1976.

Hanson, N. R. *Patterns of Discovery: An Inquiry into the Conceptual Foundations of Science*. Cambridge: Cambridge University Press, 1958.

Hardy, Daniel W. "Thomas F. Torrance." *The Modern Theologians: An Introduction to Christian Theology in the Twentieth Century*. Ed. David Ford. Oxford: Basil Blackwell, 1989, pp. 71-91.

Harre, Rom. *The Principles of Scientific Thinking*. London: Macmillan, 1970.

_____. *Varieties of Realism*. Oxford: Basil Blackwell, 1986.

Hebblethwaite, Brian. "Providence and Divine Action." *Religious Studies*, vol. 14 (1978), pp. 223-236.

Heim, Karl. *Christian Faith and Natural Science*. New York: Harper Torchbooks, 1953.

_____. *The Transformation of the Scientific World View*. New York: Harper, 1957.

_____. *The World: Its Creation and Consummation*. Philadelphia: Muhlenberg Press, 1962.

Hempel, Carl. *Aspects of Scientific Explanation*. New York: Free Press, 1965.

_____. "Deductive-Nomological vs. Statistical Explanations." *Minnesota Studies in the Philosophy of Science*, vol. III. Minneapolis: University of Minnesota Press, 1962, pp. 98-169.

_____. *Philosophy of Natural Science*. Englewood Cliffs, N. J.: Prentice-Hall, 1966.

Hempel, Carl and Paul Oppenheim. "Studies in the Logic of Explanation." *Philosophy of Science*, vol. 15 (1948), pp. 135-175.

Hendry, George. *Theology of Nature*. Philadelphia: The Westminster Press, 1980.

Hesse, Mary. *Models and Analogies in Science*. South Bend: University of Notre Dame Press, 1966.

Hesselink, I. John. "A Pilgrimage in the School of Christ – An Interview with T. F. Torrance." *Reformed Review*, vol. 38 (1984), pp. 49-64.

Hick, John, ed. *Classical and Contemporary Readings in the Philosophy of Religion*, 2nd ed. Englewood-Cliffs, N.J.: Prentice-Hall, 1970.

_____. Review of *Theological Science* by T. F. Torrance. *Expository Times*, vol. 81 (1981), pp. 57-58.

Hofstadter, Douglas. *Godel, Escher, and Bach: An Eternal Golden Braid.* New York: Vantage, 1979.

Holton, Gerald. *Thematic Origins of Scientific Thought.* Cambridge, Ma.: Harvard University Press, 1973.

Honderich, Ted. *The Oxford Companion to Philosophy.* Oxford: Oxford University Press, 1995.

Hooker, C. A. *A Realistic Theory of Science.* Albany: SUNY Press, 1987.

Hudson, W. D. "Some Remarks on Wittgenstein's Account of Religious Beliefs." *Talk of God.* Ed. G. N. A. Vessey. London: Macmillan, 1969, pp. 36-51.

_____. *Wittgenstein and Religious Belief.* London: Macmillan, 1975.

Hume, David. *Dialogues Concerning Natural Religion.* Ed. Norman Kemp Smith. Indianapolis: Bobbs-Merill, 1947.

Hyman, Arthur and James Walsh, Eds. *Philosophy in the Middle Ages.* Indianapolis: Hackett Publishing Co., 1973.

Ivry, A. "Toward a Unified View of Averroes' Philosophy." *Philosophical Forum*, vol. IV (1972), pp. 87-113.

Jaki, Stanley. *The Road of Science and the Ways to God.* Chicago: University of Chicago Press, 1978.

Johnson, Howard and Niels Thulstrup, eds. *A Kierkegaard Critique.* Chicago: Henry Regency Co., 1967.

Kaiser, Christopher. *Creation and the History of Science.* Grand Rapids: Eerdmans, 1991.

Kaufman, Gordon. *An Essay on Theological Method*, Revised Edition. Missoula: Scholars Press, 1979.

_____. *God the Problem.* Cambridge: Harvard University Press, 1972.

_____. *Systematic Theology: A Historicist Perspective*. New York Scribner's, 1968.

Kekes, John. *The Nature of Philosophy*. Totawa, N. J.: Rowan and Littlefield, 1980.

Kim, Jaegwon. "What is 'Naturalized Epistemology'?. *Contemporary Readings in Epistemology*. Eds. Michael Goodman and Robert Snyder. Englewood Cliffs, N. J.: Prentice-Hall, 1993, pp. 323-337.

Kitcher, Phillip. *Abusing Science: The Case Against Creationism*. Cambridge, Mass.: MIT Press, 1982.

Klinefelter, Donald. "God and Rationality: A Critique of the Theology of Thomas F. Torrance." *Journal of Religion*, vol. 53 (1973), pp. 117-134.

Koestler, Arthur. *The Act of Creation*. New York: Macmillan, 1964.

Kornblith, Hilary, Ed. *Naturalizing Epistemology*. Cambridge, Mass.: MIT Press, 1985.

Kourany, Janet. *Scientific Knowledge: Basic Issues in the Philosophy of Science*. Belmont, Ca.: Wadsworth, 1987.

Kuhn, Thomas. *The Essential Tension: Selected Studies in Scientific Tradition and Change*. Chicago: University of Chicago Press, 1977.

_____. *The Structure of Scientific Revolutions*. 2nd ed. Chicago: University of Chicago Press, 1970.

_____. "Theory-Change as Structure Change." *Erkenntis*, vol. 10 (July 1976), pp. 179-199.

Lakatos, Imre. "Falsification and the Methodology of Scientific Research Programmes." *Criticism and the Growth of Knowledge*. Eds. Imre Lakatos and Alan Musgrave. Cambridge: Cambridge University Press, 1970, pp. 91-195.

Langford, Thomas. "T. F. Torrance's *Theological Science: A Reaction*." *Scottish Journal of Theology*, vol. 25 (1972), pp. 155-170.

Laudan, Larry. *Progress and Its Problems*. Berkeley: University of California Press, 1977.

_____. *Science and Values*. Berkeley: University of California Press, 1984.

Lee, Edward. "Hoist on His Own Petard." *Exegesis and Argument: Studies in Greek Philosophy Presented to Gregory Vlastos*. Eds. E. Lee, A.P.D. Mourelatos, and R. Rorty. Assen: Van Gorcum, 1973, pp. 225-261.

Leplin, Jarrett, ed. *Scientific Realism*. Berkeley and Los Angeles, Ca.: University of California Press, 1984.

Loder, James. *The Transforming Moment: Understanding Convictional Experiences*. San Francisco: Harper & Row, 1981.

Loder, James and W. Jim Neidhardt. *The Knight's Move: The Relational Logic of the Spirit in Theology and Science*. Colorado Springs: Helmers & Howard, 1992.

Lohse, Bernhard. *A Short History of Christian Doctrine*. Revised American Edition. Philadelphia: Fortress Press, 1985.

Losee, John. *A Historical Introduction to the Philosophy of Science*. 2nd ed. Oxford: Oxford University Press, 1980.

_____. *Philosophy of Science and Historical Enquiry*. Oxford: Clarendon Press, 1987.

Louth, Andrew. *Discerning the Mystery: An Essay of the Nature of Theology*. Oxford: Clarendon Press, 1983.

MacIntyre, Alasdair. "The Logical Status of Religious Belief." *Metaphysical Beliefs*, 2nd ed. Eds. S. E. Toulmin, R. W. Hepburn, and A. MacIntyre. London: SCM, 1970, pp. 167-211.

MacKay, D. M. *The Clockwork Image*. Downers Grove, Ill.: Inter-Varsity Press, 1974.

_____. "Complementary Descriptions." *Mind*, vol. LXVI (1957), pp. 390-394.

_____. "Complementarity II." *Proceedings of the Aristotelian Society,* Supp. vol. XXXII (1958), pp. 105-122.

_____. "Complementarity in Scientific and Theological Thinking." *Zygon,* vol. 9 (1974), pp. 225-244.

Mascall, E. L. *Christian Theology and Natural Science.* London: Longmans, Green and Company, 1957.

Masterman, Margaret. "The Nature of a Paradigm." *Criticism and the Growth of Knowledge.* Eds. Lakotos, I. and A. Musgrave. Cambridge: Cambridge University Press, 1970, pp. 61-65.

McMullin, Ernan. "Alternative Approaches to the Philosophy of Science." *Scientific Knowledge.* Ed. Janet Kourany. Belmont:Wadsworth, 1987, pp. 3-19.

_____. "The Case for Scientific Realism." *Scientific Realism.* Ed. Jarrett Leplin. Berkeley and Los Angeles: University of California Press, 1984, pp. 8-40.

_____."The History and Philosophy of Science: A Taxonomy." *Minnesota Studies in the Philosophy of Science,* vol. 5. Ed. Roger Stuewer. Minneapolis: University of Minnesota Press, 1970, pp. 12- 67.

_____. "Introduction." *Evolution and Creation.* Ed. Ernan McMullin. Notre Dame, Ind.: University of Notre Dame Press, 1985.

_____. "Natural Science and Belief in a Creator: Historical Notes." *Physics, Philosophy, and Theology: A Common Quest for Understanding.* Eds. Robert John Russell, William Stoeger, and George Coyne. The Vatican: Vatican Observatory, and Notre Dame, Ind.: University of Notre Dame Press, 1988, pp. 49-79.

_____. "The Relativist Critique of Science." *The Sciences and Theology in the Twentieth Century.* Ed. Arthur Peacocke. Notre Dame, Ind.: University of Notre Dame Press, 1981, pp. 299-302.

_____. "Values in Science." *Proceedings of the Philosophy of Science Association*, 2 (1982), pp. 1-25.

McMullin, Ernan Ed. *Evolution and Creation*. Notre Dame, Ind.: University of Notre Dame Press, 1985.

Medawar, Peter. *The Limits of Science*. New York: Harper & Row, 1984.

Migliore, Daniel L. *Faith Seeking Understanding*. Grand Rapids: Eerdmans, 1991.

Miller, James, and Kenneth McCall, Eds. *The Church and Contemporary Cosmology*. Pittsburgh: Carnegie Mellon University Press, 1990.

Miller, R. *Fact and Method*. Princeton: Princeton University Press, 1987.

Mitchell, Basil. "Faith and Reason: A False Antithesis?" *Religious Studies*, vol. 16 (1980), pp. 131-144.

_____. *How to Play Theological Ping-Pong: And Other Essays on Faith and Reason.* Grand Rapids: Eerdmans, 1990.

_____. *The Justification of Religious Belief.* London: Macmillan, 1973.

Moltmann, Jurgen. *God and Creation*. Trans. Margaret Kohl. San Francisco: Harper & Row, 1985.

Moreland, J. P. *Christianity and the Nature of Science*. Grand Rapids: Baker Book House, 1989.

Morris, Henry. *Scientific Creationism*, 2nd ed. El Cajun, Ca.: Master Books, 1985.

Morris, Thomas V. *Our Idea of God*. Downers Grove, Ill.: Inter-Varsity Press, 1991.

_____. *The Logic of God Incarnate*. Ithaca: Cornell University Press, 1986.

Mulkay, M. *Science and the Sociology of Knowledge*. London: Allen and Unwin, 1979.

Murdoch, Iris. *Metaphysics as a Guide to Morals*. New York: Allen Lane/Penguin Press, 1992.

Murphy, Nancey. "Acceptability Criteria for Work in Theology and Science." *Zygon*, vol. 22 (1987), pp. 279-297.

_____. "Ian Barbour on Religion and the Methods of Science: An Assessment." *Zygon*, vol. 31 (1996), pp. 11-19.

_____. "Revisionist Philosophy of Science and Theological Method." Unpublished paper delivered at the Pacific Coast Theological Society, Spring 1983.

_____. *Theology in the Age of Scientific Reasoning*. Ithaca, New York: Cornell University Press, 1990.

Musgrave, Alan. "Kuhn's Second Thoughts." *Paradigms and Revolutions*. Ed. Gary Gutting. Notre Dame, Ind.: University of Notre Dame Press, 1980, pp. 39-53.

_____. "Realism Versus Constructive Empiricism." *Images of Science*. Eds. Paul Churchland and Clifford Hooker. Chicago: University of Chicago Press, 1985, pp. 197-221.

Nash, Ronald. *Faith and Reason: A Search for a Rational Faith*. Grand Rapids: Zondervan, 1988.

Neblesick, Harold. *Theology and Science in Mutual Modification*. New York: Oxford University Press, 1981.

Neidhardt, W. Jim. "Introduction." *The Christian Frame of Mind*. New Edition. Ed. and author Thomas F. Torrance. Colorado Springs: Helmers & Howard, 1989, pp. xi-xliv.

Newton-Smith, W. H. *The Rationality of Science*. London: Routledge and Kegan Paul, 1981.

Niebuhr, H. Richard. *Christ and Culture*. New York: Harper & Row, 1951.

Nielsen, Kai. "Wittgensteinian Fideism." *Philosophy*, vol. XLII (1967), pp. 191-209.

Norris, Frederick W. "Mathematics, Physics, and Religion: A Need for Candor and Rigor." *Scottish Journal of Theology*, vol. 37 (1984), pp. 457-470.

Northop, S. C. "Whitehead's Philosophy of Science." *The Philosophy of Alfred North Whitehead*. Ed. Paul Schlipp. Evanston, Ill.: Northwestern University Press, 1941, pp. 165-207.

Oppenheim, Paul and Hilary Putnam. "Unity of Science as a Working Hypothesis." *Concepts, Theories, and the Mind-Body Problem*. Eds. H. Feigl, M. Scriven, and G. Maxwell. *Minnesota Studies in the Philosophy of Science*, vol. II. Minneapolis: University of Minnesota Press, , 1958, pp. 3-36.

Palma, Robert J. "Thomas F. Torrance's Reformed Theology." *Reformed Review*, vol. 38 (1984), pp. 2-46.

Park, James L. "Complementarity without Paradox." *Zygon*, vol. 2 (1967), pp. 382-388.

Passmore, John. "Explanation in Everyday Life, in Science, and in History." *History and Theory* 2, (1962), pp. 105-123.

_____. *A Hundred Years of Philosophy*. Middlesex, England: Penguin, 1968.

_____. *Recent Philosophers*. La Salle: Open Court, 1985.

Paul, Ian. *Knowledge of God: Calvin, Einstein, and Polanyi*. Edinburgh: Scottish Academic Press, 1987.

Peacocke, A. R. *Creation and the World of Science*. Oxford: Clarendon. Press, 1979.

Peacocke, A. R., ed. *The Sciences and Theology in the Twentieth Century.* Notre Dame, Indiana: University of Notre Dame Press, 1981.

Penrose, Roger. *The Emperor's New Mind: Concerning Computers, Minds, and the Laws of Physics.* Oxford: Oxford University Press, 1989.

Peters, Ted. "Cosmos as Creation." *Cosmos and Creation: Theology and Science in Consonance.* Ed. Ted Peters. Nashville: Abingdon, 1989, pp. 45-113.

Peters, Ted, ed. *Cosmos and Creation: Theology and Science in Consonance.* Nashville: Abingdon, 1989.

Phillips, D. Z. *The Concept of Prayer.* London: Routledge and Kegan Paul, 1965.

_____. *Death and Immortality.* London: Macmillan, 1970.

_____. *Faith and Philosophical Inquiry.* New York: Schocken Books, 1971.

_____. *Religion without Explanation.* Oxford: Basil Blackwell, 1976.

Placher, William C. *Unapologetic Theology.* Louisville: Westminster/ John Knox Press, 1989.

Plantinga, Alvin. *God and Other Minds.* Ithaca: Cornell University Press, 1967.

_____. "Reason and Belief in God." *Faith and Rationality: Reason and Belief in God.* Eds. Alvin Plantinga and N. Wolterstorff. Notre Dame, Ind.: University of Notre Dame Press, 1983, pp. 16-93.

_____. *Warrant: The Current Debate.* New York: Oxford University Press, 1993.

_____. *Warrant and Proper Function.* New York: Oxford University Press, 1993.

Polanyi, Michael. *Personal Knowledge: Towards a Post-Critical Philosophy.* Chicago: University of Chicago Press, 1962.

_____. *The Tacit Dimension.* Garden City: Doubleday, 1966.

Polkinghorne, John. *One World: The Interaction of Science and Theology.* Princeton: Princeton University Press, 1986.

_____. *Reason and Reality.* Philadelphia: Trinity Press International, 1991.

_____. *Science and Creation.* Boston: Shambhala, 1988.

Pollard, William G. *Chance and Providence.* Charles Scribner's Sons, 1958.

Pollock, J. *Contemporary Theories of Knowledge.* Tottowa, N. J.: Rowan and Littlefield, 1986.

Popper, Karl. *Conjectures and Refutations.* New York: Basic Books, 1963.

_____. *The Logic of Scientific Discovery.* New York: Basic Books, 1959.

Putnam, Hilary. *Reason, Truth, and History.* Cambridge: Cambridge University Press, 1981.

_____. *"What is Scientific Realism?"* Scientific Realism. Ed. Jarrett Leplin. Berkeley and Los Angeles: University of California Press, 1984, pp. 140-153.

Quine, W. V. O. *Ontological Relativity and Other Essays.* New York: Columbia University Press, 1969.

Quine, W. V. O. and J. S. Ullian. *The Web of Belief.* New York: Random House, 1970.

Ratzsch, Del. "Grappling with Googolplexes, Gluons, and God."*Books and Religion* (Summer 1990), pp. 12, 18.

_____. *Philosophy of Science: The Natural Sciences in Christian Perspective*. Downers Grove, Illinois: InterVarsity Press, 1986.

Rescher, Nicholas. *The Limits of Science*. New York: Harper & Row, 1984.

_____. "Process Philosophy." *A Companion to Metaphysics*. Eds. Jaegwon, Kim and Ernest Sosa. Oxford: Blackwell, 1995, pp. 417-419.

Rolston, Holmes. *Science and Religion: A Critical Survey*. Philadelphia: Temple University Press, 1987.

_____. "Religion in an Age of Science; Metaphysics in an Era of History." *Zygon,* vol. 27 (March 1992), pp. 65-87.

Rorty, Richard. *Philosophy and the Mirror of Nature*. Princeton:Princeton University Press, 1979.

Rottschaefer, William. "Religious Cognition as Interpreted Experience: An Examination of Ian Barbour's Comparison of the Epistemic Structures of Science and Religion." *Zygon,* vol. 20 (1985), pp. 265-282.

Russell, Robert John. "Contingency in Physics and Cosmology: A Critique of the Theology of Wolfhart Pannenberg." *Zygon,* vol. 23 (1988), pp. 23-43.

_____. "Cosmology, Creation, and Contingency." *Cosmos as Creation*. Ed. Ted Peters. Nashville: Abingdon Press, 1989, pp. 177-209.

_____. "Religion and the Theories of Science: A Response to Barbour." *Zygon,* vol. 31 (1996), pp. 29-41.

Russell, Robert John, Nancey Murphy, and Arthur R. Peacocke, Eds. *Chaos and Complexity: Scientific Perspectives on Divine Action.* Vatican City: Vatican Observatory, 1995.

Russell, Robert John, William R. Stoeger, S. J., and George V. Coyne, S. J., Eds. *Physics, Philosophy, and Theology: A Common Quest for Understanding.* Vatican City State: Vatican Observatory, and Notre Dame, Indiana: University of Notre Dame Press, 1988.

Sagan, Carl. *Cosmos.* New York: Random House, 1980.

Salmon, Wesley. "Why Ask, 'Why?'? An Inquiry Concerning Scientific Explanation." *Scientific Knowledge: Basic Issues in the Philosophy of Science.* Ed. Janet Kourany. Belmont, Ca.: Wadsworth, 1987, pp. 51-64.

Samson, Dennis. *Scientific Theology: An Examination of the Methodology of Thomas Forsyth Torrance.* Ph. D. Diss., Southwestern Baptist Theological Seminary, 1981.

Scheffler, Israel. *The Anatomy of Inquiry.* New York: Alfred A. Knopf, 1963.

Schlegel, Richard. "Quantum Physics and Divine Postulate." *Zygon,* vol. 14 (1979), pp. 163-185.

Schlesinger, G. *Metaphysics: Methods and Problems.* Oxford: Basil Blackwell, 1983.

_____."Operationalism." *Encyclopedia of Philosophy,* vol. 5. Ed. Paul Edwards. New York: Macmillan and Free Press, 1967, pp. 543-547.

Schubert, Frank D. "Thomas F. Torrance: The Case for a Theological Science." *Encounter,* vol. 45 (1984), pp. 123-137.

Scriven, Michael. "Causation as Explanation." *Nous,* vol. 9 (1975), pp. 3-10.

_____. "Explanation and Prediction in Evolutionary Theory." *Science,* vol. 130 (1959), pp. 477-482.

_____. "Explanations, Predictions, and Laws." *Minnesota Studies in the Philosophy of Science,* vol. III. Eds. H. Feigl and G. Maxwell. Minneapolis: University of Minnesota Press, 1962, pp. 170-230.

Schoen, Edward. *Religious Explanations.* Durham: Duke University Press, 1985.

Sellars, Willard. *Science, Perception, and Reality.* New York: Humanities Press, 1962.

Shapere, Dudley. "Meaning and Scientific Change." *Scientific Revolutions.* Ed. Ian Hacking. Oxford: Oxford University Press, 1981, pp. 28-32.

_____. "The Structure of Revolutions." *Philosophical Review,* vol. 73 (1964), pp. 383-394.

Sokolowski, Robert. *The God of Faith and Reason: Foundations of Christian Theology.* Notre Dame, Indiana: University of Notre Dame Press, 1982.

Sorell, Tom. *Scientism: Philosophy and the Infatuation with Science.* London: Routledge, 1991.

Soskice, Janet. *Metaphor and Religious Language.* New York: Oxford University Press, 1985.

Spring, Beth. "A Conversation with Carl Henry about the New Physics." *Christianity Today,* Feb. 1 (1985), p. 26.

Stace, W. T. *Religion and the Modern Mind.* Philadelphia: J. B. Lippincott, 1960.

_____. *Time and Eternity.* Princeton: Princeton University Press, 1952.

Suppe, Frederick. *The Structure of Scientific Theories.* Urbana: University of Illinois Press, 1977.

Suppes, Patrick. "The Plurality of Science." *Scientific Knowledge.* Ed. Janet Kourany. Belmont: Wadsworth, 1987, pp. 317-325.

Taylor, Richard. "Causation." *The Encyclopedia of Philosophy*, vol. 1. Ed. Paul Edwards. New York: Macmillan, 1967, pp. 56-66.

Thiemann, Ronald. *Revelation and Theology: The Gospel as Narrated Promise.* Notre Dame, Indiana: University of Notre Dame Press, 1985.

Tipler, Frank. *The Physics of Immortality.* New York: Doubleday, 1994.

Torrance, Thomas Forsyth. *The Christian Frame of Mind: Reason, Order, and Openness in Theology and Natural Science.* Colorado Srings: Helmers & Howard, 1989.

_____. *Christian Theology and Scientific Culture.* New York: Oxford University Press, 1981.

_____. *Divine and Contingent Order.* Oxford: Oxford University Press, 1981.

_____. *God and Rationality.* London: Oxford University Press, 1971.

_____. *The Ground and Grammar of Theology.* Charlottesville: University Press of Va., 1980.

_____. *Reality and Scientific Theology.* Edinburgh: Scottish Academic Press, 1985.

_____. *Space, Time, and Incarnation.* London: Oxford University Press, 1969.

_____. *Space, Time, and Resurrection.* Edinburgh: Handsel Press, 1976.

_____. *Theology in Reconstruction.* Grand Rapids: Eerdmans, 1965.

_____. *Theological Science.* London: Oxford University Press, 1969.

_____. *Transformation and Convergence in the Frame of Knowledge.* Grand Rapids: Eerdmans, 1984.

Torrance, Thomas F., ed. *Belief in Science and in Christian Life: The Relevance of Michael Polanyi's Thought for Christian Faith and Life.* Edinburgh: Handsel Press, 1980.

Trook, Douglas. *The Unified Christocentric Field: Towards a Time-Eternity Relativity Model for Theological Hermeneutics in the Onto-Relational Theology.* Ph. D. diss., Drew University. Ann Arbor: University Microfilms, 1987.

van Frassen, Bas C. "To Save the Phenomena." *Scientific Realism.* Ed. Jarrett Leplin. Berkeley and Los Angeles: University of California Press, 1984, pp. 250-259.

_____. *The Scientific Image.* New York: Oxford University Press, 1980.

van Huyssteen, Wentzel. *Theology and the Justification of Faith: Constructing Theories in Systematic Theology.* Translated by H. F. Snijders. Grand Rapids: Eerdmans, 1989.

Van Till, Howard. *The Fourth Day: What the Bible and the Heavens are Telling Us About the Creation.* Grand Rapids: Eerdmans, 1986.

Van Till, Howard, Davis A. Young, and Clarence Menninga, Eds. *Science Held Hostage: What's Wrong with Creation Science and Evolutionism.* Downers Grove, Ill.: InterVarsity Press, 1988.

Vesey, G. N. A., ed. *Talk of God.* London: Macmillan, 1969.

Walsh, W. H. "Nature of Metaphysics." *Encyclopedia of Philosophy,* vol. 5. Ed. Paul Edwards. New York: Macmillan, 1967, pp. 300-307.

Weightman, Colin. *Theology in a Polanyian Universe: The Theology of Thomas Torrance.* New York: Peter Lang, 1994.

White, Alan. "The Coherence Theory of Truth." *Encyclopedia of Philosophy,* vol. 1. Ed. Paul Edwards. New York: Macmillan, 1967, pp. 130-133.

Whitehead, Alfred North. *Process and Reality.* New York: Macmillan, 1929.

_____. *Religion in the Making.* New York: Macmillan, 1926.

Winch, Peter. *The Idea of a Social Science.* London: Routledge and Kegan Paul, 1958.

_____. "Understanding a Primitive Society." *Ethics and Action.* London: Routledge and Kegan Paul, 1972, pp. 8-49.

Wittgenstein, Ludwig. *Lectures and Conversations on Aesthetics, Psychology, and Religion.* Ed. C. Barrett. Oxford: Blackwell, 1966.

_____. *On Certainty.* Eds. G. E. M. Anscombe and G. H. von Wright. Trans. Denis Paul and G. E. M. Anscombe. New York: Harper & Row, 1972.

_____. *Philosophical Investigations.* 2nd ed. Trans. G. E. M. Anscombe. Oxford: Basil Blackwell, 1968.

Wykstra, Stephen. *The Interdependence of History of Science and Philosophy of Science: Toward a Meta-Theory of Scientific Rationality.* Ph. D. diss., University of Pittsburgh 1978.

_____. "Reasons, Redemption, and Realism: The Axiological Roots of Rationality in Science and Religion." *Christian Theism and the Problems of Philosophy.* Ed. Michael Beaty. Notre Dame, Ind.: University of Notre Dame Press, 1990, pp. 119-161.

INDEX

Winch, Peter 67, 97n53,
    97n54, 97n55
Wittgenstein, Ludwig 67,
    97n54, 147n81, 215n185,
    218n213
Wykstra, Stephen, 49n71,
    53n104
Young, Davis 102n100